CAPITAL
FLOWS
AND
FINANCIAL
CRISES

CAPITAL FLOWS AND FINANCIAL CRISES

EDITED BY

Miles Kahler

A COUNCIL ON FOREIGN RELATIONS BOOK

Cornell University Press

ITHACA, NEW YORK

First published 1998 by Cornell University Press
First printing, Cornell Paperbacks, 1998

Printed in the United States of America

Capital flows and financial crises / Miles Kahler, editor.
    p.   cm.
    Includes index.
    ISBN 0-8014-3579-X (alk. paper). — ISBN 0-8014-8562-2 (pbk. :
alk. paper)
    1. Capital movements—Developing countries.   2. International
finance.   I. Kahler, Miles, 1949– .
HG5993.C364   1998
332'.042—dc21   98-38147

Cornell University Press strives to use environmentally responsible suppliers and materials to the fullest extent possible in the publishing of its books. Such materials include vegetable-based, low-VOC inks and acid-free papers that are recycled, totally chlorine-free, or partly composed of nonwood fibers.

Cloth printing   10 9 8 7 6 5 4 3 2 1
Paperback printing   10 9 8 7 6 5 4 3 2 1

Contents

Contributors

GAIL BUYSKE is a consultant specializing in financial reform in transition economies.

PABLO CABEZAS is an economist at the Budget Directorate of Chile's Finance Ministry.

BARRY EICHENGREEN is John L. Simpson Professor of Economics and Political Science at the University of California, Berkeley.

ALBERT FISHLOW is Paul A. Volcker Senior Fellow for International Economics at the Council on Foreign Relations.

MILES KAHLER is Rohr Professor of Pacific International Relations in the Graduate School of International Relations and Pacific Studies, University of California, San Diego.

RACHEL MCCULLOCH is Rosen Family Professor of International Finance in the Graduate School of International Economics and Finance at Brandeis University.

SYLVIA MAXFIELD is associate professor of political science at Yale University.

PETER A. PETRI is Carl Shapiro Professor of International Finance and dean of the Graduate School of International Economics and Finance at Brandeis University.

CARMEN M. REINHART is associate professor in the School of Public Affairs at the University of Maryland, College Park.

VINCENT RAYMOND REINHART is assistant director in the Division of Monetary Affairs at the Board of Governors of the Federal Reserve System.

JEFFREY D. SACHS is Galen L. Stone Professor of International Trade and director of the Harvard Institute for International Development at Harvard University.

DOROTHY MEADOW SOBOL is vice president in the Research and Market Analysis Group at the Federal Reserve Bank of New York.

ANDRES VELASCO is associate professor of economics at New York University and a faculty research fellow of the National Bureau of Economic Research.

Foreword

Globalization has become a word that unveils as well as masks new realities. It beckons to new features of the international and domestic landscape such as the growing power of free markets and the corresponding decline of the capacity of governments to manage their own economies. But globalization also hides old realities such as the fact that financial integration was probably as great before 1914 as it is today.

The task of sorting out these intellectual puzzles, as important to governments as to business, requires good, old-fashioned scholarship—what used to be known as hard and disciplined empirical research. Professor Kahler and his coauthors, many of the leading economists and social scientists in the world today, are to be commended and thanked for, in my opinion, avoiding the terrible twin postmodern pitfalls of abstract modeling and extended op-ed pieces. Miles Kahler, through his editing, and the authors, through their labors, have given us a welcome throwback to the period of reasonable efforts to seek truths through a combination of looking things up and using common sense.

I regret only that the book did not appear sooner. The Kahler volume would have tamped down the optimism of those who were telling us that the traditional cycles of lending and crises had become a thing of the past, and that we might be entering a period of boom and boom, not boom and bust. The Kahler volume has been proved correct by the economic crisis triggered in Asia this year. Nonetheless, its analysis remains critical as a basis for understanding what has been happening to the international economy. Of equal importance, its warning to governments comes at a most timely moment in the globalization process. In Dr. Kahler's words, decision-makers have to do a far better job of designing and maintaining "the policies that permit them to reap the benefits of financial integration while avoiding its risks. . . ."

Professor Kahler undertook this project as a Senior Fellow at the Council on Foreign Relations. He put together this volume with a traditional Council study group composed of scholars and practitioners, many of whom contributed chapters. We thank all who participated. And Council Publisher David Kellogg joins me in thanking Cornell University Press as well for its fine efforts in seeing this volume into print.

Leslie H. Gelb
President, Council on Foreign Relations
August 1998

Acknowledgments

The editor and authors wish to thank the Council on Foreign Relations for its financial support of this project and for the stimulating venue it provided the editor during his tenure as Senior Fellow for International Political Economy. We wish in particular to recognize the contribution of the Council's President, Leslie H. Gelb, and its Vice President for Studies, Kenneth H. Keller, whose counsel and guidance made this project and publication possible. The members of the planning group and the study group on private capital flows to developing and transitional economies at the Council provided commentary and criticism that transformed original drafts into polished chapters. Richard D. Erb and Susan L. Siegal, co-chairs of the Council study group, offered the leadership essential to see the project through to its conclusion. Timothy Johnson contributed invaluable organizational and programmatic support to the study group. Anonymous reviewers for Cornell University Press helped to shape final versions of each contribution. Rebecca Woolston gave essential editorial support during the final stages of the book's production. Finally, Roger Haydon, editor of Cornell University Press, oversaw a publication process whose efficiency and speed maintained the topical nature of this work.

CAPITAL
FLOWS
AND
FINANCIAL
CRISES

1

Introduction: Capital Flows
and Financial Crises in the 1990s

Miles Kahler

Capital flows to the developing economies have long displayed a boom-and-bust pattern, beginning with the first lending cycles of the nineteenth century. Rarely had the cycle turned so abruptly as it did in the 1990s, however. U.S. Treasury Secretary Nicholas Brady had hardly announced his 1989 debt reduction plan as an avenue for finally escaping the 1980s debt crisis when capital inflows to developing economies began to surge. For Latin America in particular, this rapid shift from capital famine to capital feast seemed to signal an end to the lost decade of the debt crisis. Despite lingering political and economic uncertainties in central and eastern Europe following the collapse of communism, foreign investment made its mark there as well. By 1993, private capital flows into developing economies had risen to $149 billion, a dramatic change from the annual average of $3 billion in net *outflows* from 1982 through 1989 (IMF 1995, 15).

Cautious voices warned that the new cycle of lending was dependent on transitory international conditions, particularly low real interest rates in the industrialized countries. The financial crisis and sharp recession that followed Mexico's devaluation of the peso in December 1994 seemed to confirm those warnings and to underline the volatile and possibly short-lived character of the new capital inflows. Pessimism swept away the euphoria associated with emerging markets. Skeptics proclaimed an end to the latest financial boomlet, which they compared to other speculative bubbles; Latin American bonds were analogues of Dutch tulips (Krugman 1995).

The isolation of Mexico's financial crisis and rapid recovery of investment in emerging markets in 1995–1996 suggested that the peso crisis had not signaled an end to the new pattern of capital flows. Mexico's sharp and surprising crisis and a subsequent "tequila effect" felt throughout

Latin America demonstrated, however, that developing country governments, international investors, and international financial institutions had failed to adapt to the new economic terrain.

The onset in 1997 of a new wave of financial and currency crises in a region that had been largely immune during the 1990s—the vibrant economies of Southeast and East Asia—suggested that cycles in the new era of global financial integration would persist and could become even more compressed in time. Once again, the lessons that many believed had been learned from Mexico's harsh treatment at the hands of international investors were held up to governments. Whether the new pattern of economic and financial integration can be stabilized to define a permanent change in the world economy will depend on the adaptation of national governments to the new conditions and their ability to act collectively to offset the effects of unwanted volatility. Despite progress at both the national and the systemic level, it was not clear that either adaptation or collective action was assured as the latest financial contagion unfolded in 1997.

This volume maps the new and uncertain landscape that has been revealed after two cycles of lending punctuated by the peso crisis and before a full resolution of the 1997 Asian currency and banking crises and suggests policy changes that will be required in a world of large-scale, market-driven financial flows. This chapter and those that follow emphasize several features of private capital flows to developing and transitional economies during the 1990s. Barry Eichengreen and Albert Fishlow situate the lending cycles of the 1990s in the history of previous periods when capital flows to developing areas surged and then declined in the face of financial crises. The patterns and intermediaries of capital flows in different eras have produced different dilemmas for governments in their attempts to win the benefits of capital inflows while maintaining domestic economic stability. Governments have attempted to influence capital flows through policy change; at the same time, they have been constrained by the prospective behavior of those investing. Sylvia Maxfield examines the composition of investors and the constraints that their behavior imposes on national governments and assesses existing evidence for the constraints that capital mobility imposes on governments.

National policy responses have diverged in the face of the new flows, and governments have demonstrated strikingly different capabilities in coping with capital account instability. Andres Velasco and Pablo Cabezas, and Carmen Reinhart and Vincent Raymond Reinhart evaluate lessons drawn from the Mexican peso crisis and the successful and unsuccessful experiences of other governments during the 1990s.

Rachel McCulloch and Peter Petri, Dorothy Sobol, and Gail Buyske reinforce the portrait of diverse responses to financial integration through descriptions of regional and national variations hidden beneath the deceptive umbrella of "emerging markets." Whether considering the emerging bank-industrial combines of Russia that have discouraged foreign direct investment, or the credible commitments to open economic policies that McCulloch and Petri link to portfolio capital flows, all of these authors also point to the importance of financial liberalization and the stance of governments toward foreign capital in determining larger trajectories of national political economy. These contributors illuminate the consequences of the new lending for national models of economic development and reflect on the probability of the success of these models in the new international context. The differential ability of governments to attract capital through policy change also reflects on the development prospects of the poorest economies, which have attracted relatively little of the burgeoning capital flows of the 1990s.

In the final chapter Jeffrey Sachs considers whether a new international policy response is required in this world of rapidly shifting capital movements. Because another large-scale, bilateral package of financial assistance was unlikely following the Mexican episode, observers have proposed alternatives that range from a purely market-based approach (creditors and borrowers negotiating with little government intervention) to an international bankruptcy model that would require more radical transformation of existing international rules. Recent financial disarray in Asia has confirmed some of these international policy changes and highlighted the need for others.

Capital Flows in the 1990s: Old and New Patterns

The rapidly increasing *volume* of capital flows to developing countries from 1990 to 1994 marked a sharp break from recent experience; the *composition* of that new lending was also marked by new features. In the 1970s, the last cycle of lending had diminished the role of official flows (bilateral and multilateral); in the 1990s, aid and official lending declined from 60 percent of total flows in 1990–1994 to a mere 11 percent of the total in 1990–1994 (Truman 1996). As Fishlow and Eichengreen describe, however, the rising share of private capital was no longer intermediated by commercial banks, as it had been two decades before. Instead, foreign direct investment and portfolio investment (bonds and equity) increased both absolutely and in relative importance. These portfolio flows reflected the growing securitization of global finance since the 1980s. Both foreign direct investment and equity portfolio flows surged because of deeper economic reforms that had taken hold first in developing economies and then in economies transiting from planned to market economies. Privatization provided opportunities for both forms of investment; financial deregulation and regulatory reforms offered a new political and legal framework attractive to foreign investors.

Regional differences persisted in the new lending boom. As Petri and McCulloch describe, despite rapidly growing portfolio flows to East and Southeast Asia, portfolio investment did not overtake the dominant position of foreign direct investment in the region. In striking contrast to the regulation and barriers of the recent past, attracting foreign direct investment had become a "top policy priority" for governments in Asia. Portfolio flows were more significant in Latin America. Although most developing regions benefited from the new flows, regional concentration was also readily apparent. East and Southeast Asia and Latin America attracted the bulk of both foreign direct investment and portfolio flows; South Asia, the Middle East, and sub-Saharan Africa lagged far behind.

Sobol's analysis of three economies in eastern and central Europe—Poland, Hungary, and the Czech Republic—illustrates both regional variation and differences among national economies in the pattern of capital inflows over time. Poland and Hungary had been mired in the debt crisis of the 1980s; Poland completed a debt reduction package with its commercial bank lenders only in 1994. As economic reforms proceeded after 1989, the three economies experienced the same shift from bank lending to foreign direct investment and equity portfolio investment that occurred in other regions. Sobol also documents growth in foreign direct investment that was associated with privatization programs in the Czech Republic and Hungary. Portfolio investment arrived later. Access to international bond markets was at first restricted to sovereign borrowers, but larger firms also began to participate. With the creation of stock markets in each country during the 1990s, equity portfolio investment, encouraged by emerging market mutual funds, also began to increase.

In the buoyant atmosphere of the emerging markets boom, capital inflows were viewed positively by economic policy makers throughout the developing world. New sources of finance enhanced prospects for successful economic reforms and renewed economic growth. The inflows were also seen as a mark of international approval for difficult policy changes. Alternative explanations for the inflows, less flattering to borrowers and their new policy regimes, were often overlooked. Interest rates in the industrialized countries were at historically low levels during the early 1990s. If interest rates explained a large share of the capital flows to developing economies, then a shift toward tighter monetary policies in the industrialized countries could sharply reduce the scale of capital outflows to emerging markets (Calvo, Leiderman, and Reinhart 1992). Portfolio capital flows slowed in 1994 as the Federal Reserve began to raise U.S. interest rates, providing an early confirmation of these views.

The financial crisis that followed the devaluation of the Mexican peso in December 1994 was the sharpest signal that the new era of capital flows could carry high risks for national economies. The spreading financial contagion in East and Southeast Asia that began with the Thai financial crisis and devaluation in July 1997 confirmed that even economies with high rates of growth and consistent and open economic policies could be jolted by the sudden withdrawal of foreign investment. Capital inflows could, as Reinhart and Reinhart remark, be too much of a good thing. The peso crisis, with its regional tequila effect, and the 1997 financial dominoes in Asia also caused observers to question prevailing, benign assumptions that these capital flows would persist without further adaptation of national policies combined with periodic international crisis management.

National Policies and the New Financial Environment

Drawing clear-cut lessons from the Mexican peso crisis has been difficult. As Eichengreen and Fishlow observe, the crisis that closed (or inflected) this cycle of lending to emerging financial markets was limited to one country, even though the tequila effect forced policy changes on other governments that depended on capital inflows. The peso crisis, however, may have been limited to Mexico because of the financial support package mobilized in its aftermath by the U.S. government and international financial institutions. Arguments continue over what would have happened in the absence of the U.S.-led international response.

Even if Mexico is not taken to be unique in its dependence on capital inflows, its susceptibility to political and economic shocks, or its policy missteps, the relative weight assigned to those causes of financial instability also remains controversial. On the one hand, an unsustainable current account deficit and policy slippage suggest that the Mexican government could have averted a crisis of this depth with policy changes taken earlier or more forcefully. On the other hand, the rapid reversal of market sentiment and an apparent overreaction by investors, given Mexico's economic fundamentals, suggest the analogy of a self-fulfilling bank run—a panicky "rush for the exits"—as an important alternative explanation for Mexico's experience (Sachs, Tornell, and Velasco 1996).

The authors of this volume compare Mexico and its peso crisis of 1994–1995 with other developing countries that have experienced similar capital inflows and have managed them with different and more successful results. From that array of experience, a consensus emerges on how governments can cope with the new financial world, a world in which apparently benign capital flows can reverse rapidly, with destabilizing effects. As

Velasco and Cabezas point out, the issue is not the volume of capital flows per se, but the fact that foreign capital flows enter a particular national policy environment. In their contrasting portraits of Chile and Mexico, the attitudes of governments toward those flows are themselves an important variable. Although Chile and Mexico had both entered liberalizing trajectories and embraced market-oriented reforms, Mexico welcomed foreign portfolio capital with little hesitation; Chile kept the influx at arm's length. Chile's economic reforms were more mature than Mexico's, a feature that also served to stabilize capital flows.

Apart from these broad contrasts in the longer-term environment, Mexico's immediate policy choices diverged from those of Chile and other countries whose developing economies surmounted the shocks of 1994–1995 more successfully. In the contest between a policy mix emphasizing credibility and one emphasizing flexibility, Mexico and Argentina, given their experiences with inflation, chose credibility. Deploying the exchange rate as an anti-inflationary anchor has received the most attention and criticism following the peso crisis. Velasco and Cabezas note that Chile's flexible crawling peg (targeting the real exchange rate) traded somewhat higher inflation for greater policy flexibility. Sachs also supports the prevailing, post-peso crisis skepticism regarding a pegged exchange rate, arguing that usefulness as a policy instrument is limited in time. Even in circumstances of high inflation, a credibility-enhancing exchange rate peg should be transformed over time to a more flexible system. In Sachs's view, the new fashion for currency boards, except in the case of very small, very open economies, should also be avoided. Of course, such economic rules of thumb will not prevent exchange rate decisions based on political calculations. Those concerns over the political costs of devaluation appear to have played a role in Mexico's futile efforts to maintain its exchange rate under intense pressure.

Other policy measures chosen to deal with capital surges offer similar dilemmas for national governments. Tightening fiscal policy is a blunt instrument. As Reinhart and Reinhart point out, in Thailand and other rapidly industrializing countries, its short-term usefulness may collide with pressing longer-term needs for infrastructure development. Revaluation of the exchange rate, as Reinhart and Reinhart suggest, is a rarer policy choice because it can impose heavy adjustment costs on the economy through abrupt exchange rate movements following capital surges and outflows.

Sterilization of capital inflows is perhaps the most common policy response in the short run, but its risks increase rapidly if it is continued for too long. By promoting the accumulation of government debt, its fiscal impact may become large and adverse. Sterilization, when coupled with poor internal debt management, increases susceptibility to financial crisis. Velasco and Cabezas point out the stark differences between Mexico and Chile in this regard. The Chilean government did not issue large amounts of short-term debt in the face of capital inflows. Mexico's short-term government debt grew substantially during 1994; the dollarization of a growing proportion of that debt, in the form of *tesobonos*, added yet another element of instability to its position by late 1994. Drawing on Mexico's unhappy experience, Sachs argues that central banks should discourage dollarization of accounts in the domestic banking system as well as the dollarization of the government's own short-term debt.

The new era of financial volatility has also encouraged reevaluation of a policy measure consigned to the Dark Ages of statist intervention and international closure: capital controls. Here once again the contrast between Chile and Mexico is clear. Chile marshaled an array of controls to limit short-term inflows; Mexico designed few impediments to capital mobility. Several authors argue that the record of the 1990s confirms at least the temporary effectiveness of controls directed toward capital inflows. On this reading of the evidence, the relatively modest controls imposed by Chile were able to restore some measure of national monetary autonomy and change the composition of flows toward longer maturities. The volume of inflows, however, could be only temporarily diminished. A mirror image of controls on capital inflows might appear to consist of the liberalization of capital outflows. But as Reinhart and Reinhart point out, such a policy change may have an unintended and unwanted effect: the encouragement of even greater capital inflows because of this positive signal to foreign investors.

In the new policy consensus, few recommendations to national governments are unqualified or easy to implement. The spread of speculative assaults against pegged currencies in Asia in 1997 sharpened negative views of fixed exchange rates. Nevertheless, the shift from credibility to flexibility in exchange rate management may be a treacherous one, as the Mexican government in 1994 and successive Asian governments in 1997 discovered, unless the change is well prepared and accompanied by other strong and positive policy signals to foreign investors. As Velasco and Cabezas admit, even a judicious use of flexible exchange rates may impose an inflationary cost.

Most of the other policy fixes are in fact policy dilemmas, accompanied by risks or shortcomings when applied at the wrong time or for too long. Reinhart and Reinhart emphasize the interactive effects of different policy responses that often undercut the effectiveness of otherwise sound policy choices. Living in the brave new world of large capital inflows and outflows cannot be based on an easy-to-use list of policy nostrums; policy makers must learn to cope with the management of competing risks, which is unfamiliar terrain for most of them.

At least one policy thread could be detected as running from the Mexican crisis to the successive national crises across the Pacific three years later: inadequate regulation of financial institutions. The authors of this volume are unanimous in concentrating attention on the unalloyed benefits of intensified scrutiny of financial institutions during periods of large-scale capital inflows. The link to fixed exchange rates is also clear, particularly in the Mexican and Thai crises. A government's credibility in defending the exchange rate had the perverse effect of convincing lenders and borrowers that they ran no exchange rate risk; exchange rate flexibility, on the other hand, would have forced a more cautious stance and encouraged the development of hedging by private actors.

The reform of banking and securities regulations has been a key part of national efforts to attract the new capital inflows.[1] Unfortunately, financial liberalization and privatization have too often meant underregulation of financial institutions. As a result, lending booms are often followed by financial crisis. As Velasco and Cabezas make clear in the Mexican case, the deterioration in bank balance sheets not only added another element of risk to the Mexican crisis, but bank weaknesses also constrained policy makers in the months before December 1994, preventing a tightening of monetary policy. The importance of reducing the vulnerability of the banking system to capital flow reversals leads Sachs and others to recommend that banks in these economies operate under prudential standards more rigorous than the current international standards set by the Bank for International Settlements.

The constraints on effective regulation, however, are largely political. Regulation of financial institutions and foreign investment is far more than a matter of economic prescription; it is also an intensely political process. In her chapter, Buyske draws attention to the political economy of capital market regulation during these new cycles of lending. Her account of Russian capital markets makes clear that opposition to foreign investment persists, even in an era of widespread financial liberalization. Foreign investment may be a boon for national economic welfare, but it implies threatening competition for entrenched domestic industries. In the Russian case, those industries have powerful ministerial protectors that can hinder or cause delays for a regulatory regime that is friendly to foreign investors. Other groups have a strong interest in continuing lax regulation of financial markets, despite the risks that such lack of oversight poses for the economy as a whole. The Russian Federation Commission of Securities and Exchanges has struggled to develop more transparent, regulated financial markets with political support that has often been reduced to a

---

1. For a recent account of securities market regulation in Latin America, see Stetson and Stolper 1996.

core group of liberalizers around the president. The plight of Russian regulators could undoubtedly be replicated in many other emerging financial markets. If better regulation is designed to attract foreign investors and those investors are seen as unwelcome competitors, then the progress of regulatory reform is likely to be slow.

Regulatory outcomes are also dependent on the supply of regulation by international actors to consumers of regulatory reform in the developing and transitional economies. Many host governments lack the expertise, resources, and time to adequately absorb emerging international norms of regulation. Philip Wellons (1996) has argued that the regulation of securities markets in developing and formerly planned economies will improve if suppliers devote more attention to legal reforms that complement regulatory changes, to enforcement and implementation of agreed regulatory reforms (rather than simply designing those reforms), and to the specific needs of consumer governments that lack financial sophistication. Successful regulatory reform not only enhances the ability of governments to attract inflows of portfolio capital, reforms also reinforce the ability of governments to ride out inevitable fluctuations in those flows.

Investor Behavior and the Autonomy of Host Governments

The abrupt reversal of investor sentiment and capital flows that precipitated the Mexican peso crisis confirmed for many observers that the actions of the new international investors were driven by short-term yields. (Widespread speculation against the peso by *Mexican* investors in December 1994 indicates that short-term motivations were not limited to London or New York.) Edwin M. Truman summarizes this view of the new portfolio investors:

> Unlike many direct investors, portfolio investors often have relatively near-term horizons—that is, the future that concerns them is a relatively brief period of time—regardless of the maturity of the underlying instruments. Unlike direct investors and traditional commercial bank lenders, they assume that they can liquidate their investments fairly quickly in well-developed trading markets. Moreover, near-term relative rates of return are important, as perhaps are considerations of capital gains and losses, for some instruments. (Truman 1996, 201)

Maxfield challenges this view of the homogeneous international investor. Her analysis of investor behavior fails to support simple generalizations that international portfolio investors have uniformly short time horizons, are impatient, and respond rapidly to internal political and economic events in the host country. Her findings suggest that national policy makers have more slack in making choices than the more extreme statements of financial globalization would have us believe. McCulloch and Petri support Maxfield's broad finding in their analysis of the determinants of stock market capitalization in East and Southeast Asia. Trade linkages are identified as the most powerful predictor for the development of a strong equity market, because "an open economy is more likely to allow future repatriation of capital and to retain a favorable policy regime" (McCulloch and Petri, this volume). The significance of such policy parameters suggests that the new domestic and foreign investors may be more attuned to longer-run determinants of national policy regimes rather than hair-trigger responses to short-term policy mistakes. Further disaggregation of emerging market investors would illuminate the relative importance of yield-oriented investors, whose behavior most constrains government policy.

McCulloch and Petri also lend support to those who hold that prudent national policies can reduce the risk of a sharp equity market decline and enhance national abilities to cope with a decline's consequences. Over time, the mix of investors is likely to shift further toward those whose primary interest in these equity markets is diversification rather than higher yields, investors who are likely to offer more stability in external financing. Yields in emerging equity markets are likely to converge over time toward the yields available in industrialized-country markets, as information premiums, restrictions on market access, and lack of availability decline. Early investors driven by short-term yields may be succeeded by investors whose behavior will reduce volatility in equity markets as they commit to these economies for the longer term.

The evolving composition of international investors and the learning curve of national governments hold out the promise that governments may, over time, influence the characteristics and stability of capital flows. Certain policy measures such as capital controls may suffer from erosion over time, but other, longer-run regulatory and policy measures that enhance the credibility of policy commitments and attract investors interested in portfolio diversification and long-term returns may also be effective. Following the Mexican peso crisis, investor discrimination among developing-country financial markets became clearer; the International Monetary Fund (IMF) remarked on the reliance of institutional investors on "a broader array of macroeconomic and financial indicators" as well as measures of the soundness of financial infrastructure (IMF 1996, 8).

Initial responses to currency and financial shocks in Asia during 1997 sent mixed signals regarding growing investor discrimination, however. Thailand and South Korea, hardest hit in the latest wave of retrenchment, shared a weak financial structure, one that was particularly prone to sudden collapses of confidence by domestic and international investors. The pressures felt in 1997 by such widely separated economies as Russia and Brazil might at first glance indicate an undiscriminating and general withdrawal from emerging financial markets. On the other hand, Brazil's pegged exchange rate, viewed as overvalued by many observers, and Russia's fragile political and economic conditions set them apart from other countries that had received large capital inflows. Much of Latin America was far less affected in 1997 than it had been in 1995 following the peso crisis. Fiscal policies had become more stringent, foreign debt had been restructured, and, most important, financial systems had been strengthened through regulatory reform and an opening to foreign participation (Friedland and Torres 1997).

Overall, the portrait of the 1990s presented here is not one of international investors swayed primarily by short-term political and policy shocks or of governments straitjacketed in their policy choices. As investor learning continues, that pessimistic portrait is likely to capture a smaller share of the capital flows to developing and transitional economies. Familiarity with these financial markets and economies will increase. As information about them becomes less costly, discrimination should also increase, which will lower tendencies toward herd behavior and contagion.

Capital Flows and Development: Missing the Cycle, Reacting against It

Capital flows in the 1990s resembled past cycles of lending in another important respect. Although many developing countries benefited from the inflows, the main beneficiaries were highly concentrated among rapidly industrializing and largely middle-income economies. Data on capital flows to developing countries during 1996 indicated that nearly three-fourths of private capital went to a dozen countries; over half went to six countries (China, Mexico, Thailand, Malaysia, Brazil, and Indonesia). With the exceptions of China and India (the former a major exception), the poorest developing countries received only about 3 percent of private capital flows. This pattern of concentration was only reinforced by a steady decline in public government grants and low-interest loans directed to the developing countries (Wessel 1997). Although private capital flows more than compensated for shrinking official development assistance to rapidly industrializing and middle-income countries, the poorest countries were slowly losing out on both public and private flows.

Multilateral financial institutions confronted the plight of the poorest developing countries in their debt initiative for the poorest and most heavily indebted countries. The initiative was proposed by the World Bank and the IMF to reduce the high levels of debt owed by the poorest countries to the multilaterals and industrialized-country governments. Reducing debt overhang might encourage private investment, as it had in Latin America after the Brady plan debt reductions. Nevertheless, the need for additional measures to insert these economies into the evolving international financial system is apparent. The World Bank's International Finance Corporation has announced plans to encourage private investment in the poorest countries or regions of the developing world, which is a modest effort in the direction of introducing these small and troubled economies to private investors. Developing sound financial institutions in these economies would also strengthen their international links, but delivery of financial sector reform to the poorest countries is often hindered by these countries' own existing deficit of expertise. Regional collaboration could assist in this regard and might also reduce the deterrent posed by the small economic scale of many poor economies. Unfortunately, the poorest regions—sub-Saharan Africa, South Asia, and parts of the Middle East—have also lagged in developing the means for regional economic cooperation. Whether this cycle of lending breaks from past patterns and moves beyond concentration on a relatively small number of successful industrializers may be the most significant marker of its status as a sea change in the international economy.

Apart from the threat of further marginalization that the concentration of capital flows poses for the poorest developing countries, the widespread acceptance of foreign capital in the 1990s also suggests broader effects on the political economy of development. The volatility of those flows and the macroeconomic instability that they may induce could undermine market-oriented reforms that are in place throughout the developing and transitional economies. The fear of such a backlash in Mexico and the rest of Latin America was one of the motivations for intervention to moderate the effects of the peso crisis. Despite a recession that set back Latin American recovery from its previous debt crisis, few signs of a populist resurgence appeared. Similar fears pervaded Southeast Asia in 1997, even though the most likely outcome was a slowing of robust economic growth rather than a recession. Although East and Southeast Asia displayed less economic inequality than Latin America, the political systems of the region were often less democratic and, even when democratic, less responsive to the demands of economic adjustment and political protest. In the absence of economic gains for wider sectors of the population and continued political opening, economic downturns induced by financial volatility could produce a backlash against both further economic opening and the regimes that have sustained policies of liberalization.

The financial turmoil of 1997 posed in sharpest form whether acceptance of foreign capital and financial liberalization will undermine models of economic development that have enjoyed wide attention since the 1980s, particularly the "Asian model," which is built on close and collusive relations between government and business. Buyske's description of the efforts by Russian banks to dominate key sectors of Russian industry with the support of the Russian government (to the exclusion of foreign investors) is reminiscent of such state-led models of development. As Buyske points out, such a collusive model runs counter to the opening of a national economy to foreign investment. The competitive pressure that foreign capital may exert on such incipient domestic bargains may be one of its most important consequences for longer-term trajectories of industrialization. As Thailand, Indonesia, and South Korea confronted programs of economic adjustment under the supervision of the IMF, the most controversial provisions were not the traditional mainstays of IMF programs—fiscal and monetary stringency—but demands that the old way of doing business—politically motivated and often corrupt—should be changed. If pressure from international institutions and financial markets serves to undermine these deeply rooted patterns of government-business relations, the results will be one of the most important legacies of large-scale capital flows to these economies.

Systemic Risks and International Response

The Mexican peso crisis stimulated a widespread debate on desirable national policies in the face of the new capital flows, and the characteristics and likely behavior of investors. Those arguments, however, were far more conclusive—at least in pointing up persistent dilemmas—than readings of the international implications of the crisis. Some observers such as Truman (1996) saw at least four elements of systemic risk in the crisis: a threat to the banking systems of countries other than Mexico, a risk from financial and psychological contagion effects to the international financial system, a more remote danger to global economic activity had international economic circumstances been less buoyant, and finally, the negative effects that the crisis might have had on market-oriented reforms in Mexico and elsewhere.

Other analysts discounted the global risks inherent in the Mexican crisis; despite a widespread but relatively short-lived tequila effect, no other economy endured the deep crisis that Mexico experienced. As Fishlow and Eichengreen remark, the Mexican crisis differed substantially from the crises that had ended other cycles of lending in this century. The run from the peso was not seen to pose a substantial risk to financial systems in the industrialized economies, nor was it a precursor to a wider global or regional crisis in lending, such as the cascading national crises of the 1930s or the 1980s. This relatively benign outcome, however, may have been the result of U.S. intervention. The Clinton administration extended, despite considerable domestic opposition, a package of bilateral financial support that was complemented by resources from the IMF. Whether the regional or global effects of the Mexican crisis would have been more extensive in the absence of that intervention remained a crucial and unknowable counterfactual.

A final twist was added to the post-Mexico debate over desirable international action by widespread acknowledgment that a program of financial support on the scale mobilized by the United States was highly unlikely in any future crisis. Political resistance had been great in the United States, even though the loans were directed to a country that shared a long border and deep economic interdependence. European skepticism was even more marked. IMF involvement on this scale was opposed on the grounds that the peso crisis was national or at worst regional in scope, not the precursor of global financial contagion.

The political aftereffects of the Mexican rescue suggested that lowering systemic risk in the future would depend on preventive policy measures at the national level (as described earlier), or multilateral measures of support that would borrow to a greater or lesser degree from existing institutional designs. The principal alternative was a model of negotiation between international creditors and national governments, without significant international intervention or the contribution of public resources. This would be a return, in effect, to the model in place before the Great Depression, the last era of large-scale portfolio lending to developing countries.

The arguments for public intervention in the Mexican peso crisis and the 1997 financial crises in Asia are summarized by Eichengreen and Fishlow: the risks of contagion, which are difficult to estimate, and the existence of multiple equilibriums as a contributor to crisis. In this view, the appropriate analogy is not the failure of an insolvent firm, but a bank run on a sound institution by panic-stricken depositors. In such cases, rapid supply of liquidity may stave off a far worse crisis in the real economy and restore financial stability at lower cost. The price, as critics of such intervention stress, is the moral hazard of encouraging both governments and private investors to pursue riskier strategies in the future, given the implicit insurance of an international bailout.

Sachs has proposed the most radical revision of existing practices and institutions for dealing with a threat of default on national debt obligations. Summarized in his contribution to this volume, his proposed reforms draw an analogy to domestic bankruptcy procedures. Sachs argues for a new system to deal with financial workouts that would "reduce moral hazards," "ensure the effective functioning of the debtor government at all stages of the financial workout," and "create mechanisms for coordinating the actions of creditors." Because the current arrangements do not meet these criteria, new mechanisms are needed to parallel the core features of domestic bankruptcy procedures: automatic standstills in debt servicing, new loans that are assigned priority for repayment, and a means of final reorganization that does not permit free riding or holdouts among the creditors.

To many of those who favor improved international crisis management, Sachs's proposals are unsatisfactory. In their view, the bankruptcy analogy does not hold up, because in the case of a country there is no equivalent for the value of a firm, and, unlike incompetent managers, governments cannot be removed by international means. The use of an American bankruptcy model raises barriers to international agreement on reform, because national models and acceptance of bankruptcy vary (Eichengreen and Portes 1995, 38–42). Eichengreen and Portes offer a more limited menu of reform that is directed to countries whose debt takes the form of "widely held, highly liquid, foreign-currency-denominated bonds." Efficient negotiations between private creditors and governments would be shored up. Governments would provide necessary assistance to alleviate organizational problems among the bondholders, which would complement and reinforce the bondholders' committees. Public capabilities would also be reinforced to avert a wider financial crisis in the event of an impasse in creditor-debtor negotiations. New crisis management roles and additional resources are proposed for the IMF. This agenda for reform attempts to deal with the crucial issue of speed of response; it is also tailored for a world in which a massive public bailout—from the IMF or bilateral sources—is highly unlikely.

As described above, a final dimension of financial crisis has risen on the international agenda since the peso crisis and receives attention in Sachs's chapter: banking crises that may accompany and exacerbate the financial woes of developing-country borrowers. The malaise of national banking systems was at the core of the Mexican, Thai, and South Korean financial crises. As Sachs notes, the international rules governing banking supervision are strained when domestic banks have large liabilities that are denominated in foreign currencies. The sudden withdrawal of those funds during a financial crisis may require international lending to support the banking system. Before such lending can be carried out with any confidence, however, much tougher prudential requirements are needed in developing and transitional financial systems. Banking systems in such economies operate in newly liberalized environments; however, the regulatory expertise and oversight required in the new environment often lags far behind. Banks, which occupy central roles in domestic financial systems, often lack an adequate capital base and are unable to evaluate credit

risk (when politics does not override their desire to make such an evaluation). Because weak banks are often conduits for volatile international capital flows, they can amplify a financial crisis and provide a key channel for
international contagion as well (Wessel, Frank, and Smith 1997).

The absence of widespread contagion following the Mexican peso crisis,
the rapid recovery of the Mexican economy and its reentry into international capital markets, and the renewal of large outflows of capital to
emerging financial markets temporarily reduced estimates of systemic risk.
Modest reforms were endorsed to deal with hazards in the new pattern of
international lending. At the Halifax Summit in June 1995 the Group of
Seven (G-7) industrialized countries proposed a number of steps to deal
with risks to the international financial system that had been exposed by
the Mexican peso crisis. At the request of the G-7, a working party of the
Group of Ten (G-10) was established to suggest procedures that would
contribute to the resolution of future financial crises; its report was submit-
ted in May 1996. The measures recommended, some of which are already
in place, dealt with both crisis prevention and crisis management. In addition, the 1996 Lyons Summit added to the international agenda the issue
of strengthening financial systems in countries entering the international
capital markets.

Crisis prevention measures centered on an enlarged role for the IMF in
improving the amount and quality of financial information available to private investors, governments, and multilateral institutions, and a stiffening
of IMF surveillance of its members' economic policies. Implementation of
the first is easier to evaluate than implementation of the second. In April
1996 the IMF established Special Data Dissemination Standards. Since the
IMF could not compel its members to make public additional national economic data, new standards of data provision monitored by the IMF provide
a different route to the same goal. Those countries that seek access to international capital markets and have not subscribed to the new standards
may experience market-based pressures to bring their standards of data
collection and dissemination into line. The IMF also claims to have
changed its surveillance of members' economic policies by broadening the
scope of its regular Article IV consultations to include capital account and
financial system issues. This ensures the continuity of surveillance and
achieves a new level of frankness and transparency in dialogues with national governments (Adapting IMF Surveillance 1997).

Although the G-10 working party report seemed to tilt toward encouraging market-led crisis management, efforts have been made since 1995 to
expedite crisis decision making at the IMF and expand the financial resources at its disposal. The IMF adopted an emergency-financing mechanism that would "front load" IMF resources during a crisis and grant faster
access to those resources. The New Arrangements to Borrow, comprising

lines of credit from both the industrialized G-10 and dynamic industrializing economies, will roughly double the resources available to the IMF under the long-standing General Arrangements to Borrow. In addition, the members of the IMF agreed to increase their quotas by 45 percent, which directly increases the resources available to the IMF. Finally, the IMF, in collaboration with the World Bank and the Bank for International Settlements, has addressed the issue of financial system fragility in borrowing countries, aiming to establish a concerted international strategy that will reinforce regulatory oversight.

Skeptics endorsed some of these initiatives but wondered whether the international financial establishment is fighting the last war. The concentration on better and more timely information as a key element of crisis prevention was called into question by one financial market participant who argued that "in 1994 . . . and contrary to common belief, lack of information does not seem to have been a major problem" (Fraga 1996, 54). Others suggested that preparing for the next Mexico and emphasizing an unproven risk of widespread contagion will lead only to costly overinsurance. The likeliest crises in this view will be country specific and directly related to policy errors in the countries involved. As investors become more discriminating over time, the risks of herd behavior and contagion will continue to decline (Cline 1996, 13).

In addition to determining whether the right lessons are learned from the experience of the 1990s and previous lending cycles, implementation of even this modest program of reforms was partial and halting. The U.S. contribution to the agreed IMF quota increase remained blocked by political opposition in the U.S. Congress. The urgent need for regulatory reform of financial systems proved difficult to negotiate and even more difficult to implement. International pressure may have only a limited effect in such a politicized sector, as contributions to this volume amply demonstrate. Even if each of the proposed changes is implemented, international decision making may not be able to overtake the increased speed with which contemporary international financial crises are precipitated. Modest increases in decision-making efficiency will hardly overcome the obstacles of consensus rules at the IMF and the unwillingness of some key members to acknowledge global risks and responsibilities.

Finally, even these measured steps toward public intervention in future crises have stirred opposition by private financial institutions that endorse a "hands-off" approach by governments. The Institute of International Finance (IIF), representative of major international banks, has objected to an expanded role for the IMF in dealing with future crises. The IIF was particularly hostile to the suggestion that the IMF might "lend into arrears" during a crisis, that is, offer support to governments that had not resolved disputes over payments to their private creditors. That suggestion, contained in the 1996 G-10 report, would clearly tilt debt negotiations toward borrowing governments. The response of the banks was only one signal of the domestic political conflicts that could appear in future interventions.

The surprising spread of financial crisis in Asia in 1997 provided an early test of these global initiatives. The initial response of the United States to the request of Thailand for external assistance was to avoid direct participation, leaving the negotiation and external financial support to the IMF and other regional governments, most notably Japan. The response of the region to this American stance came with a Japanese proposal to establish an Asian monetary fund, which was immediately viewed by the IMF and the U.S. government as a threat to global management of financial crises and a "soft money" alternative to IMF conditionality. At the Manila meeting of Asia-Pacific finance and central bank deputies in November 1997 the Japanese initiative was rejected in favor of regional financing that was explicitly treated as a necessary supplement to the first-tier financing (and conditionality) of the IMF. The Manila meeting also provided a first indication of policy responses to perceived weaknesses in the international mechanisms put in place since the peso crisis. The assembled finance ministers endorsed enhanced regional surveillance of economic policies, a clear sign that regional contagion effects had produced a willingness to intrude on "domestic" economic policy making that could threaten neighboring economies. In addition, the meeting endorsed more rapid response on the part of the IMF to the fast-breaking crises in the new financial era; initiatives undertaken since the peso crisis were judged inadequate. Finally, the recurrent and central theme of strengthening domestic financial systems was emphasized. Using external advice and peer pressure to move forward the process of financial regulatory reform would be a key agenda item for the near future.

In light of the Asian crises, U.S. Treasury Secretary Robert Rubin made clear that the additional data provided by governments under post-1995 IMF programs remained insufficient. Rubin urged even more transparency on the part of central banks in disclosing their foreign exchange commitments and the balance sheets of their national banking systems. Rubin's suggestions were hardly greeted with enthusiasm by governments and central banks that had long treated their operations as politically sensitive and immune from external scrutiny. The failure of the IMF to change Thai policies as its exchange rate crisis loomed in late 1996 also called into question the intensified surveillance that the IMF claimed had been put into place after the Mexican crisis. In advance of a crisis and in the absence of additional public comment and revelation, the levers that the IMF could deploy to shift the course of governments were not clear.

The completion of the financial support package for South Korea suggested that the model established in the Mexican crisis, modified from case to case, would persist. The IMF's lead position, which would require additional resources provided by quota increases, other international financial institutions, and national governments, was ensured. The policy changes endorsed were becoming clearer from case to case. The crises in Thailand and South Korea, like that in Mexico before, did not result from excesses in fiscal and monetary policy or large-scale public indebtedness. These crises resulted instead from private sector indebtedness that became untenable with the collapse of an exchange rate peg, a collapse that endangered the banking and financial systems. The IMF moved rapidly to stabilize exchange rates by restoring confidence through large packages of financial support and also moved to take on the much more contentious, longer-term task of renovating and restructuring financial institutions. The very predictability of the IMF-led bailout model, however, only reinforced the fears of those who saw increased moral hazard with each new financial package. The risks assumed by foreign investors and banks were implicitly reduced, which could lead to even more risky behavior in the future.

A New International Economy or a New Cycle of Lending?

Two years after the Mexican peso crisis, the claims of pessimists had appeared confounded. In December 1996—three years early—Mexico repaid all of the $12.5 billion borrowed from the United States. The Mexican economy, after suffering a sharp recession in 1995, had rebounded, although the severe social costs of the peso crisis lingered for the working class and the poor. Mexico's repayment to the United States was made possible by its reentry into the international capital markets, where it had once again become a large-scale borrower. Mexico was not alone; Latin America also recovered rapidly from the tequila effect. After a recession in 1995 following the peso crisis, growth resumed in early 1996, and Latin American borrowers reclaimed their pre-peso crisis position in financial markets. Foreign direct investment to the region reached a record $30.8 billion in 1996. Despite the economic downturn and continuing high levels of economic inequality, there was little evidence of a political backlash against market-oriented reforms in the region.

The resurgence of capital flows to the developing and transitional economies was an even sharper rebuff to those who had labeled the 1990s surge in lending a bubble or a fad. In 1996 the volume of bond issues to developing-country borrowers reached $73 billion, up 53 percent over the preceding year. This was the highest volume ever recorded for developing countries (World Bank 1997, 5). Stock markets in the emerging markets also recovered strongly after their slump in 1995, and new equity issues surged. Overall, the flow of private capital to the developing economies in 1996 was 20 percent higher than for the preceding year. The new pattern of lending in the 1990s—despite its relative novelty—seemed to have demonstrated its resilience.

The contagion of financial crisis in Asia that began in Thailand and spread from Southeast Asia to Hong Kong and Korea in 1997 ended the recovery from the peso crisis and lent new ammunition to those who saw a decade-long pattern of compressed cycles of lending and crisis. Those re-current crises, it seemed, could be surmounted only by repeated commitment of public resources on an ever-growing scale. The Korean rescue in late 1997 produced the largest IMF-led package to date: $57 billion, contributed by the IMF, the World Bank, the Asian Development Bank, and national governments.

Despite the disruption of capital flows by these crises and the uncertainties surrounding both national and international responses to the new financial environment, the contributors to this volume offer broad support for the view that the new capital flows represent a permanent change in the world economy rather than a temporary and faddish infatuation with emerging markets. The integration of developing economies into the global financial system, historically a volatile, stop-go process, seemed to have attained a new stability, one that might see shallower troughs and less dizzying peaks in foreign investment. That stability, as these authors suggest, would be based on several broad trends. The credibility of market-oriented policies in most developing and transitional economies meant that demand for capital was rooted in a wide array of largely private borrowers, rather than sovereign ones. Despite the dilemmas posed by inflows of capital, beneficial policy choices could be made in the face of the new global financial environment; governments were not stripped of all autonomy, although their margin for error may have been reduced. Those national choices could shape the use to which foreign capital was put—the crucial distinction among developing economies—as it had been in previous lending booms.

The supply side was also likely to become more stable over time. As McCulloch and Petri argue, the rationale for emerging market investment is diversification as well as the returns that can be expected in rapidly growing economies. Investors that had not ventured previously into these markets were announcing large investment commitments. The state treasurers of California, Connecticut, and Ohio announced plans to invest more than $10 billion of their public pension funds in Asian equities over two years (Tam 1996). The announcement was only one indication of the entry of investors who were likely to commit for the longer term.

The stabilizing effects of these trends on the part of borrowers and investors would not prevent periodic crises, however. Whether one of those crises—based on policy errors, investor overreaction to shocks, or both—could spiral into a wider contagion that would affect investor attitudes toward all developing economies could not be disproved on the basis of the Mexican crisis of 1994–1995 or the initial outcomes in Asia during 1997. Assuring the confidence of investors and nudging government toward prudent policies in the new environment had become the central task of multilateral institutions and industrialized-country governments in the 1990s. If they were successful, the integration of the developing and transitional economies, with all of the economic benefits that flow from that integration, could proceed apace.

The dilemmas of both national governments dealing with the mixed blessing of capital inflows, and multilateral institutions seeking to both encourage and moderate the behaviors that produced the new lending were only one part of a process of global economic integration. All of the players were grappling with an international economy that had remained government managed until recently and was now evolving rapidly to a market-based mode of governance. The ascendancy of financial markets and the creation of new forms of interdependence are unprecedented. Financial integration before 1914 may have been as great or greater, but the expectations placed on governments by their electorates were far lower than the demands of the 1990s. Whether governments will be able to design and maintain policies that permit them to reap the benefits of financial integration while avoiding its risks (in the form of sharp economic cycles and wider financial crises) cannot be predicted. The consequences of failure, however, can easily be seen in the unhappy conclusions to previous cycles of lending.

References

"Adapting IMF Surveillance to a Changing Global Economy." 1997. *IMF Survey* 26 (8):113–116.

Calvo, Guillermo A., Leonardo Leiderman, and Carmen M. Reinhart. 1992. "Capital Inflows to Latin America: The 1970s and the 1990s." Working paper, International Monetary Fund, Washington, D.C.

Cline, William R. 1996. "Crisis Management in Emerging Capital Markets." In *From Halifax to Lyons: What Has Been Done about Crisis Management?* edited by Peter B. Kenen, 7–25. Princeton, N.J.: International Finance Section.

Eichengreen, Barry, and Richard Portes. 1995. *Crisis? What Crisis? Orderly Workouts for Sovereign Debtors.* London: Center for Economic Policy Research.

Fraga, Arminio. 1996. "Crisis Prevention and Management: Lessons from Mexico." In *From Halifax to Lyons: What Has Been Done about Crisis Managment?* edited by Peter B. Kenen, 46–55. Princeton, N.J.: International Finance Section. Department of Economics, Princeton University.

Friedland, Jonathan, and Craig Torres. 1997. "Latin America Now Benefits from Lessons of '94." *Wall Street Journal,* October 29, sec. C1.

IMF (International Monetary Fund). 1995. *Private Market Financing for Developing Countries.* Washington, D.C.: International Monetary Fund.'

———. 1996. *International Capital Markets: Developments, Prospects, and Key Policy Issues.* Washington, D.C.: International Monetary Fund.

Krugman, Paul. 1995. "Dutch Tulips and Emerging Markets." *Foreign Affairs* 74 (4):28–44.

Sachs, Jeffrey, Aaron Tornell, and Andres Velasco. 1996. "Financial Crises in Emerging Markets: The Lessons from 1995." *Brookings Papers on Economic Activity* 1:147–215.

Stetson, Anne, and Antonia E. Stolper. 1996. *Reform and Renewal: Current Regulatory Developments in Latin American Capital Markets.* New York: Association of the Bar of the City of New York.

Tam, Pui-Wing. 1996. "Asia Attracts Pension Funds of Three States." *Wall Street Journal,* September 3, sec. B9A.

Truman, Edwin M. 1996. "The Mexican Peso Crisis: Implications for International Finance." *Federal Reserve Bulletin* (March):199–209.

Wellons, Philip. 1996. "Regulatory Reform and Coordination in Emerging Financial Markets." Paper presented to the Council on Foreign Relations Study Group on Private Capital Flows to Developing and Transitional Economies, October, New York.

Wessel, David. 1997. "Capital Flow to Developing Nations Surges 20%." *Wall Street Journal,* March 24, sec. B9A.

Wessel, David, Robert Frank, and Craig S. Smith. 1997. "Next Economic Crisis May Stem from Woes of the World's Banks." *Wall Street Journal,* May 7, sec. A, pp. 1, 6.

World Bank. 1997. *Financial Flows and the Developing Countries: A World Bank Quarterly* 4 (2).

2

Contending with Capital Flows:
What Is Different about the 1990s?

Barry Eichengreen and Albert Fishlow

Recent financial difficulties in Mexico and Asia have been widely seen as the latest in the series of debt crises that have punctuated lending by the industrialized countries to the developing world. This characterization of the historical record implies, of course, that smooth capital transfers are the norm and disruptions to international financial flows are the punctuation marks. The opposite might also be argued: debt-servicing difficulties, the suspension of voluntary lending, and calls for third-party intervention—the constituents of which are called debt crises—are the normal state of affairs. Thus the three short, post–World War I periods when large quantities of international portfolio investment took place— 1924 to 1929, 1976 to 1981, and the 1990s to date—were the exceptions. Either way, the repetition of events prompts a search for parallels and policy precedents.

Those who insist that history repeats itself would nonetheless acknowledge that it never repeats itself in the same way. This observation is pertinent to the three post–World War I episodes of large-scale foreign lending and to the crises that followed. Perhaps the most prominent difference across these episodes lies in the method of finance. Although trade credits, fixed-interest securities, and direct foreign investment (DFI) were important in each period, the three episodes can be differentiated from one another by the distinctive financial market institutions and arrangements that mediated the major part of the flow of funds.

In the 1920s the U.S. bond market was for the first time the vehicle for portfolio capital flows from industrial to developing countries. Government bonds were underwritten by investment banks in New York and marketed to institutional and private investors. During the second half of the decade, a large secondary market developed for the bonds of industrial and industrializing economies. For a country seeking access to foreign capital, the critical steps were to establish a relationship with a reputable investment bank and to arrange a bond flotation, whereas the key to retaining access was to ensure that the bonds subsequently traded at prices close to their par values.

In response to the defaults of the 1930s, the bond market fell into disuse. After an extended hiatus during which little portfolio lending took place, commercial banks entered the market in the second half of the 1960s. The volume of bank lending to less-developed countries (LDCs) increased enormously during the "recycling boom" that followed the oil shock of 1973. Money-center banks originated and syndicated dollar loans to developing countries; in contrast to the preceding episode of bond finance, the banks themselves held these obligations. With the subsequent rise of securitization and a secondary market in LDC debt, this process of bank intermediation increasingly resembled the bond finance that had preceded it. Critical differences remained, however. One was the failure to subject the decision to extend a bank loan to the government of a developing country to the market test. Rather, bank loan officers made the decision of their own volition. It had only a muted effect on the market valuation of the bank's equity.[1] This was in contrast to the era of bond finance, when each bond issue had to float on its own bottom. At that time, a large number of individual investors decided whether to subscribe to each bond issue, thereby subjecting it to a market test.

Following the 1982 debt crisis and the subsequent effort at remedy launched by the Baker Plan in 1985, when commercial banks engaged in limited amounts of concerted lending, the banks withdrew from lending to the governments of developing countries. At the end of the 1980s, when large-scale lending resumed, the new conduit for capital transfer was equity markets. Trade credits, fixed-interest securities, and DFI remain important vehicles (as they were during the two earlier waves of foreign lending), but an unprecedented volume and share of capital flows to developing countries began to take the form of equity purchases by individual investors. These were made available through their institutional representatives: mutual and pension funds. To a greater extent than in the 1920s or in the 1970s and early 1980s, these are investments in private and semiprivate companies rather than in government obligations. They are residual claims to the profits that remain after debts with higher seniority have been serviced and promise a return denominated not in dollars but in local currency.

These differences in the structure of lending by developed to developing countries have had an important influence on the course and conse-

---

1. This point should not be overdrawn. Megginson, Poulsen, and Sinkey (1995) identify a statistically significant, if small, negative effect of the announcement of syndicated loans to Latin American borrowers on the stock prices of the issuing banks.

quences of debt crises in the twentieth century. They conditioned the responses of lending and borrowing governments, of multilateral organizations, and of market participants alike.

We develop these points by highlighting three differences among the crises of the 1930s, 1980s, and 1990s. The first is their scope. Whereas the 1930s' crisis was global, that of the 1980s was more selective, affecting several regions (Latin America, eastern Europe, and Africa, but not East Asia), and those of 1995–1997 were isolated in that they were limited to a single country (e.g., Mexico) or a single region (e.g., Asia). In part these differences are attributable to the severity of the macroeconomic shock. In the 1930s the crisis was global because the Great Depression was global; all capital-importing countries were rocked by the collapse of the commodity markets on which external debtors relied to generate foreign exchange, and by the debt deflation and high real interest rates that disrupted financial markets. Not even countries with light debt loads and flexible economic structures were immune. The crises of the 1980s and 1990s were less general because the macroeconomic shocks that contributed to them were smaller. Real interest rates rose, as in the 1930s, but production and imports in the industrial world did not collapse.

In addition to the severity of global economic disturbances, intervention by creditor-country governments and multilateral institutions affected the scope of the three crises. This is the second difference. In the 1920s, when money-center banks floated but did not themselves hold significant quantities of bonded debt, default did not jeopardize the stability of creditor-country banking systems. Consequently, default elicited little response by creditor-country governments concerned for the stability of their financial systems. In the 1980s, by contrast, the risk to creditor-country banking systems prompted the industrial countries to support early and decisive intervention by the International Monetary Fund (IMF). In 1995–1997 there was also intervention, but it operated through the leadership of regional powers such as the United States (in the case of Mexico) and Japan (in the case of Thailand), as well as through multilaterals such as the IMF. Once again, crises in the developing world pose a threat to the stability of financial institutions in developed countries, but that threat is more selective than it was in the 1980s in terms of which intermediaries are at risk and which countries are affected. The Mexican crisis posed a threat mainly to Wall Street firms with heavy exposure to Mexican debt, whereas the Asian crisis was a problem mainly for Japanese banks with heavy commitments in Thailand. Such specificity resulted in a regional response.

The third difference between episodes lies in the response of the borrowing countries themselves, which took the form of import substitution in the 1930s, fiscal adjustment in the 1980s, and monetary adjustment in the 1990s. In part the different responses reflected different external conditions. In the 1930s the global nature of the crisis and the absence of intervention to contain its spread prompted developing countries to de-link themselves from the international system. With the collapse of global financial and commodity markets, the capital importers resigned themselves to life without foreign funds. That also meant reduction of external obligations, which was accomplished through policies of import substitution, reducing dependence on foreign markets and foreign capital. In the 1980s, import substitution was less attractive because export markets remained buoyant even when portfolio lending was suspended. But the sharp curtailment of lending to LDC governments forced those governments to institute budget cuts. Fiscal correction became the principal vehicle for external adjustment. In the 1990s, foreign capital flowed heavily to private and semipublic enterprises; therefore, governments did not make use of foreign funds to finance their budget deficits to the same extent, and hence, there was less need for fiscal correction.[2] But because most equity claims were denominated in the currency of the borrowing country, foreign investors were exceedingly sensitive to the specter of devaluation. Adjustment was therefore effected through the use of monetary as well as fiscal instruments. Mexico and Thailand both raised interest rates to reassure equity investors of their commitment to sound currency policies.

But external conditions do not provide the entire explanation for the differing responses of capital-importing countries. Domestic policies were no less important in the periods leading up to each of the three crises. In the 1990s many countries sought to sterilize capital inflows through the pursuit of restrictive monetary policies. Governments resisted the temptation to finance deficit spending with increased supplies of money. Instead, they accumulated international reserves in record quantities, acquiring a cushion that could be used when inflows dried up. (But as the Mexican and Thai cases both illustrate, not all countries used that cushion productively to buy time for adjustment.) The crisis of 1982, by contrast, was preceded by a period of rapid inflation, generated largely by the need to finance budget deficits. Without a cushion of reserves, adjustment was necessarily drastic, and harsh fiscal retrenchment was essential. The late 1920s more closely resembled the 1970s than the 1990s. Fiscal policies expanded as capital flowed in; borrowing countries accumulated budget deficits rather than international reserves. But whereas prices rose rapidly on the eve of the 1982 crisis, they fell alarmingly in 1931. In the 1980s it was possible for countries to price their exports back into international markets by curtailing their inflation rates; in the 1930s, when falling prices

---

2. This is not to say that fiscal retrenchment was unimportant. But in the countries at the center of our story, it had a small effect compared with the last time. For example, while under President de la Madrid, the Mexican fiscal adjustment was on the order of 10 percent of gross domestic product (GDP), this time it appears to be closer to 2 percent. The Thai budget was already in balance when that country's crisis struck.

were already severely straining mortgage markets, financial institutions, and labor market conventions, the scope for adjustment was more limited.

In the remainder of this chapter we elaborate these arguments from a historical vantage point. Each main section focuses on one of the three twentieth-century episodes of large-scale lending to developing countries. The goal of each section is to highlight distinctive institutional features of the operation of the lending process and to link them to the response to crises. In the conclusion we synthesize our findings and glean the policy implications.

The Era of Bond Finance

By the 1920s there was nothing new about the use of bond finance to transfer funds to developing countries. The bond markets of London, Paris, Berlin, and Amsterdam had been the vehicles for massive amounts of capital transfer to the emerging markets of the United States, Canada, Australia, Latin America, and Russia in the century preceding World War I.[3] The prewar record was checkered; lending to these and other countries was interrupted by defaults in the 1820s, 1850s, 1870s, and 1890s. But although lending was sometimes interrupted, there was no extended hiatus like the one that began in the 1930s, because each wave of default was confined to a relatively small number of countries. Reflecting this fact, creditor-country experience was reasonably satisfactory, especially in Britain, where capital markets functioned with a minimum of government interference, and export-oriented infrastructure projects were financed in overseas regions of recent settlement. Results were least satisfactory for countries such as France, whose government sought to use international investment as a foreign policy lever to encourage investors to finance the fiscal ambitions of Russia, Egypt, and other interventionist states.

The global debt crisis of the 1930s was unprecedented in scope, superseding the more limited defaults of the nineteenth century. Understanding this crisis requires first comprehending what changed between the prewar and interwar period, setting the stage for global defaults.

Changes in the structure and operation of the markets are not hard to identify. In fact, they affected the origin and destination of foreign funds, the structure of the intermediation process, and the uses to which foreign finance was put. Many accounts focus on the rise of New York relative to

---

3. There is a vast literature on pre–World War I foreign lending, synthesized by Fishlow (1985) in "Lessons from the Past: Capital Markets in the 19th Century and the Interwar Period," in M. Kahler, ed., *The Politics of International Debt* (Ithaca: Cornell University Press, 1985), pp. 37–94.

London and the continental European financial centers as a source of foreign funds.[4] The United States, traditionally a recipient of international capital, first shifted from net capital importer to net capital exporter in the 1890s. During World War I it sprinted to the head of the pack of lending countries. The United States was the one major industrial country whose economy was not severely disrupted by the war; it was the one place where saving naturally exceeded investment, and therefore it was an obvious source of foreign funds.

Prior to the war, U.S. lending predominantly comprised direct investment in railways, sugar mills, and mining ventures in the Western Hemisphere. The war years saw large-scale, officially sanctioned bond flotations on behalf of France, Britain, and other Allied governments. But it was the sale of U.S. government bonds as much as foreign flotations that awakened the American bond market from its dormancy. Whereas in 1914 there had been no more than 200,000 bond buyers in the country as a whole, wartime Liberty Loan campaigns raised that number to the millions (Stoddard 1932, 43). Once jarred from its slumber, the bond market was awake for good. Estimates for 1897 show that more than 90 percent of U.S. foreign investment was direct; by 1930 the share of portfolio investment had risen to more than 50 percent.

U.S. financial intermediaries took aggressive steps to compete in this market. They had to secure an agreement with a foreign government or corporation to underwrite a bond issue, and they had to place the bonds with investors at prices that yielded an acceptable profit margin. The inexperience of many U.S. banks may have contributed to subsequent difficulties; Mintz (1951) shows that financial institutions that were newly entering the market for foreign debt were disproportionately associated with issues that defaulted in the 1930s.

Financial innovation was a concomitant of rapid expansion. In the 1920s investment trusts played much the same role as emerging-market mutual funds in the 1990s. They pooled the subscriptions of their clients, placed their management in the hands of specialists, and issued claims entitling holders to a share of their earnings.[5] They facilitated position-taking in foreign securities by investors who would have been otherwise deterred by transaction and information costs. Commercial banks established bond departments and securities affiliates, much in the manner that commercial banks in the 1990s created their own mutual funds.

It is hard to ascertain how well or poorly this process worked independent of the unsatisfactory outcome whose causes we are seeking to com-

---

4. See, for example, Mintz (1951).
5. The role of investment trusts is relatively neglected in the literature; two contemporary discussions were written by Speaker (1924) and Robinson (1926).

prehend. Senator Hiram Johnson, head of the congressional 1931–1932 foreign bond investigation, argued that these structures created pervasive incentive problems. Those who placed their money in investment trusts, he and other critics alleged, were given an exaggerated sense of the extent of portfolio diversification and underestimated the risks. Those who purchased foreign bonds through the bond departments and securities affiliates of commercial banks failed to realize that these investments entailed risks unlike those attached to U.S. government securities. The banks, for their own reasons, were loath to advertise the risks. Underwriting divisions pressed securities affiliates and bond departments to place the issues they originated; between 1922 and 1931 the number of national banks with securities affiliates grew more than tenfold. They opened ground floor branch offices to encourage walk-in business and advertised their wares in the pages of *Harper's* and the *Atlantic Monthly*. Having created this infrastructure, bond departments and affiliates then pressed the underwriters to make additional bonds available for placement.

Come the 1930s, this process was viewed with considerable disenchantment:

> Up to the slump of 1920, these new clients sought the branch-offices. After the slump, the branch-offices sought them. They did so through hosts of young salesmen, carefully schooled in "high pressure" methods of breaking down "sales resistance." Their keynote was pressure—all down the line. The home office kept the branch-offices "on their toes" by a stream of phone calls, "flashes," "pep-wires," and so forth. The branch managers kept the young salesmen all "burned-up" with "pep-talks," bonuses, and threats of getting fired. Everybody in authority demanded "results"; which meant, more sales. Every salesman must sell his "quota." What he sold, how he sold it, and whom he sold it to, did not much matter. Verily, business had got into banking; or, rather, "banking," in the old sense of the word, had been kicked out of doors by business." (Stoddard 1932, 106)[6]

When foreign governments sought access to the New York market, they found a ready reception. Many had frequented the City of London or the Paris Bourse before the war; Argentina, Brazil, Australia, and Canada were among the leading borrowers of the 1920s. They were joined by the newly truncated Germany and the successor states of the Austro-Hungarian Empire, which were among those that had suffered the most severe wartime devastation and had the heaviest reconstruction costs. Some, such as Germany, were saddled with reparation burdens that placed heavy short-term

---

6. Recent research casts some doubt on the extent to which securities affiliates were really at fault. See Krosner and Rajan 1994.

drains on their balance of payments, encouraging them to seek external financing to bridge the gap. The high interest rate policies adopted by their central banks to limit reserve losses in turn encouraged foreign investors to purchase their high-yielding securities. As would again be the case in the 1970s and 1990s, the development of new markets in countries in fragile political positions was integral to the lending process.

Reparations and infrastructure investments had to be financed out of government budgets. Central, state, and municipal governments borrowed abroad to finance their operating expenses. While funds sometimes were used for the construction or modernization of roads or port facilities that served to enhance export competitiveness, more commonly they were devoted to paying public employee salaries and transfer payments that were unlikely to augment export revenues. Clearly, if exports suddenly turned down, debt service would become a very serious problem.

Events in the center also shaped the flow of lending. U.S. interest rates (as proxied by the yield on domestic medium-grade bonds) peaked in 1923 and trended downward through 1928. The decline in yields encouraged U.S. investors to seek more remunerative returns abroad. After 1925 the yield on Lary's sample of foreign bonds consistently exceeded that on domestic medium-grade securities (Lary 1943). U.S. foreign lending rose steadily to its peak in 1927–1928. Thus, the surge of lending in the 1920s can be understood only as a combined result of financial innovation, the investment trust and bond market revolution, and the downward trend in U.S. interest rates.

Figure 2.1 shows the evolution of debt service relative to exports after 1924. Following Eichengreen and Portes (1989), it distinguishes countries for which default starting in 1931 was minimal or absent, from those that defaulted on a substantial share of their external debts.[7] Debt service relative to exports was higher for the heavy defaulters all through the 1920s and rose quickly during the period of peak borrowing, 1926 through 1928. Figure 2.2 shows these same data for Latin America and central and eastern European debtors.[8] The Latin American debt ratio was consistently higher (not so much because of higher-debt stocks, the data suggest,

---

7. The heavy defaulters were Brazil, Bulgaria, Chile, Colombia, Costa Rica, Germany, Greece, Hungary, Poland, and Uruguay. The light defaulters were Argentina, Australia, Austria, Belgium, Canada, Czechoslovakia, Denmark, Finland, France, Italy, Japan, New Zealand, Nicaragua, Norway, Spain, and Venezuela. Figures reported are unweighted averages of country statistics. Cline (1995) notes that this categorization weights the light-defaulter category toward relatively advanced industrial countries, an asymmetry that is important to keep in mind when interpreting the results.
8. Latin America includes Argentina, Brazil, Chile, Colombia, Costa Rica, Uruguay, Nicaragua, and Venezuela. Central and eastern Europe include Bulgaria, Germany, Hungary, Poland, Austria, and Czechoslovakia.

Figure 2.1 Foreign debt service to exports (%).

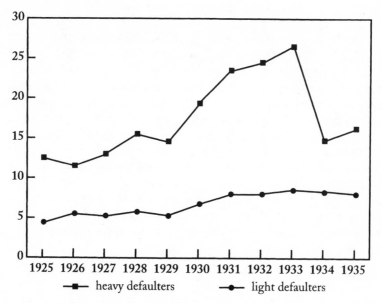

Source: United Nations 1948a, 1948b, 1953; Mitchell 1975, 1983, 1995.

Figure 2.2 Foreign debt service to exports (%).

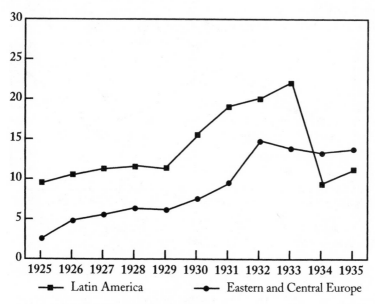

Source: United Nations 1948a, 1948b, 1953; Mitchell 1975, 1983.

as higher interest rates). This heavier burden is consistent with the fact that Latin American defaults historically began first.[9]

In a period when capital inflows were strengthening the balance of payments, it was possible for countries to accumulate international reserves. Under the gold standard of the 1920s, reserves rose automatically as economies expanded, because central banks were required to limit the growth of their monetary liabilities to a specified multiple of their international reserves (typically 250 percent or 300 percent). But nothing prevented central banks from accumulating reserves at a more rapid rate than mandated by the gold standard statutes. Whereas figure 2.3 shows that industrial production (and, by implication, the demand for money) grew in the second half of the 1920s at the same rate for both light and heavy defaulters, figure 2.4 shows that gold holdings rose more quickly for the light defaulter, as if they took advantage of circumstances to accumulate a cushion of reserves.[10] But with many countries mechanically following the gold standard rules, the growth of excess reserves was modest and provided an

Figure 2.3 Industrial production index (1929 = 100).

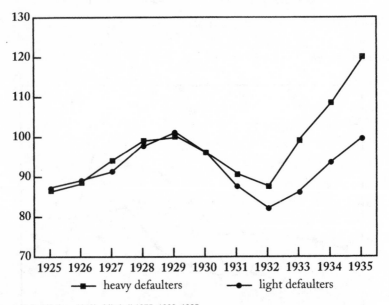

Source: United Nations 1948b; Mitchell 1975, 1983, 1995.

9. It is worth noting that these debt-service-to-export ratios of 10 to 15 percent were modest by the standards of the 1980s and 1990s.
10. The changes in reserves in Latin America and central and eastern Europe move in close parallel through the end of the 1920s.

Figure 2.4 Changes in gold reserves (million U.S. dollars).

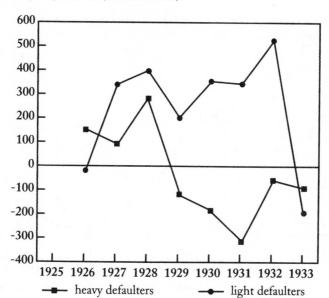

—■— heavy defaulters   —●— light defaulters

Source: League of Nations.

inadequate support when international financial and commodity market conditions deteriorated toward the end of the decade.

What happened starting in 1928 is sufficiently well known to permit a brief summary. The Federal Reserve Board, concerned about the heights scaled by the Wall Street stock market boom, raised interest rates in a series of steps. Suddenly domestic bills and bonds became more attractive than foreign investments. Net portfolio lending by the United States declined from more than $1 billion in 1927 to less than $700 million in 1928, with virtually all lending in 1928 concentrated in the first half of the year. Bond flotations on behalf of Germany and South America were hit particularly hard. With the cost of servicing dollar loans running at about $900 million a year, lending through the middle of 1928 had proceeded at a rate sufficient for new capital inflows to finance service on the outstanding debt. When new lending dried up in the second half of the year, the entire bill came due.

This interruption to lending came on top of a decline in the relative price of nonfood primary commodities. Figure 2.5 shows that this relative price had been trending steadily downward for five years. The decline accelerated in 1929–1930 with the slump in industrial production in Europe and the United States and the increase in the relative supply of these raw

Figure 2.5 Commodity prices (1929 = 100) relative to manufactured goods.

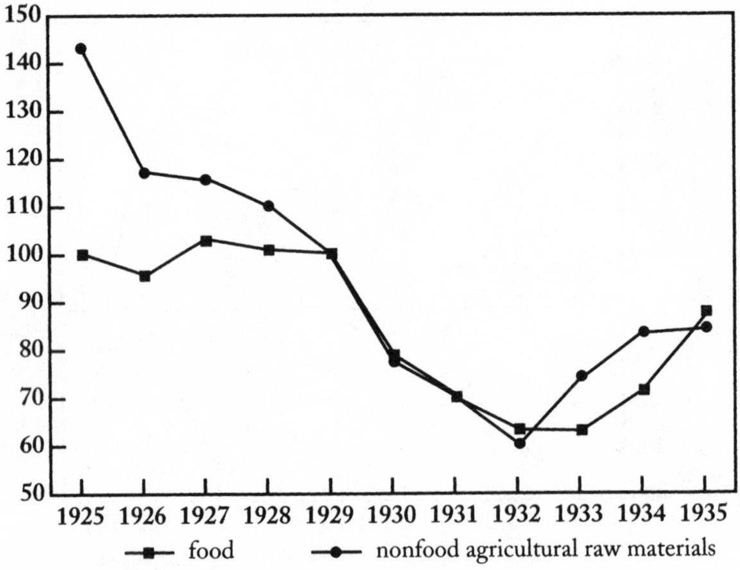

Source: Grilli and Yang 1988, app. I, cols. 5, 7, and 8.

material inputs. The terms of trade of the heavy defaulters deteriorated dramatically in 1929–1930 (Eichengreen and Portes 1989, fig. 4.3). Measured in terms of wholesale prices, the terms of trade of Latin American countries fell more sharply than those of eastern European debtors starting in 1929 (figure 2.6). Together, figures 2.5 and 2.6 underscore the importance of the commodity composition of trade. For Latin American countries that exported mainly primary products, the deterioration in export-market conditions was persistent and began to reverse itself only in 1933; for Germany, Austria, Czechoslovakia, and the other more industrialized countries of central and eastern Europe, terms-of-trade movements were relatively moderate. The depth and persistence of the slump in the industrial world, and its repercussions on primary commodity markets, clearly had much to do with the severity of the debt servicing difficulties of Latin American countries.

The wave of protectionism that started in the United States in 1930 compounded these difficulties. A debate exists over the effect of the Hawley-Smoot tariff (which had itself been imposed partly to aid farmers whose plight reflected the same global commodity-price trends noted in the preceding paragraph) on the Great Depression in the United States. However, there is no question that by switching U.S. demands away from

Figure 2.6 Terms-of-trade index (1929 = 100) wholesale prices relative to those in the United States.

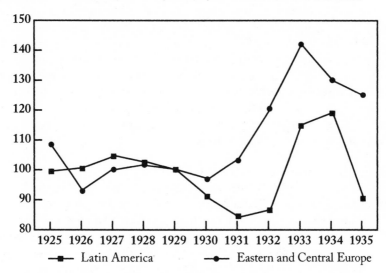

—■— Latin America   —●— Eastern and Central Europe

Source: United Nations 1948a, 1948b; Mitchell 1975, 1983.

imported goods in general and imported raw materials in particular, the tariff and similar ones in other industrial countries compounded the primary producers' problems.

The debtors' response was to hold on as long as possible. Countries that were ultimately forced to default first sought to finance their deficits by running down their reserves (figure 2.4). When the constraints of the gold standard began to bind, they imposed restrictions on various categories of international gold and capital flows and used this room for maneuver to depreciate their exchange rates. Governments cut public spending, raised taxes (especially import duties), and applied export bounties. These measures worked to strengthen the balances of trade of countries that could no longer finance deficits via capital imports. Argentina, Austria, Australia, Brazil, Bulgaria, Colombia, Germany, Greece, Hungary, Poland, and Venezuela all strengthened their trade balances in 1929. But the further deterioration of international commodity markets and the rise of industrial-country protection in 1930 dealt their efforts a further blow. Bolivia suspended service on its sovereign debts in March of 1931. During the rest of the year much of Latin America defaulted. Only Argentina, with close financial and commercial ties to the United Kingdom, and the small Central American republics dependent on the United States remained solvent. In 1932 default spread to southern and eastern Europe, and 1933 was dominated by default by Germany, the world's largest debtor.

Import substitution was the natural response. The collapse of primary commodity prices and the imposition of tariffs in the industrial world prevented developing-country debtors from exporting their way out of their bind. The depression and the attempt to respect the requirements of the gold standard had already forced severe monetary and fiscal retrenchment. Adjustment to the new circumstances of the 1930s therefore took place by substituting away from imports. Currency devaluation turned domestic spending toward homespun goods. Tariffs and quotas, often supplemented by exchange controls, were used to stifle imports. Governments extended credit on favorable terms to import-competing industries to promote their growth.

The import-substitution strategy was associated with reasonably smooth recovery from the crisis of the early 1930s. (Figure 2.7 distinguishes between Latin America and Eastern Europe.) Eichengreen and Portes (1989, fig. 4.3) and Cline (1995) caution that this result need not carry over to other times. Many Latin American countries possessed an array of labor-intensive industries characterized by limited domestic production and ample opportunity for rapid expansion. Import substitution was attractive not only because of the difficulty of penetrating export markets but also because of the scope it provided for expanding domestic supplies of imported goods. Later, when the easy opportunities for import-substituting industrialization

Figure 2.7 Industrial production index (1929 = 100).

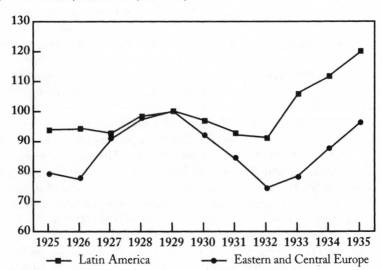

Source: United Nations 1948b; Mitchell 1975, 1983.

had been exhausted, further pursuit of such policies ran up against skill and technology constraints.

The readjustment of defaulted debts involved a protracted process of negotiation. Then, as now, negotiations were complicated by the existence of a large number of investors. A football stadium would have been needed to seat the thousands of bondholders whose assent to the terms of settlement would have been required as a prerequisite for regaining capital-market access. While getting scores of commercial banks to agree on the terms of a rescheduling or a concerted lending program involved significant transaction costs in the 1980s, the transaction costs entailed in debt negotiations in the era of bond finance were more formidable still.

To an extent, this problem was managed by the intervention of bondholders' representative committees. In Britain, the Corporation of Foreign Bondholders had been in existence since 1868. A private entity, it solicited subscriptions from bondholders and negotiated settlement terms with the debtor. When it announced that the debtor had negotiated in good faith and endorsed the offer as the best that could be expected, bondholders were asked to validate the agreement by registering their opinion with the council or by cashing a coupon with the debtor. Stock market sanctions were then withdrawn, in principle reopening the capital market to the debtor.

Bondholders could and did withhold their consent. There was enough dissent over the terms of settlement and enough debt still in default in neighboring countries that few debtors regained significant bond market access until after World War II. In the United States the process worked even less smoothly. Reflecting the country's late emergence as an international creditor, an organization comparable to the Corporation of Foreign Bondholders (the Foreign Bondholders Protective Council) was established only in 1934. Until then, bondholders had to rely on ad hoc committees that lacked the reputation and authority to negotiate effectively.

This process proceeded with a minimum of government intervention.[11] Starting in 1933, the Roosevelt administration attached priority to the reconstruction of international trade and refused to use sanctions as leverage on behalf of private investors. The British government was somewhat more interventionist. It used the 1932 Ottawa Agreements and the Roca-Runciman Treaty negotiations with Argentina to secure favorable treatment of sterling debts. It threatened to impose clearing arrangements on Germany following that country's default in 1933, leading the latter to re-

---

11. Admittedly, the Foreign Bondholders Protective Council had been established partly with the impetus of the U.S. State Department. But the state department's concern had been not so much to aid American investors as to deflect their demands for assistance.

sume service on its sterling debts. But such intervention was the exception to the rule.[12]

There were also attempts to coordinate the intervention of national governments through international institutions. The first such scheme proposed to endow the Bank for International Settlements (BIS) with resources to extend credit to countries seeking to reorganize their debts. Hubert Henderson, an adviser to the British government, proposed in 1931 to authorize the BIS to issue "International Certificates" to help finance countries' debt-service payments and other balance-of-payments obligations. Another 1931 plan, proposed by Montagu Norman, governor of the Bank of England, and Robert Kindersley, one of the bank's directors, would have created a new international facility, also possibly housed at the BIS, to make loans to countries unable to obtain finance through normal channels. At the 1933 World Economic Conference organized by the League of Nations, the British proposed the creation of a multilateral "normalization fund" to channel funds to countries seeking to reorganize defaulted debts.

None of these proposals bore fruit. Default on private investments, interwar policy makers repeated, was a private matter. While bank failures were widespread, banks in the creditor countries held only limited amounts of foreign debt; from their point of view, sovereign default was only a minor factor in the financial instability of the 1930s. The fear that banking systems might collapse prompted a variety of unprecedented actions, but extraordinary assistance for sovereign debtors was not one of these. To the extent that high finance was a convenient whipping boy for the economic crisis of the 1930s, there was little popular sympathy for investment trusts and other institutional investors with a stake in foreign debt, especially in the United States.

The Era of Bank Finance

The impact of the debt crisis of the 1980s, unlike that of the 1930s, was more regionally focused. The IMF group of fifteen heavily indebted countries includes ten from Latin America. Therefore we emphasize the experience there, while providing some commentary on other continents.

In the mid-1960s, as output flagged and inflation mounted even in countries that were relatively successful practitioners of import substitution, Latin America sought new policies. Tariffs, which had reached extraordinarily high levels, were slowly reduced. Crawling peg exchange

12. This is the conclusion, for instance, of the Royal Institute for International Affairs (1937).

rates were introduced in Chile, Colombia, and Brazil as a means of assuring competitiveness in the midst of continuing inflation. Starting in the second half of the 1960s attempts to promote nontraditional exports led to the adoption of special export subsidy programs. The period as a whole was marked by the relatively rapid expansion and diversification of trade.

Entirely different patterns of development evolved in East Asia and Africa. The former undertook significant reconstruction and embraced a new strategy of rapid export growth joined with substantial increases in savings. Eventually this combination proved extraordinarily successful and initiated the long period of Asian growth that has just come into question. But time was required for the response. From 1960 through 1970, the weighted average annual growth rate in East Asia was not much higher than the 5.7 percent attained in Latin America. Indeed, in the period from 1965 to 1973, it actually was lower.

For Africa the 1960s were a final period of postwar expansion. Rather than finding a new model, as was true in Asia, or experimenting, as Latin America did with state impulses to development, the continent saw more of the same. Africa soon began experiencing negative rates of per capita income growth, from which it has begun to emerge only recently. Similarly, for much of South Asia the 1960s were a period of disappointingly slow growth.

Substantial private capital inflows first became available to developing countries toward the end of the 1960s. The Eurodollar market pursued new borrowers and found them primarily in Latin America. Governments had the luxury of financing additional imports and public sector outlays without the need for private retrenchment. Domestic policies retreated from the regulation that had become widespread during import substitution. Prices were allowed a larger role in the allocation of resources.

Military governments, whose domain expanded in these years, still saw a role for the public sector. The Brazilian miracle of the late 1960s and early 1970s was a clear descendant of the earlier era of import substitution, not to be confused with the outward-oriented policies pursued by South Korea and Taiwan. The home market still dominated, thereby affording advantage to Brazil and Mexico, the largest Latin American countries, both of which managed their highest rates of expansion in this period. Even Argentina, despite its failed attempt at stabilization under military rule in 1969, succeeded in achieving its peak growth rates in these years.

This period of adaptation, which saw an improvement in growth performance regionwide, was brought to an end by the disequilibrium ushered in by the oil price rise in 1973. The post-oil-shock experience in Latin America was conditioned by the almost universal willingness of governments to take on debt in order to sustain imports. Again, the Latin American model deviated from the Asian model, which was dominated by an acceptance of immediate price increases rather than reliance on debt finance.

Debt looked like a winning strategy in a world where real interest rates were low, as they remained until the late 1970s. But there was a shift from debt-led growth in the years before 1973 to debt-led stagnation thereafter. Even when accompanied by continuing growth, the strategy was precarious. It led to a marked increase in debt exposure that proved decisive at the end of the decade when interest rates rose and new capital inflows were curtailed.

In the meantime, countries took advantage of borrowing. In the Southern Cone, led by a newly militarized regime in Chile receiving guidance from the "Chicago Boys," monetarism was the rage. Its downfall was associated with an excessive capital inflow that became impossible to sustain in the 1980s. Mexico was a substantial borrower, relying on newfound oil resources as a magnet for capital; after the second surge in oil prices in the midst of the Iran-Iraq conflict, there was essentially no limit to the external finance available to the country. In Brazil, balance-of-payments deficits financed domestic expansion, albeit at decelerating rates and with rising inflation. Expanding debt inhibited growth but also deterred devaluation because of the implications of increased service payments on outstanding obligations. Only Colombia was able to avoid indebtedness, with rising coffee prices and receipts from illicit drug traffic providing needed resources. Its problem became accommodation to an external boom rather than adjustment to a substantial oil tax.

In the period after the first oil shock, Latin America as a whole showed a deceptive ability to adapt—or rather, a lack of necessity to do so. Foreign finance was readily available. Growth remained high, reinforcing military rule throughout much of Latin America. The precariousness of the situation was revealed only after a new rise in oil prices, an abrupt increase in real interest rates, and a recession among members of the Organization for Economic Cooperation and Development (OECD) coincided in the early 1980s. But, contrary to what Angus Maddison has argued, it was not that governments had continued to follow blindly the original import substitution bias of the 1950s. Maddison states that, "The economic growth performance of Latin America since 1973 has been abysmal. . . . there has . . . been a certain continuity in economic policy attitudes since the 1930s, and the liberal international order which was created by OECD countries and has influenced policy in Asia has left them virtually untouched" (Maddison 1985, 53).

In fact, the major factor contributing to instability in these countries was that they had shown a capacity to depart from earlier policy commitments. What influenced the outcome was their asymmetric opening to the world economy, combining vast financial flows with much more limited trade penetration.

Fiscal distortions also reduced these countries' room for maneuver. For growth to continue in the late 1970s, the governments of Brazil and Mexico had to resort to rising deficits and the nationalization of economic activity. Stop-go macroeconomic policies were only a prelude to the stop-stop policies that became necessary in the 1980s. A situation of renewed external dependence and rapid change in the international economy offered an illusion of permanence.

The strategy did not work badly for a time. Growth continued. Investment ratios remained respectable. The marginal propensity to save out of external borrowing was, on the whole, the same or greater than the propensity to save out of domestic income. There seems to have been no difference in this regard between Indonesia and Korea on the one hand and Brazil and Mexico on the other. Nor do the Asian countries, particularly Korea, seem to have been spared entirely from mistakes in investment.

The real difference lay in the response to the second oil shock. Latin American countries, particularly the Southern Cone and the oil exporters, continued to borrow and paid the consequences when rising real interest rates and accompanying industrial-country recession brought matters to a head. Table 2.1 provides a comparative perspective, distinguishing four negative effects on the balance of payments. First is the terms-of-trade effect; second is the rise in real interest rates; third is the impact of reduced OECD growth on the exports of developing countries; and fourth is the shift in the willingness of commercial banks to continue to lend, measured as the change in the ratio of capital flows to gross product.

Two conclusions emerge. One is the greater impact on Latin America, Colombia excepted, of interest rates and capital supply as opposed to terms of trade and OECD recession effects.[13] The more open East Asian economies were buffeted by deteriorating trade conditions, whereas Latin America was more sensitive to financial shocks.

The second and critical point is the importance of measuring shocks relative to exports rather than gross national product (GNP). Upon doing so, as in Table 2.1, one can see the immediate necessity of attending to the balance-of-payments crisis that did in Latin America; imports declined by $40 billion (more than 40 percent in volume terms) between 1981 and 1983.

When Mexico defaulted (appropriately enough, on Friday, August 13, 1982), the countries of the Western Hemisphere were plunged into difficulties that persisted until very recently. Growth ceased, and what was proclaimed by some to be another temporary balance-of-payments adjust-

---

13. The reason is straightforward: the former depend on the debt:GNP ratio rather than the export:GNP ratio.

Table 2.1 The impact of external shocks, 1981–1983

	Ratio to GNP					Ratio to exports[f]
	Import and export prices[a]	Interest Rates[b]	OECD recession[c]	Capital supply[d]	Total[e]	Total
Latin America						
Argentina	0.006	−0.025	−0.009	−0.047	−0.075	−0.64
Brazil	−0.044	−0.025	−0.005	−0.022	−0.093	−1.37
Chile	−0.097	−0.034	−0.016	−0.026	−0.173	−0.80
Columbia	−0.057	−0.004	−0.012	0.023	−0.050	−0.31
Mexico	0.018	−0.035	−0.008	−0.020	−0.045	−0.42
Peru	−0.001	−0.039	−0.017	−0.027	−0.030	−0.13
Venezuela	0.131	−0.034	−0.020	−0.162	−0.085	−0.31
East Asia						
Indonesia	0.141	−0.012	−0.018	−0.021	0.132	0.53
Korea	−0.068	−0.027	−0.022	−0.011	−0.128	−0.43
Malaysia	−0.047	0	−0.038	0.112	0.027	0.05
Philippines	−0.076	0.012	−0.014	−0.024	−0.129	−0.70
Taiwan	−0.154	−0.004	−0.038	−0.014	−0.182	−0.35
Thailand	−0.087	−0.007	−0.016	−0.004	−0.114	−0.52

Sources: Import and Export Prices: Economic Commission for Latin America; IMF.
Interest Rates: *World Debt Tables;* OECD.
OECD Growth Rates and Capital Flows: IMF, Asian Development Bank.
[a] Price effect: percentage change in export price index times export/income ratio 1977–79 minus percentage change in import price index times import/income ratio 1977–79.
[b] Interest rate effect: change in nominal implicit interest rate on medium- and long-term debt, adjusted for change in US wholesale price index, between 1977–79 and 1981–83 times net debt/GNP ratio in 1980.
[c] OECD recession effect: change in OECD growth rate between 1977–79 and 1981–83 times import volume elasticity of 1.5 times export/income ratio, 1977–79.
[d] Capital supply effect: ratio of capital inflow, exclusive of exceptional financing and adjusted for net errors and omissions, to income in 1981–83 minus ratio in 1977–79.
[e] Sum of all effects.
[f] Sum of all effects relative to GNP times export/GNP ratio, 1977–79.

ment turned into the region's longest period of negative development in the century. At the end of 1993, national income per person, including the negative effects of a 36 percent terms-of-trade decline, stood at about 90 percent of its 1980 value (Economic Commision for Latin America 1992, 39). By contrast, the 1980s were a period of vigorous expansion in much of Asia.

Latin American adjustment passed through four stages.[14] First there was a phase of drastic balance-of-payments correction between 1981 and 1984,

---

14. For a summary of the literature up to the new commitment to debt reduction, see Fishlow 1988. For the subsequent evolution of the Brady accords, see IMF *International Capital Markets* various years.

when the continent's imports fell by 45 percent. So rapid was the decline that *World Financial Markets* could speak of "lasting resolution of the LDC debt problem" (*World Financial Markets* 1984, 1). Instead, difficulties worsened in the second phase. The banks were not inclined to lend more but rather were committed to reducing their exposure to the region. Latin America was forced to deal with the crisis through a more fundamental realignment than had been imagined.

The third phase began with the Baker Plan in 1985, which was a tripartite strategy dependent on the banks, international institutions, and country adjustment. As this effort failed to secure needed bank support, it eventually gave way to the Brady Plan, which allowed, for the first time, substantial reduction of country indebtedness to banks. The policy became a reality in 1988 when Citibank wrote down its developing-country loans; it was confirmed the following year by the settlement of the outstanding Mexican debt at a price of about 65 cents to a dollar. Other countries soon settled at parallel discounts, larger for smaller countries such as Bolivia and Costa Rica, and comparable for those holding large stocks of debt.[15]

A fourth phase of restructuring has followed. Beginning in 1991 there was a sudden and unanticipated flow of capital into the region, which we discuss further in a later section. Latin America was again a place for foreign funds to go. This progression from import surplus to export surplus, back to new import surplus traces the evolution of the region's external accounts, shown in figure 2.8. Note the decline of the Latin American ratio of current account to gross domestic product (GDP) after 1982, and its subsequent rise after 1990. Note also the contrast with Asia, which mirrored the Latin American decline beginning in 1983 but had an earlier recovery and a spontaneous adjustment after 1991. During this latter period, when capital flooded into Latin America, the Asian countries were able to reduce their deficits autonomously.

What remains to be described is the restructuring of domestic economies, which has shown itself in three areas. First, there has been a shift in government fiscal capability, and with it a decline in inflation rates. Brazil was virtually the last country in the region to introduce its new currency, the real, on July 1, 1994, and to mount a serious effort to limit inflation. Second, there has been a significant change of ownership, from public to private. And third, there has been a reduction of tariffs and quotas and greater reliance on internal productive capability.

15. The various relief packages did not reduce debt drastically; indeed, the IMF estimated that only about 8 percent of total obligations were reduced. Note, moreover, that the external debt of the region mounted to some $490 billion at the end of 1993, almost three times exports. Although total interest payments as a percentage of exports have declined, rising interest rates would greatly complicate the situation. (See ECLA 1992, tables 20 and 23; IMF 1994, 95.)

Figure 2.8 Current account balance/GDP (%). *Note:* 1982 GDP weights.

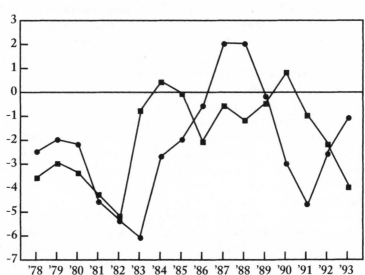

Source: IDB various years; IMF *International Monetary Statistics* various years .

The change in fiscal capability and inflation is major, as is evident in figure 2.9. In most countries it has been a continuous process, especially over the last three years, of increasing government command of revenues and expenditures. The fiscal balance has also benefited from lower international interest costs. Overall, the region's fiscal balance swung from a deficit of the order of 3 percent of GDP in 1989 to a surplus of 1 percent in 1993 (ECLA 1992, tables 20 and 23; IMF 1994, 1995). More than two-thirds of the countries in the region saw some improvement.

This recovery was due mainly to increased public sector revenues. Still, the somewhat skeptical position of the Economic Commission for Latin America requires recognition:

In only a few countries . . . can the fiscal accounts be said to be structurally balanced. For this to be the case, current income must be solidly backed by a stable tax base, which in turn is consistent with a level of current spending that can support the normal functioning of government administration and the provision of basic social services. The tax base must also be able to support the public investment required to revamp and develop infrastructure necessary for economic growth and enhanced social equity. (ECLA 1992, 2)

Figure 2.9 Fiscal deficit/GDP (%). *Note:* 1982 GDP weights (negative numbers indicate a surplus). Indonesia excluded from 1992.

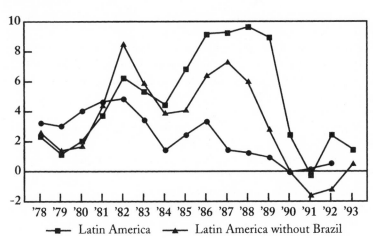

Source: IMF *International Financial Statistics* various years. 1992–1993 data for Brazil from ECLA 1993.

It is too early to tell whether such caution is justified. But the stabilization efforts of recent years, if continued, promise to respond to a major need of countries in the hemisphere. It is no accident that price inflation has been dramatically reduced. Excluding Brazil, inflation in Latin America, as measured by consumer prices, fell to only 19 percent in 1993, less than half its 1991 value, and extraordinarily lower than the more than 1,000 percent registered in 1990 (ECLA 1992, 1, table 5). For the first time in the post–World War II period the region has made a commitment to fiscal soundness. Figure 2.9 illustrates this in the plot of the ratio of the fiscal deficit to GDP for the Latin American and Asian countries. The stability achieved in Asia is clear. After a decline forced by lack of foreign finance in 1982 and 1983, Latin American deficit ratios increased again before finally declining in the late 1980s. And Brazil has finally shown movement toward greater stability with its real plan.

Latin America thus has emerged from the 1980s with greater fiscal discipline. Contributing to it has been a willingness to entrust the private sector with more responsibility and control. Sales of nationalized enterprises have accounted for sizable revenues, from 1 percent to 4 percent of total government receipts in recent years. Airlines, telephone and telegraph operations, steel facilities, and countless other enterprises have been turned over to private hands. In contrast with the 1970s, when external debt assisted the state in financing its needs, a radically different model has emerged. For the new strategy to work, however, private investment must be sustained and rationalized. If the shift to private hands is simply a one-time event, the benefits will not be realized.

Thus, privatization should not be viewed simply as an aspect of fiscal reform. It encompasses a broader conception of the role of the state. Enterprises that are sold should not merely be those able to yield an immediate return to public authorities. Rather, the objective must be to improve economic efficiency continuously.

A third important policy modification has occurred in the governments' strategy for promoting domestic production. Latin America began the post-1950 period committed to import-substituting industrialization. Import barriers were erected to allow domestic sectors to develop. Already by 1960 it was evident that protection was not working; only Brazil and Mexico, with their large domestic markets, had succeeded in growing. But it was not until the balance-of-payments crisis of the 1980s that all countries in the region moved to freer trade.

Tariff reductions have been spectacular. Virtually everywhere the value of domestic production subject to restriction has been reduced substantially and the average tariff lowered significantly.[16] A sharp decline in real exchange rates has also been undertaken to reduce imports and encourage exports. Unfortunately, the inflow of capital has resulted in a significant exchange rate appreciation in many countries in recent years. This movement may be contrasted with the stability of the Asian real exchange rate in the first half of the 1990s (see figures 2.10 and 2.11.)

This Latin American appreciation has contributed to the sharp rise of imports since 1990. Between 1990 and 1993, the region's imports grew from $94 billion to $148 billion, an average annual increase of almost 15 percent. The only large country whose behavior was at variance with this pattern is Brazil, which continued to repress imports until 1993 but sharply increased its foreign purchases subsequently.

Latin America is thus a different region from a decade ago. The fiscal situation has improved. Inflation is under control for the first time since the 1950s. Bloated public sectors have been compressed, and the increased efficiency of tax collection has yielded additional revenues for public authorities much in need of them. Trade barriers have been substantially removed, and a commitment to greater competitiveness has emerged. These changes are due to the brute force of the adjustment forced on the region. No longer do people have faith in the ability of state managers to plan. Instead, as elsewhere around the globe, reliance on markets is now the rule.

---

16. It now stands at little more than 20 percent, compared to close to 50 percent before tariff reduction began (ECLA 1993, table 13).

Figure 2.10 Real exchange rate index: Latin American wholesale prices relative to those of the United States (1990 = 100).

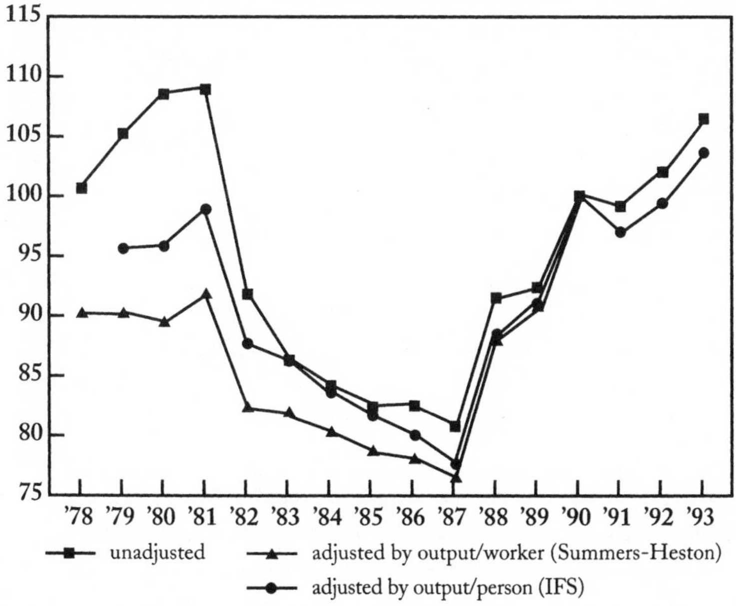

Note: 1982 GDP weights. Productivity adjustments are relative to United States.
Source: Summers and Heston 1991.

The Era of Equity Finance

The age of equity finance can be dated from the end of the 1980s.[17] The international diversification of investment portfolios by pension funds and life insurance companies in the United States, prompted by regulatory changes, was one factor. Another was the liberalization of financial markets and growth of mutual funds—and the reluctance of the money-center banks to commit funds again to emerging markets. These combined to initiate a wave of equity investment to Latin America and Asia.[18] Investment was further encouraged by declining U.S. interest rates, which enhanced the creditworthiness of indebted countries and encouraged mutual fund managers to search for yield overseas. Various observers—Calvo, Leider-

17. A good review of the trends is in Tesar and Werner 1995.
18. In a parallel with the 1920s, Hale remarks that the surge of lending in the 1990s and the negative reaction to the 1994 peso devaluation were "magnified by the moral hazard problems resulting from Wall Street's big investment in emerging market research and investment banking departments. Many firms had downplayed Mexico's exchange rate vulnerability because they were afraid that it might jeopardize the deal flow required to cover their expensive overhead at a time when Wall Street's domestic business was in recession." (Hale 1995).

Figure 2.11 Real exchange rate index: Asian wholesale prices relative to those of the United States (1990 = 100).

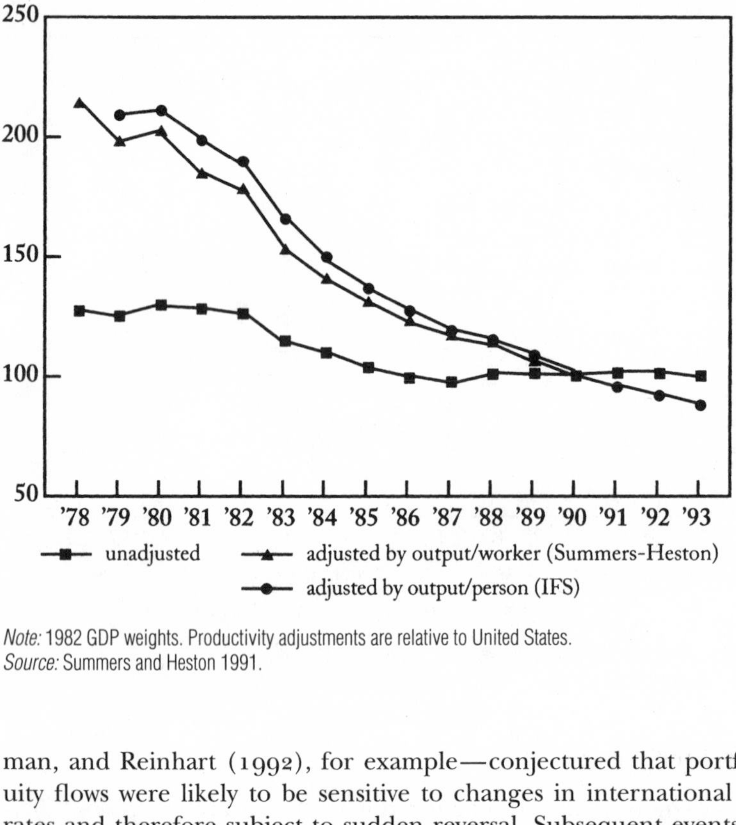

Note: 1982 GDP weights. Productivity adjustments are relative to United States.
Source: Summers and Heston 1991.

man, and Reinhart (1992), for example—conjectured that portfolio eq-uity flows were likely to be sensitive to changes in international interest rates and therefore subject to sudden reversal. Subsequent events proved them correct.

Capital inflows to Latin America matched and then exceeded those reached during the peak of bank lending (1978–1981), with $24 billion in 1990, $40 billion in 1991, $64 billion in 1992, $69 billion in 1993, and $42 billion in 1994. The flow was more modest relative to GDP or exports, reflecting the growth of the recipient economies in the interim; whereas the balance on capital account reached 7.4 percent of GDP in 1981, it was "only" 3.8 percent in 1991 (Calvo, Leiderman, and Reinhart 1992, table 1). Mexico and Bolivia were the only Latin American countries for which inflows as a share of GDP substantially exceeded the levels reached ten years before, in the first case reflecting the enthusiastic reception accorded the North American Free Trade Agreement (NAFTA), in the second reflecting the difficulties in which the Bolivian economy had been mired a decade earlier. Flows to Asia similarly exceeded the levels reached the previous decade, absolutely if not as a share of GDP.

What is less widely appreciated is the continued importance of trade credits, bonds, and DFI in the 1990s. As late as 1991, flows of DFI into Asia and Latin America were four times as large as portfolio equity. In 1992 the ratio fell, but only to three times as large. DFI was associated with deregulation and privatization in a way that had no parallel in the 1920s or the 1970s.[19] There was an important contrast between Asia and Latin America, with the latter relying less heavily on DFI and more on foreign investment in equity and bonds.

In the 1990s, as in the 1920s and 1970s, foreign lending was encouraged by declining interest rates in the center.[20] Falling rates in the United States encouraged a search for yield by mutual fund portfolio managers attracted to emerging markets. They enhanced the creditworthiness of developing countries already saddled with a burden of floating-rate debt. Chuhan, Claessens, and Mamigni (1993) conclude that external factors explain about half of the variation in bond and equity flows from the United States to six Latin American countries, and somewhat less of the variation for Asia. The lower share for Asia may reflect the greater weight of DFI insensitive to interest rates in the region's capital inflows; in addition, Latin American countries had a higher share of variable-rate debt (57 percent in 1993, according to IMF estimates), which heightened the region's sensitivity to global interest rates. Calvo, Leiderman, and Reinhart (1993) reach an analogous conclusion. Fernandez-Arias (1994) similarly finds that lower international interest rates explain the largest share of the variation in recent capital inflows to developing countries. The exceptions are Mexico, where an improving investment climate played the dominant role, and Argentina, where improving country creditworthiness was key. Countries such as Peru experienced increased capital inflows as early as 1990, when they were still experiencing severe financial difficulties, consistent with this view of the strong influence of external effects.

This surge of lending was curtailed in the second half of 1994. The research mentioned earlier suggests that the series of interest rate increases undertaken by the U.S. Federal Reserve played an important role. The parallel with 1928–1929 and 1981–1982 is unmistakable.

In addition, 1994 was marked by a series of unsettling events in Mexico, the single largest importer of capital. The size of Mexico's current account deficit, the failure of investment to keep pace with capital inflows, and the

---

19. The recent wave of DFI is also distinctive for the extent to which it is concentrated in sectors newly exposed to international competition, in contrast with the situation in the 1920s when it was concentrated mainly in extractive industries, and in the 1970s when it was used to jump tariff walls (Stevens 1994).

20. In this context, foreign lending should be understood to include the repatriation of flight capital. that is, the foreign assets of domestic investors.

high real exchange rate already had some observers worried.[21] (For statistics see table 2.2.) Then came a peasant revolt in the southern state of Chiapas and the assassination of Partido Revolucionario Institucional (PRI) presidential candidate Luis Donaldo Colosio in March. Superimposed on rising U.S. interest rates, Mexico was suddenly a less attractive place in which to invest.

A decline in capital inflows from 8 percent of GDP to zero would have required a difficult adjustment under the best circumstances. However, 1994 was an election year, so Mexican officials preferred to delay. They used their international reserves to prevent the peso from depreciating more rapidly than permitted by the country's crawling band; one-third of the total was used to fend off the attack on the peso that followed Colosio's assassination. The Bank of Mexico allowed an expansion of domestic credit at an annual rate of about 20 percent to sustain consumption and support a weak banking system. Off-budget spending by the government's development bank further primed the pump.

When Ernesto Zedillo was inaugurated as president on December 1, 1994, he found the cupboard bare. Some days before, an apparent agreement by the Salinas government to devalue the peso was vetoed by departing Finance Minister Pedro Aspe. What made the situation worse was Mexican speculation in anticipation of a devaluation; IMF numbers indicate some $4.6 billion of capital outflow by nationals just prior to the devaluation in mid-December. The Bank of Mexico again intervened but withdrew from the market when reserves fell to $6 billion. On December 20 it widened the peso's trading range, effectively devaluing the currency by 15 percent, which only incited further outflows. The next day the peso was allowed to float and sank like a stone, soon falling below seven pesos to the dollar. Meanwhile the Mexican stock market tumbled.

Notwithstanding reference to "the tequila effect," this crisis was largely limited to one country. Difficulties there may have been in Argentina and Brazil, but neither country suffered a Mexico-style crisis. Other Latin American countries, such as Chile and Colombia, were little affected by the Mexican affair. Thailand and Hong Kong, which had done the least to limit capital inflows in the preceding period, experienced some difficulty when portfolio investment reversed direction, but although both raised interest rates, neither was forced into a major policy reorientation.

However hard it may be to deny that contagion exists in financial markets[22] and that the Mexican affair negatively affected the willingness of

---

21. See, for example, Dornbusch and Werner 1994. Mexican investment as a share of GDP did rise modestly from 1989 to 1991 but not subsequently. The real effective exchange rate, calculated as the Mexican consumer price index divided by a trade-weighted average of trading partner CPIs multiplied by their respective dollar currency prices, rose by some 25 percent between 1991 and 1994.

22. As documented by Barry Eichengreen, Charles Wyplosz, and Andrew Rose (1996).

Table 2.2

Mexico: economic indicators, 1989–1993

	Average of four years before start of inflows	1989	1990	1991	1992	1993	Average 1989/93
Balance on the capital account							
Billions of U.S. dollars	−1.0	3.6	6.7	20.6	24.7	23.6	15.8
As a percent of GDP	−0.4	1.7	2.7	7.3	7.6	6.6	5.2
Current account							
As a percent of GDP	−0.7	−2.9	−3.2	−4.7	−7.1	−6.3	−4.8
International reserves							
Change, billions of U.S. dollars	−0.5	0.7	3.3	7.6	1.4	6.2	3.8
Savings and investment (as a percent of GDP)							
Change in investment	0.2	0.5	1.5	2.6	−0.7	0.7	0.9
Change in saving	−0.7	0.4	0.0	−2.0	−1.6	1.3	−0.4
Other macroeconomic indicators (percent changes)							
Real GDP	−0.2	3.3	4.4	3.6	2.6	0.4	2.9
Private consumption	1.0	7.3	6.0	3.8	4.9	−2.7	3.9
Inflation	97.5	20.0	26.7	22.7	15.5	9.8	18.9
Money	80.4	30.6	47.9	91.6	70.2	18.1	51.7
Real exchange rate	5.6	−0.3	−5.3	−9.8	−8.0	−5.8	−5.8
Stock prices in U.S. dollars	45.3	67.8	24.9	102.4	20.0	46.9	52.4

Source: Calvo, Leiderman, and Reinhart 1993.

investors to lend to other industrializing economies, in contrast to the 1930s and 1980s the Mexican crisis was more limited geographically and in extent (Calvo and Reinhart 1995). One reason is that U.S. interest rates were trending down, reflecting some slowing of growth in the United States. This enhanced the credit worthiness of indebted countries and again encouraged the search for yield by U.S. portfolio managers. But a more fundamental reason is the extent of policy reform in the developing world. In contrast to the early 1980s, government budgets are in balance. Savings rates are respectable, although admittedly more so in some places than in others. In countries that suffered high inflation during the previous decade, a new anti-inflation consensus emerged. Policy credibility may be far from perfect, but it is much improved relative to the inheritance of the 1980s, providing some insulation from destabilizing shocks.

This new policy stance has had significant macroeconomic benefits. In Chile and Colombia, to take two examples, the real exchange rate has been kept stable out of concern for export competitiveness. Throughout Latin America, import controls have been removed. Deregulation and privatization have increased the responsiveness of exports. This flexibility allows economies to cope more easily with shocks, as even Mexico illustrates through the massive correction of its current account deficit and unprecedented expansion of exports.

Hence, the Mexican crisis could be perceived as the consequence of an unfortunate conjuncture of economic and political circumstances unique to Mexico rather than a reflection of inconsistent policies in emerging markets generally. Mexico's singular dependence on capital imports reflected its proximity to the United States and the successful conclusion of NAFTA negotiations. Its rapid monetary expansion in the six months leading up to the crisis was a result of electoral politics. Its low savings rate reflected the recent liberalization of consumer goods imports and encouragement of domestic demand. Its reluctance to adjust the exchange rate in the period preceding the election, as had been done prior to every previous presidential inauguration since 1976, reflected the policy's special sensitivity in light of NAFTA, as well as the retiring president's candidacy to head the newly founded World Trade Organization.

Notwithstanding the fact that the incoming Zedillo administration inherited significant handicaps, criticizing its attempts to manage the crisis became popular sport. Among its shortcomings was a failure to recognize how the situation had been transformed by the advent of equity finance. Arguably, equity investors are more sensitive to expectations than are bondholders and banks. Portfolio equity flows, even more than other investments, are driven by expected capital gains, encouraging investors to herd in and out of markets. This makes mutual fund investors highly sensitive to changes in international interest rates, something the Mexican authorities failed to assimilate. It also means that the groundwork for policy changes such as devaluation has to be laid carefully to avoid surprising investors in a way that leads them to conclude that everything gold has turned to dross.[23] Failure to do this accounts for the market's negative reaction to Mexico's devaluation.[24] The Zedillo administration then confounded the problem by attempting to treat Mexico's new creditors like the creditors of the 1980s. It assumed a continuing business relationship, as Mexico once had with the banks, where one did not exist.

For all these reasons, the crisis when it came was severe. Whether it justified the exceptional support extended by the Clinton administration and the IMF is too large a question to answer here. The arguments against Mexican rescue are two. One is that the United States has little economic interest in Mexico (Schwartz 1995). Mexico in 1994 took only 10 percent of U.S. merchandise exports, amounting to less than 1 percent of U.S. GDP. It is hard to argue that U.S. prosperity, either generally or specifically, hinges on the Mexican market. To the extent that illegal immigration will be promoted by economic difficulties south of the border, increased border surveillance, it is said, is a more direct and efficient method for dealing with the problem than a $50 billion bailout.

This view defines U.S. interest in Mexico narrowly. It ignores the political reaction in Mexico to paramilitary operations along the border, minimizes the potential for growth in U.S.-Mexican trade and investment, and attaches no value to bilateral cooperation in the Caribbean and Central

---

23. Hale (1995) describes the contrast as follows:

The . . . vulnerability which the peso crisis has exposed is the greatly increased sensitivity of securitized capital flows to adverse news events compared to commercial bank lending and foreign direct investment, the primary sources of private capital for developing countries before the 1990s. Managers of mutual funds and pension funds have different attitudes toward currency devaluations than commercial banks or multinational companies. Commercial banks with dollar loans do not object to currency depreciation in developing countries with large trade deficits because they can improve the credit rating of the country by boosting exports at the expense of domestic consumption. Multinational corporations also can benefit from a currency devaluation if they are using the country as an export base. The portfolio managers of mutual funds and pension funds operate under different constraints. Although they understand that currency devaluations are sometimes a necessary component of an economic restructuring program, they do not like unpredictable exchange rate holdings in cases where they are large holders of debt and where the equity market is dominated by companies oriented toward domestic consumption.

24. Here the contrast with Brazil is striking. Brazil introduced more flexibility into its exchange rate early in 1995 but phased in the new regime, first shifting the existing band and then widening it. While the markets' reception of the new Brazilian policy was not entirely positive (the real plunged to its new floor the day after the band was shifted), the reaction soon stabilized. One reason was the much greater reserve level when Brazilian policy altered.

America. It ignores the fact that a full-scale meltdown could have led to the perceived failure of the U.S.-promoted model of liberalization and privatization, with negative repercussions throughout the developing world.

The second argument against intervention is moral hazard. The analogy with deposit insurance is direct, because the U.S. bailout can be interpreted as an extension of insurance from the U.S. Treasury to depositors in Mexican banks (Hoskins 1995). Aid like that provided by the United States, if extended with regularity, can encourage risk taking by the recipient government. That Mexico has had a financial crisis in every election year since 1976 and received assistance from the U.S. Treasury or the Federal Reserve Board since 1982 ($1.8 billion in 1982, $3.5 billion in 1988, and $20 billion in 1994) can be taken as evidence of this danger. The caveat is that attaching stringent policy conditionality to the loan may mitigate this danger.

The arguments in favor of the bailout are also two. One is contagion: default by Mexico could have spread to other countries, setting back reform and liberalization in Argentina, Brazil, Thailand, and other semiindustrialized nations. The counterargument is that widespread policy reform in Latin America and elsewhere in the developing world would have caused investors to pause before generalizing Mexico's problems. The second justification for the bailout is predicated on the existence of multiple equilibriums. In this view, the markets' overreaction to the Mexican devaluation unnecessarily aggravated the crisis. Timely intervention prevented the markets from shifting the country from the good to the bad equilibrium. Sachs (1994) compares flight from the peso and from Mexican debt to a self-fulfilling bank run. Mexico had nearly $30 billion of *tesobonos* (dollar-denominated public debts that began to be issued in 1994) due in 1995. Although the *tesobono* stock totaled only some 10 percent of 1994 GDP, it was large relative to the Bank of Mexico's reserves and hence vulnerable to a self-fulfilling run.[25] As long as investors renewed their maturing *tesobono* subscriptions, nothing prevented the government from servicing them indefinitely. But each potential creditor realized that if other creditors refused to roll over their *tesobonos,* Mexico could be forced to default even if its low debt:GDP ratio implied long-term solvency. The December 20 devaluation provided a focal point for investors to coordinate such action.[26] Their failure to roll over maturing *tesobonos* pushed the Mexican authorities to the brink of default. It forced them to raise interest rates to extraordinary heights and caused the exchange rate to plummet to the point where

25. Models of self-fulfilling debt runs include those by Calvo (1988); Alesina, Prati, and Tabellini (1990); and Giavazzi and Pagano (1990).

26. The work of Rogers (1992a, 1992b) is consistent with this hypothesis. It shows that a plausible proxy for default risk (the ratio of dollar- to peso-denominated bank deposits) increases with the peso's expected rate of depreciation.

public support for economic reform was jeopardized. Lender-of-last-resort intervention by the United States can be justified on the same grounds as central bank support for an illiquid but solvent bank.[27]

This position is given even greater weight by Mexico's early return to the capital market in July of 1996; an initial $500 million issue was doubled as a consequence of great investor interest in two-year floating-rate notes. To be sure, a substantial 5 percent premium over the London Interbank offered rate also played a role, but Mexico's sharp domestic adjustment program—made possible by the rescue—was equally important.

Cognizant of Sir Walter Raleigh's caution that historians following too close on the heels of events risk being kicked in the teeth, we are reluctant to say too much about the East Asian crisis of 1997. An early reading does suggest, however, that it is consistent with many of our generalizations regarding the era of equity finance. Equity investment played a prominent role in Thailand in the run-up to the crisis; it responded to East Asia's track record of fast economic growth, to the search for yield by U.S. and European portfolio managers cognizant of high valuations on developed country equity markets, and to the ongoing internationalization of portfolios by American households, insurance companies, and pension funds. Thailand, like Mexico, sought to sterilize these inflows, but with incomplete success. In Thailand as in Mexico a weak government delayed the imposition of painful adjustment measures, hoping against hope that the need for them would go away. Reflecting the importance of equity investment, Thailand, like Mexico, then responded to investors' loss of confidence by radically raising interest rates and to the collapse of domestic demand by boosting exports.

Thailand's crisis, like Mexico's, was limited in geographic scope. While there was contagion within Asia, the crisis had only limited repercussions elsewhere, such as in Brazil and a few eastern European countries with Thai-style current account deficits. As in 1995, this reflected the benign interest rate environment and the fact that the crisis took place against the backdrop of global, buoyant economic growth, and investment-friendly policies in a broad range of countries. As in 1995, the initial thought was that the rescue should be spearheaded by the country with the largest economy in the region, in this case Japan, although Tokyo deferred to the IMF when it came time to negotiate conditionality. (We return to this point later.) The crisis gave rise to discussions about the establishment of an Asian stabilization fund to facilitate regional responses to regional problems.

27. However compelling this story, it is also possible to argue that the negative reaction of investors reflected the disarray in Mexican policy and fears that trade union and business support was absent. Although the idea of multiple equilibriums is suggestive, it requires further substantiation.

Admittedly, Thailand's crisis also differed from Mexico's.[28] Thailand had a high private savings rate, Mexico a low one. Thailand had been growing rapidly in the period leading up to the crisis, whereas Mexico had hardly been growing at all. The problem in Mexico centered on the government's reliance on short-term, foreign-currency-indexed debt. In Thailand the crux of the problem was the weakness of the banking system, which created uncertainties for foreign investors (who saw banking problems as putting a damper on the real estate and stock markets and worried whether they would be able to retrieve their money from insolvent financial institutions), for the government (for which bank insolvencies implied fiscal liabilities), and for the economy (for which bank insolvencies meant disintermediation, asset-price deflation, and slower growth). To be sure, Thailand had external debt, and Mexico had insolvent banks, but the relative importance of the two problems was quite different.

Notwithstanding these differences, there are also impressive parallels. In neither case were the traditional causes of balance-of-payments crises, namely excessively expansive monetary and fiscal policies, at the root of the problem. Mexico's budget was broadly balanced; most estimates put the country's consolidated budget deficit for 1994 at no more than 2 percent of GDP. Although the central bank was reluctant to raise interest rates in response to reserve losses in the last three quarters of 1994, inflation and monetary growth were moderate by Mexican standards. There was no significant acceleration in either, relative to the preceding years of financial stability. In particular, the growth of the M1 money supply slowed from 18 percent in 1993 to 6 percent in 1994. And even those who insist that excessive growth in domestic credit was part of the problem would admit that it was only a part.

In Thailand, the government budget was in surplus in the period leading up to the crisis. Thai inflation exceeded inflation in the countries to which the currency was pegged, leading to some real appreciation, but this inflation differential was slight. In the five years ending with 1996, inflation never once reached 6 percent on an annual average basis. Consistent with this, the monetary aggregates rose at the rate of 15 percent per year, not obviously excessive for an economy growing at 9 per cent. Problems of competitiveness resulted from the heavy weight of the U.S. dollar in the Thai authorities' basket peg and the appreciation of the dollar relative to the yen and the European currencies in 1996–1997. But the point is that the domestic economic policy variables to which the IMF customarily directs its attention, namely money growth and the budget deficits, were at best subsidiary concerns in Thailand as they were in Mexico two and one-half years before.

28. Our discussion of Thailand relies on Eichengreen and Portes 1998.

The most striking parallel between the two cases was the current account, which was in deficit to a level of 8 percent of GDP. In both cases this reflected an excess of private investment over private savings (in turn reflecting the fact that the government budget was close to balance), and reliance on foreign financing to fill the gap. Together, these two experiences clearly confirm that current account deficits are not a problem when they reflect private-sector decisions rather than public-sector behavior. They force one to ask why the markets did not draw back sooner and more smoothly before events got out of hand.

Rather than hanging one's argument on investor myopia, one can point to two factors common to Mexico and Thailand that encouraged persistent large-scale capital inflows: the exchange rate peg and the belief that banks could not be allowed to fail. These two implicit commitments provided investors an irresistible incentive to indulge in the relatively high interest rates offered by Thai financial institutions.

A final parallel between the Mexico and Thailand situations is that both cast doubt on the notion that crises necessarily erupt in response to wholly unanticipated events (because if the events that precipitated them had been anticipated, the crises would have broken out earlier). To be sure, in both cases the unexpected occurred: in Mexico the Colosio assassination, in Thailand various political battles within the government and between the government and the opposition. But in neither instance were investors wholly unaware of mounting problems. In the case of Mexico they had been warned by expert commentators many months before the crisis. The curtailment of capital inflows fully six months before the crisis, and the Bank of Mexico's consequent need to support the exchange rate through the expenditure of reserves are evidence that not everyone naively believed that all was copacetic. In the case of Thailand, the baht experienced three episodes of speculative pressure in the second half of 1996 and in January–February 1997, and short-term capital inflows fell off over the course of 1996. Total capital imports declined from $22 billion in 1995 to $17 billion in 1996. Moody's downgraded Thailand's short-term debt rating in September. In both cases, then, there was plenty of unease six months to a year before the eruption of the full-fledged crisis. But opinion was divided, and as long as that remained so, the government could hold out.

The other striking fact about Thailand is that the authorities pursued most of the policies recommended by expert commentators for a government confronted with large-scale capital flows. Thailand tightened monetary policy. It maintained a tight fiscal policy; the 1996–1997 budget targeted a surplus of 0.5 percent of GDP, and in February the Cabinet proposed further cuts in government outlays of 0.8 percent of GDP and in public enterprise expenditures (on infrastructure) of 1.2 percent of GDP. To limit the impact of capital inflows on domestic liquidity, it auctioned

Bank of Thailand bonds. It raised reserve requirements on nonresident baht accounts and on short-term foreign borrowing by the banks. It imposed constraints on the banks' credit:deposit ratios. Loans denominated in foreign currencies made to sectors that did not produce foreign exchange were defined as no longer acceptable as eligible bank assets.

Thailand's experience reveals the difficulty that countries with small economies have when attempting to shape policy to manage large capital inflows. Tightening monetary and fiscal policy was painful in a period when economic growth was decelerating. For a variety of well-known political reasons, large expenditure reductions are difficult to effect in short periods. Whereas higher interest rates may damp down domestic demand and inflation, they will only attract additional foreign funds. Sterilization operations increase the budgetary burden on the government, which acquires low-yielding foreign assets in return for issuing higher-yielding domestic debt. Raising reserve requirements on the banks increases bank costs. For all these reasons, it may not have been feasible for Thailand to call for further adjustment.

In addition, of course, Thailand made two critical mistakes. First, it clung to a policy of pegging its exchange rate within a narrow band. Pegging encouraged capital inflows because foreign investors were not deterred by exchange risk. Thailand, like Mexico, revealed the well-known tendency for government officials, once committed to a currency peg, to regard devaluation as an admission of failure and to cling to the peg for too long.

The second problem lay in the management of the financial system. Until the autumn of 1996, offshore banks (Bangkok International Banking Facilities) were allowed to borrow funds abroad and on-lend them to Thai residents without limit. The government allowed the banks to maintain lax disclosure requirements and asset classification procedures (permitting them to disguise the actual extent of their property loans). In contrast to the policies in advanced industrial economies, Thai banks were not obliged to disclose their nonperforming loans, which encouraged management to delay in provisioning for loan losses. The government allowed the banks to purchase finance companies, which are less regulated and more sensitive to interest rate changes.

As if this was not enough, the banking crisis interacted with the flaws in exchange rate management. Massive capital inflows encouraged by the apparent absence of exchange risk were one factor leading to the deterioration in asset quality. Banks flush with funds scrambled to place them. The volume of loanable funds outstripped the capacity of competent loan officers to administer them.

And when capital markets finally turned around, devaluation threatened to provoke the meltdown of the banking system. Thai banks, mistakenly thinking that the exchange rate was locked, had failed to hedge their foreign currency exposure. Thai borrowers, mistakenly thinking the same, had failed to hedge their loans denominated in foreign currencies. Hence, devaluation threatened to push first borrowers and then lenders into insolvency. As the government came under pressure to aid distressed banks and firms, currency traders, who anticipated domestic credit creation, again push the baht down. This further increased distress among unhedged banks and firms, auguring more political pressure, more credit creation, and more currency depreciation, again worsening the condition of the banks. This positive feedback threatened to generate multiple equilibriums like those described in our earlier discussion of Mexico. The international rescue package was intended to prevent a complete meltdown of Thailand's banking system and a complete collapse of its currency. It was designed to prevent Thailand from shifting to an even worse equilibrium in which the costs of adjustment were greater than necessary.

Policy Implications

It is too early to distill definitive policy implications from the events of the last three years. But we hazard some provisional thoughts about options for managing international capital flows in the future.

It is clear from recent events that international capital markets can turn on a dime. Capital flows can scale high levels relative to the GDPs and domestic financial markets of developing countries and can reverse direction abruptly. They are sensitive to global economic conditions and industrial-country interest rates. Events in individual countries can disrupt the flow of external finance to other borrowers. For all these reasons, developing countries are vulnerable to capital-account shocks not of their own making—more than ever, given the increasing importance of interest rate and expectation-sensitive portfolio equity flows.[29] And adjustment to those shocks can be painful on both political and economic grounds.

What policy response should this recognition prompt? Mexico attempted to obtain assistance bilaterally, appealing to the United States, whereas Thailand's initial approach was to Japan, not to the IMF. One important lesson of these episodes is that bilateral solutions are not feasible. Politicians in countries such as the United States and Japan do not savor the responsibility of having to administer the conditionality attached to bilateral loans. IMF conditionality can become politicized, but the conditions attached to bilateral loans are inevitably more political still. (Recall the Mexican reaction to suggestions from north of the border that Pemex

29. This is evident once again in the wake of the Mexican crisis, which has been marketed by a surprisingly rapid resumption of lending to emerging markets. No explanation for this pattern would be adequate without reference to the decline in U.S. interest rates associated with decelerating economic growth.

revenues be used to back intergovernmental debts. Similarly, imagine the reaction in Thailand had the Japanese attempted to dictate the Thai government's economic strategy, given the intensity with which memories of Tokyo's World War II policies are held.) In addition, while markets move swiftly, politicians do not, especially when the question is aid to foreigners. The Clinton administration may have been able to move relatively swiftly in 1995, but only by taking exceptional measures. Its recourse to the Exchange Stabilization Fund antagonized the Congress and such action will not be as easy in the future. And the United States is unlikely to evince the same willingness to shoulder the risks of a fire-brigade operation for a country more distant from its own borders. Clearly, an alternative to bilateralism is needed.

Some would rely on more timely publication of economic statistics as a way of strengthening market discipline. If the markets are better able to identify countries whose positions are approaching unsustainability, rising interest rates and declining capital flows will force governments to act more quickly. Because information is a public good, however, incentives to provide it may be inadequate . This has led the IMF to establish a Special Data Dissemination Standard to be met by countries actually or prospectively borrowing on international capital markets, for posting up-to-date economic and financial statistics on the Internet, and to put pressure on its members to meet it. There is an analogy with financial disclosure requirements for domestic firms floating securities, as well as a Securities and Exchange Commission with the power to open firms' books and verify that the information disclosed is accurate.

Even with IMF guidance, however, it is not clear that the markets will react by smoothly raising the price and restricting the availability of credit to the debtor. Historical experience suggests that the markets, when they react, tend to overreact, with periods of complacency suddenly giving way to an overwhelming sense of crisis. This means that crises will occur, and that IMF-led assistance will be needed to prevent devaluation or the high interest rates needed to defend the currency from producing a complete financial and economic meltdown. Some recommend in addition that the IMF "blow the whistle" on countries whose policies heighten the risk of a crisis, publicly if necessary. It can be argued that the IMF, by virtue of the leverage associated with its lending capacity, is well positioned to play this role. Of course, there are reasons to question whether the IMF is in a better position than the markets to recognize signs of impending danger. Traders, after all, have considerable profits at stake.[30] In addition, the IMF rightly worries that a public warning that causes the markets to draw back may ag-

---

30. At the same time, the virtual unanimity that more and better information is necessary enables portfolio fund managers to find an excuse for their poor predictions. Once there is

gravate economic problems in the borrowing country and jeopardize any IMF Structural Adjustment Program in place. In other words, a mandate for the IMF to issue early warning signals may not be incentive compatible. These concerns were much in the minds of IMF management when the institution warned Thailand—more than once—of the risks it was running in the year leading up to July 1997. It did not go public with those warnings and was the subject of severe criticism in some circles for having taken that approach.

Sudden, even violent, reversals of capital movements may, for all these reasons, be endemic to the markets. Governments can buy insurance against them by tightening fiscal policy, which will damp down private-sector demand and, by lowering interest rates, discourage capital inflows (the opposite of the effect of sterilized intervention). The urgency of public pension reform in countries experiencing large capital inflows is often cited in this connection. In practice, however, pension reform is contentious and protracted. More generally, it is hard to fine-tune fiscal policy with the precision needed to manage sudden swings in capital flows.[31]

The other way for countries to insure themselves against the domestic costs of a sudden capital outflow is to use taxes and taxlike devices to regulate inflows.[32] Restrictions or taxes, for example, can be placed on the ability of banks to borrow offshore. This method can be thought of as an open-economy variant of the standard types of prudential regulation to which all national banking systems are subject.

The fact that governments are the lenders of last resort in the event of banking crises leads them to adopt measures designed to limit the exposure of banks to various kinds of risks that could bring down the country's financial system. In developing economies open to international financial markets, a leading source of such risk is offshore borrowing by banks, particularly borrowing in foreign currency. This link was evident recently in both Mexico and Argentina, where the weakness of the banking system and its vulnerability to a sudden reversal in the direction of capital flows fed on one another. In Malaysia, for example, limits on non-trade-related swap transactions were imposed on commercial banks in 1992. The central bank discouraged inflows in early 1994 by limiting banks' holdings of foreign funds, raising the cost of holding foreign deposits, imposing ceilings on the net external liabilities of domestic banks, and prohibiting the

---

fuller information, the next crisis will fail to be foreseen for other, also initially profitable, reasons. So fuller knowledge alone will not suffice to avoid future difficulties.

31. Even countries such as Thailand and Mexico, which were able to engineer sharp fiscal corrections, did not succeed in heading off large capital inflows and preventing the emergence of substantial current account deficits.

32. It is also possible to discourage inflows by taxing or controlling outflows, because foreign investors will be discouraged by impediments to repatriating their funds.

sale of short-term financial instruments to foreigners.[33] As a result, the inflow of portfolio capital was dampened.

In November 1994 India sought to curb capital inflows by ordering firms that were raising funds on international capital markets to keep the money abroad until it was needed for specific projects, and by banning firms' use of warrants (which give investors the right to buy shares at a fixed price at a future date). The Mexican crisis had little effect on any of these countries, in contrast with the temporary reaction in neighboring Thailand, which did not limit capital inflows in this way (Glick and Moreno 1995).

In Latin America, Chile restricted capital inflows starting in 1991. The Chileans required firms borrowing foreign currency to deposit a 20 percent reserve in a non-interest-bearing account with the central bank for a period of one year. In 1992 the reserve requirement was raised to 30 percent. Colombia imposed a similar requirement, at a rate of 47 percent, in September 1993. The non-interest-bearing deposit is to be maintained for the duration of the foreign loan and applies to all loans of eighteen months or less, except for trade credit. In August 1994 Colombia, in response to continued capital inflows and complaints by exporters about their loss of competitiveness, extended the deposit requirement to all loans of sixty months or less (again, excepting trade credit) at a cascading rate that fell from 140 percent for funds of thirty days or less to 42.8 percent for five-year funds. In addition, foreigners were prohibited from investing in the Colombian bond market. In October 1994, in response to the real appreciation caused by the combination of a fixed nominal peg and large capital inflows, Brazil imposed a 1 percent tax on foreign investment in the stock market and raised the tax on Brazilian companies issuing bonds overseas from 3 to 7 percent. Having eased this requirement in the wake of the Mexican crisis, Brazil acted again in August 1995 to check a rapid accumulation of reserves.[34]

It is noteworthy that the Mexican crisis had little impact on Chile and Colombia, whose capital inflows disproportionately took the form of DFI, in contrast with Argentina, which had not limited inflows significantly. Foreign investment amounted to one-third of Argentine stock market capitalization prior to the Mexican crisis, but the comparable figure for Colombia was one-twentieth. Admittedly, these countries also differed in other

33. The effectiveness of these measures was arguably enhanced by the announcement that they were temporary (which encouraged foreigners to delay their investments rather than attempt to evade the controls). In fact, some Malaysian controls were relaxed or removed when the volume of international lending fell off in the second half of 1994.

34. The Brazilian tax on equity investments by foreigners, paid at the time of purchase, will therefore fall more heavily on short-term investors and is designed to encourage a buy-and-hold strategy.

respects. Chile's success in raising its domestic savings rate also helped it to limit its dependence on foreign capital; this is in contrast with Mexico and Argentina, where the savings share of GDP fell in the years following the resurgence of lending.[35] But controls on inflows surely helped the first set of countries weather the storm.

The diverse experiences of these countries confirm the feasibility of measures to stem capital inflows. Such policies can moderate inward foreign investment without repulsing investors and causing the country to lose all access to the capital market. Controls on outflows are less obviously expeditious. If investors fear that a large devaluation is coming, they have a strong incentive to get their money out in advance, and even severe controls on outflows may prove much less than watertight. It is better, in this view, to use modest taxes and controls on inflows to limit the magnitude of the adjustment that will have to be undertaken when the flow reverses than to attempt to use even draconian controls on outflows to fight a losing battle once that reversal has begun.[36] The debate over the efficacy of controls has gained new urgency in the wake of the recent East Asian crisis and with the impending amendment to the IMF Articles of Agreement to give the IMF jurisdiction over its members' efforts to establish capital account convertibility. It is a debate to which more thought needs to be given, and quickly.

There is still another way to organize international help, but this comes after the fact. We refer to various schemes that seek to provide a means of permitting international bankruptcy, in analogy to domestic access to this possibility (Eichengreen and Portes 1996; Sachs 1994; Group of Ten 1996; IIF 1996; Macmillan 1995; U.S. General Accounting Office 1997). To the extent that the purpose of bankruptcy procedures is to freeze payments, such an option already exists insofar as countries can invoke it unilaterally; we saw this in the 1980s when several countries suspended debt service payments. But other provisions of bankruptcy proceedings—assigning seniority to new money and implementing a plan to restructure the firm's operations—have no analogue in the sovereign setting. Schemes to create a full-fledged international bankruptcy court therefore encounter very serious obstacles. Such a court would not possess the power to seize collateral, nor would it "replace" the government of a country in the way that bankruptcy courts in the United States can replace the management of a reorganized firm. Moral hazard would therefore be severe. Bankruptcy

---

35. This factor does not similarly complicate efforts to evaluate the effects of controls in Malaysia and Thailand, because the savings share actually rose in Thailand while falling in Malaysia over the four years following the reinitiation of lending.
36. This is in line with the controversial conclusion of the IMF's *International Capital Markets* (1995), "Background Paper V," which suggests that controls on inflows may be more efficacious than those on outflows.

statutes in different countries differ significantly, making it unlikely that governments could agree on the structure of a plan. Modest reform to enhance the orderliness of workouts may be feasible (as proposed by Eichengreen and Portes 1996), but not the development of a full-fledged bankruptcy procedure.

International capital flows have much to recommend them. But in a world of distortions, there is an argument for marginal interventions to limit their magnitude. Investors dislike controls that raise questions about a government's commitment to open markets, as do international institutions, which fear that they will be adopted instead of, rather than in addition to, policy reforms (IMF 1994). These are legitimate fears. But those who laud the benefits of open markets and caution that governments can abuse the privilege of intervening in their operation are under an obligation to offer alternatives. In particular, they should be in the forefront of those calling for an expanded IMF role in crisis management and for new procedures to deal in a more orderly fashion with debt crises when they occur.

References

Alesina, Alberto, Alessandro Prati, and Guido Tabellini. 1990. "Public Confidence and Debt Management: A Model and a Case Study of Italy." In *Public Debt Management: Theory and History,* edited by R. Dornbusch and M. Draghi. Cambridge: Cambridge University Press.

Calvo, Guillermo A. 1988. "Servicing the Public Debt: The Role of Expectations." American Economic Review 78:647–661.

Calvo, Guillermo A., Leonardo Leiderman, and Carmen M. Reinhart. 1992. "Capital Inflows to Latin America: The 1970s and the 1990s." Working Paper, International Monetary Fund, Washington, D.C.

———. 1993. "Capital Inflows and Real Exchange Rate Appreciation in Latin America." IMF Staff Papers, No. 40, pp. 108–151, International Monetary Fund, Washington, D.C.

Calvo, Sara, and Carmen M. Reinhart. 1995. "Capital Inflows to Latin America: Is There Evidence of Contagion Effects?" World Bank and International Monetary Fund Photocopy.

Chuhan, Punam, Stijn Claessens, and Nlandu Mamigni. 1993. "Equity and Bond Flows to Latin America and Asia: The Role of External and Domestic Factors." Policy Research Working Paper, No. 1160. Washington, D.C.: World Bank.

Cline, William R. 1995. *International Debt Reconsidered.* Washington, D.C.: Institute for International Economics.

Corbo, Vittorio, and Leonardo Hernandez. 1994. "Macroeconomic Adjustment to Capital Inflows." Policy Research Working Paper, No. 1377. Washington, D.C.: World Bank.

Dornbusch, Rudiger, and Alejandro Werner. 1994. "Mexico: Stabilization without Growth." *Brookings Papers on Economic Activity* 1:253–313.

ECLA (Economic Commission for Latin America). 1992. "Preliminary Overview of the Latin American and Caribbean Economy, 1993." *Notas sobre la Economia y el Desarrollo,* No. 537/38.

——. 1993. *Estudio Económico, 1991.* Vol. 1. Santiago, Chile: Economic Commission for Latin America.

Eichengreen, Barry, and Richard Portes. 1989. "Dealing with Debt: The 1930s and the 1980s." In *Dealing with the Debt Crisis,* edited by Ishrat Hussain and Ishac Diwan. Washington, D.C.: World Bank.

——. 1996. *Crisis? What Crisis? Orderly Workouts for Sovereign Debtors.* London: Centre for Economic Policy Research.

——. 1998. "Managing Financial Crises in Emerging Markets." In *Maintaining Financial Stability in a Global Economy.* Kansas City, Mo.: Federal Reserve Bank of Kansas City.

Eichengreen, Barry, Charles Wyplosz, and Andrew Rose. 1996. "Contagious Currency Crises: First Tests," *Scandinavian Journal of Economics* 98 (4):463–484.

Fernandez-Arias, Eduardo. 1994. "The New Wave of Private Capital Inflows: Push or Pull?" Policy Research Working Paper, No. 1312. Washington, D.C.: World Bank, 1994.

Fishlow, Albert. 1972. "Origins and Consequences of Import Substitution in Brazil." In *International Trade and Development,* edited by L. de Marco. New York: Academic Press.

——. 1985. "Lessons from the Past: Capital Markets in the 19th Century and the Interwar Period," In *The Politics of International Debt,* edited by M. Kahler. Ithaca, N.Y.: Cornell University Press.

——. 1996. "Some Reflections on Comparative latin American Economic Performance and Policy." In *Economic Liberalization: No Panacea,* edited by Tariq Banuri. Oxford: Oxford University Press.

Giavazzi, Francesco, and Marco Pagano. 1990. "Confidence Crises and Public Debt Management." In , edited by Rudiger Dornbusch and Mario Draghi, eds. Cambridge: Cambridge University Press.

Glick, Reuven, and Ramon Moreno. 1995. "Responses to Capital Inflows in Malaysia and Thailand." *Weekly Letter, Federal Reserve Bank of San Francisco* 95 (14):1–3.

Grilli, Enzo R., and Maw Cheng Yang. 1988. Primary Commodity Prices, Manufactured Goods Prices, and the Terms of Trade of Developing Countries: What the Long Run Shows." *World Bank Economic Review* 2:1–47.

Group of Ten. 1996. "The Resolution of Sovereign Liquidity Crises," abridged version. Reprinted in *From Halifax to Lyons: What Has Been Done about Crisis Management?* Essays in International Finance, No. 200, edited by Peter Kenen. Princeton, N. J.: International Finance Section, Department of Economics, Princeton University.

Hale, David. 1995. "Emerging Markets After the Mexican Crisis." Kemper Financial Services, Inc., Chicago. Photocopy

Hoskins, Lee. 1995. "Mexico: Policy Failure, Moral Hazard and Market Solutions." In *Shadow Open Market Committee, Policy Statement and Position Papers, March 5–6. Public Policy Studies Working Paper Series*. Rochester, N.Y.: William E. Simon Graduate School, University of Rochester.

Hussain, Ishrat, and Ishac Diwan, eds. 1989. *Dealing with the Debt Crisis.* Washington, D.C.: World Bank.

IDB (Interamerican Development Bank), *Annual Report.* Various years. Washington, D.C.: Interamerican Development Bank.

IIF (Institute of International Finance), 1996. *Resolving Sovereign Financial Crises*. Washington, D.C.: Institute of International Finance.

IMF (International Monetary Fund). 1994. *World Economic Outlook*. Washington, D.C.: International Monetary Fund.

——. 1995. *World Economic Outlook*. Washington, D.C.: International Monetary Fund.

——. *International Capital Markets*. Various years. Washington, D.C.: International Monetary Fund.

——. *International Financial Statistics*. Various years. Washington, D.C.: International Monetary Fund.

——. *International Monetary Statistics*. Various years. Washington, D.C.: International Monetary Fund.

Kahler, Miles, ed. 1985. *The Politics of International Debt*. Ithaca, N.Y.: Cornell University Press.

——. 1988. "From Crisis to Problem: Latin American Debt, 1982–87." In *Coping with the Latin American Debt*, edited by R. Wesson. New York: Praeger Publications.

Kenen, Peter B. 1993. "Reforming the International Monetary System: An Agenda for Developing Countries." In *The Pursuit of Reform*, edited by J. J. Teunissen. The Hague: Forum on Debt and Development.

Krosner, R. S., and R. G. Rajan. 1994. "Is the Glass-Steagall Act Justified? A Study of U.S. Experience with Universal Banking before 1933." *American Economic Review* 84:810–832.

Larrain, Felipe B. 1995. "Exchange Rates and Reserve Management with Large Capital Inflows: Latin America in the 1990s." Catholic University of Chile, Santiago, Chile. Photocopy.

Lary, Hal B. 1943. *The United States in the World Economy.* Washington, D.C.: Government Printing Office.

League of Nations. Various years. *Statistical Yearbook*. Geneva: League of Nations.

Macmillan, Rory. 1995. "Towards a Sovereign Debt Work-Out System," *Northwestern Journal of International Law and Business* 16:57–106.

Maddison, Angus. 1985. *Two Crises: Latin America and Asia, 1929–38 and 1973–83*. Paris: Organization for Economic Cooperation and Development.

Megginson, William L., Annette B. Poulsen, and Joseph F. Sinkey Jr. 1995. "Syndicated Loan Announcements and the Market Value of the Banking Firm." *Journal of Money, Credit, and Banking* 27:465–485.

Mintz, Ilse. 1951. *Deterioration in the Quality of Foreign Bond Issues in the United States, 1920–1930*. New York: National Bureau of Economic Research.

Mitchell, Brian R. 1975. *European Historical Statistics*. London: Macmillan.

———. 1983. *International Historical Statistics: The Americas and Australasia*. London: Macmillan.

———. 1995. *International Historical Statistics: Africa, Asia and Oceania, 1750–1988*. London: Macmillan.

Robinson, Leland Rex. 1926. *Investment Trust Organization and Management*. New York: Ronald Press.

Rogers, John H. 1992a. "The Currency Substitution Hypothesis and Relative Money Demand in Mexico and Canada." *Journal of Money, Credit, and Banking* 24:300–318.

———. 1992b. "Convertibility Risk and Dollarization in Mexico: A Vector Autoregressive Analysis." *Journal of International Money and Finance* 11:188–207.

Royal Institute for International Affairs. 1937. *The Problem of International Investment*. London: Oxford University Press.

Sachs, Jeffrey. 1994. "Do We Need an International Lender of Last Resort?" Harvard University, Cambridge, Mass. Photocopy.

Schwartz, Anna J. 1995. "Trial and Error in Devising the Mexican Rescue Plan." In *Shadow Open Market Committee, Policy Statement and Position Papers, March 5–6. Public Policy Studies Working Paper Series*. Rochester, N.Y.: William E. Simon Graduate School, University of Rochester.

Speaker, Lawrence M. 1924. *The Investment Trust*. Chicago: A. W. Shaw.

Stevens, Guy V. G. 1994. "Politics, Economics, and Investment: Explaining Plant and Equipment Spending by U.S. Direct Investors in Argentina, Brazil, and Mexico." International Finance Discussion Paper No. 490, International Finance Division, Board of Governors, Federal Reserve System, Washington, D.C.

Stoddard, Lothrop. 1932. *Europe and Our Money*. New York: Macmillan.

Summers, Robert, and Alan Heston. 1991. "The Penn World Tables (Mark 5): An Expanded Set of International Comparisons." *Quarterly Journal of Economics* 106:327–368.

Tesar, Linda L., and Ingrid M. Werner 1995. "U.S. Equity Investment in Emerging Stock Markets." *World Bank Economic Review* 9:109–129.

United Nations 1948a. *Public Debt.* Lake Success, N.Y.: United Nations.

——. 1948b. *Statistical Yearbook.* Lake Success, N.Y.: United Nations.

——. 1953. *Public Debt.* Lake Success, N.Y.: United Nations.

U.S. General Accounting Office, 1997. *International Financial Crises: Efforts to Anticipate, Avoid and Resolve Sovereign Crises.* Report to the Chairman, Committee on Banking and Financial Services, House of Representatives, 105th Congress. Washington, D.C.: Government Printing Office.

World Financial Markets. 1984. October–November.

3

Effects of International Portfolio Flows on Government Policy Choice

Sylvia Maxfield

"We have to learn about these capital flows and how they might actually matter to governments and national interests."

—John Woolley (1994)

Through modern history, capital flows from capital-rich to relatively capital-scarce countries has taken many forms. The experience of commercial bank lending beginning in the late 1960s and ending with the wave of near defaults that ensued in 1982 dominates recent memory. Since the late 1980s there has been a large increase in securitized lending to and in developing countries. This means investors in Organization for European Cooperation and Development (OECD) countries are purchasing stocks and bonds issued by governments, agencies, or corporations in countries as far-flung as Ghana, Peru, and Kazakhstan. Net capital flows to developing-country equity markets rose from $1.3 billion in 1989 to $52 billion in 1993 (Hale 1994, 21).

The contributors to this book analyze the rise of private international capital flows, focusing on global historical trends, causes and consequences of the contemporary worldwide trend, and specific regional situations. This chapter constitutes a first step in exploring the political consequences of the global rise in private capital flows for emerging market countries. The analysis is concerned specifically with the ways and extent to which economic policy choice may be constrained. Such constraint has indirect consequences for consolidation of democracy, which the following pages do not explicitly address. If the economic policy choices of government leaders in emerging market countries are heavily constrained by the

Kent Eaton provided excellent research assistance. The section "American Depository Receipt Price Determination and Investor Information Use" draws on joint work with Joshua Hoffman. I am grateful for comments on an earlier version from Miles Kahler and participants in the Council on Foreign Relations Study Group on "Emerging Markets."

potential for private capital outflows, prospects for democratic consolidation could be compromised if electoral support and democratic legitimacy depend on the ability to make policy choices that respond to voter demands (Page 1997).

Analyst after analyst is skeptical of the benefit of portfolio investment (stock and bond purchases) as a source of financing for capital-short developing countries. "The market," editorializes the *Columbia Journal of World Business*, "ruthlessly penalizes governments that cannot . . . balance macroeconomic and political priorities" (Erdman and Brandmeyer 1994, 5). Hale (1994, 24) reports analysts' views "that the recent upsurge of capital flows to the developing country stock markets is only a bubble and that investors will ultimately experience as unhappy an outcome as did the U.S. banks who made loans to Latin America during the 1970s." A *New York Times* business reporter warns that even relatively sophisticated markets "experience wild swings as government policies change" (Eaton 1994, 35). "Will these flows," queries the business press, "which can leave countries overnight at the first sign of instability, leave governments that were not able to balance macroeconomic and social reform lost for another decade?" (Erdman and Brandmeyer 1994, 5). Financial guru Felix Rohatyn (1994, 51) predicts that, if confidence is destroyed in emerging markets, "political reform and economic growth in the developing world will be badly hampered." The Canadian business press chastises investors in emerging markets urging, them "to learn to invest responsibly and not to impose unrealistic expectations" (McMurdy 1994, 43).

In short, observers contend that international portfolio investors are impatient; the price of hosting such investment is reduced policy autonomy that can complicate consolidation of democracy. The purpose of this chapter is to evaluate the logic of this claim. Future success in understanding the extent and type of influence that international financiers exercise over economics and politics in emerging market countries requires the disaggregation of international financial asset holders by product and investment objective. Different classes of investors will constrain emerging market governments' policy choices differently. This is because investor motivations vary. Since the rise of private portfolio investment beginning in the late 1980s and until recently, the predominant investors in emerging market stocks and bonds have used mutual funds and so-called hedge funds that borrow (use leverage) to raise the yields from trading stocks, bonds, and currencies. These investors tend to be yield-oriented and respond to short-term changes in yield rather than signals of a fundamental change in the host country's political economy. They have short time horizons because investors in mutual or hedge funds can redeem their funds if any particular money managers' return fails to perform as well as or better than the industry average.

Evidence from existing studies and new tests reported here suggest that in the contemporary private investment boom, capital flows to emerging market countries do not respond to information about changes in host country economic policy or prospects for political stability. Either most investors do not have such information or they base their investment decisions on other factors. This evidence is consistent with the predominance of yield-oriented investors whose decisions are driven by comparing the short-term, risk-free return in OECD countries, usually the United States and emerging market countries. If capital flows and proxies for capital flows do not correspond closely to economic and political news from the borrowing country, we must rethink arguments suggesting that growth in international portfolio flows *directly* restricts the economic policy choices of emerging market government leaders.

Emerging Market Investor Frameworks

The determinants of international portfolio investment in emerging markets or, put differently, the decision frameworks of the investors should inform any hypothesis about the impact of such international capital flows on politics and policy in the "host" countries. Considerable effort has been made to evaluate the extent to which (1) motivations of portfolio investors are short or long term and (2) portfolio investment flows correspond more closely to factors external or internal to recipient countries. Investors with short time horizons are purveyors of "hot," volatile money. Flows more nearly determined by factors external to host countries are "pushed," and those more nearly determined by internal factors are "pulled."

Investors are pushed into emerging markets by low yields or high prices in other markets and assets. Investors can also be pushed by a more or less collective view of an emerging market asset based on rumor or technical factors unrelated to factual events in the country (or countries). A common truism on Wall Street trading floors illustrates this logic: Buy on rumor, sell on fact. In these cases, investment decisions have relatively little relation to factors affecting asset prices and yields from within the country. In contrast, price and yield expectations shaped by events internal to an emerging market country, such as prospects for privatization or exchange rate stability, can pull investors into that country.

As table 3.1 shows, international portfolio investors in emerging markets could be characterized in four ways, depending on their time horizons and the importance of push or pull factors in driving their decisions. The implications for policy autonomy in each case are different. To the extent that push factors predominate in explaining patterns of international port-

Table 3.1 Types of emerging market investors

	Push	Pull
Short term	Yield orientation	Price and value orientation
	Mutual fund managers	Hedge funds
	Directly constrains only host country interest rates and exchange rate policy	Can start *or* mitigate impact of herd behavior
	Aggravate herding	Should constrain policy but timing of their actions is unpredictable
Long term	Yield orientation	Diversification and value goal
	Commercial bank loan officers in 1970s	Pension funds and insurance companies
	Virtually no constraint on borrowing-country policy until default looms	Salutary long-term constraint on general policy direction and performance in host country

folio investment in emerging markets, the inflow of such capital will constrain national policy only when rates of return on substitute investments are relatively high. If the surge of the early 1990s, for example, is explained primarily by low U.S. interest rates, host countries should not expect to attract or keep portfolio investment capital by virtue of "good" national policy.

Investors with Short Time Horizons, Pushed into Emerging Markets by Low Yields on Less Risky Investments

If push factors predominate and portfolio investment capital is volatile on a day-to-day, week-to-week basis, host country policy will be more constrained as differentials in rates of return on substitute investments narrow. When OECD interest rates are low, presumably because global supply of capital outpaces demand, returns on investments in less risky OECD environments may not satisfy investors. When global interest rates are low, investors are forced to look at non-OECD investments to find a desirable yield. We can say that they become less risk averse when global liquidity is high. Generally speaking, mutual fund managers fit into this category. If they do not keep yields high, they face redemption of the money they manage.

Inflows of volatile capital predominantly seeking the highest relative yield will constrain policy choices of emerging market governments in a particular way: through interest and exchange rates. To the extent that flows are dominated by investors of this type, developing countries seeking to continue attracting or to retain existing capital must match changes in international interest rates while protecting exchange rate stability. If they do not do so, they risk sudden capital outflows.

A dramatic example of this phenomenon involves the Mexican peso crisis of 1994. The U.S. Federal Reserve raised interest rates several times beginning early in 1994. The Mexicans were heavily dependent on continued foreign capital inflow at that time. A rise in Mexican interest rates to mirror the U.S. increase was inconvenient for two key reasons. First, it was an election year and many middle-class Mexicans had recently taken on considerable floating-rate consumer debt. Second, and related, the local banking system was in crisis, and an interest rate increase would have revealed the magnitude of the problem and cast doubt on the governing party's reform achievements. The Mexicans failed to raise rates, and foreign investors in Mexican bonds began to consider alternatives. Inflows from equity investments slowed, as did the flow of foreign direct investment.

The shortfall of capital inflows raised concerns about the stability of the macroeconomic policy mix involving a somewhat overvalued exchange rate, relatively loose monetary and fiscal policy, and a large current account deficit. As a result, downward pressure on the peso mounted. Instead of devaluing just after the midsummer elections, policy makers bet that capital inflows would help sustain the exchange rate until the economy's productivity and export performance narrowed the current account gap. The lesson of the Mexican story is consistent with the suggested hypothesis. With U.S. interest rates rising, the Mexican government did not have any leeway to delay domestic interest rate increases. Had they raised rates, the electoral fortunes of the Party of the Institutionalized Revolution (PRI) could have been hurt. But the most important point to take away from this anecdote is that had U.S. interest rates not risen in 1994, the Mexican gamble, which involved delaying their own interest rate hike, might have paid off. The Mexican's policy leeway would have been greater and the constraints imposed by financial internationalization less, if U.S. interest rates had remained low and stable.

Relative yield-oriented investors may be less concerned about host-country policy than about policies affecting interest rates in developed countries. Borrowers can pursue poor policy at little cost if international conditions are favorable. When international liquidity tightens, these yield-oriented portfolio inflows will constrain host-country interest and exchange rate policy. To the extent this type of investor dominates north to south capital flows, they place developing and transitional economies at the mercy of factors beyond their control.

Investors with Short Time Horizons and Some Appreciation of Host-Country Fundamentals

Short-term investors can focus more on price than relative yield, seeking to maximize capital gain as opposed to accrual over time of dividends and interest. These investors will try to distinguish between price declines based on market irrationality and price declines associated with a change in the direction of the country's economic policy and performance. These investors have an appreciation for the opportunity afforded by volatility, and their behavior could help dampen market cycles fed by herd behavior, if they believe the market has misjudged fundamentals. these investors can, however, also cause a capital stampede if they believe that the market has missed a change in fundamentals. These investors make their money trading and taking large bets on future price movements.

Roughly speaking, hedge funds fall into this category. Hedge funds rely on money placed under their management privately. They are not as vulnerable to redemptions as mutual funds because of the private placement. Many hedge funds manage a mix of proprietary and nonproprietary money. It is not as simple for owners of hedge funds as it is for mutual fund investors to change who manages their money. This should give the typical hedge fund money manager a slightly longer time horizon than the mutual fund money manager.

An example of how this type of investment constrains emerging market governments lies in the Thai financial crisis of 1997. Thai economic policy had suggested fundamental deterioration in the country's creditworthiness for well over a year, but capital inflows continued. Recognizing a divergence between market actions and fundamental conditions or the "value" of Thai financial assets, hedge funds began to speculate on a fall in value in mid-1997. This touched off a stampede of capital from Thailand and the rest of Asia. To prevent this, Thailand would have had to avoid policy imbalances that made it vulnerable to speculative attack. Capital flows from this kind of investor are constraining in an unpredictable way. Poor domestic policy will bring an investor reaction, but the timing is uncertain.

Patient Investors Pushed by International Conditions

If push factors predominate and capital is patient, there is little constraint on national policy. The commercial bank lending boom of the late 1970s highlights this logic. Emerging markets could borrow without limit from commercial banks, with virtually no regard for national policy and performance, because of tremendous excess liquidity in the international banking system. Under these circumstances capital flowing from capital-rich to capital-scarce environments carried little conditionality, and many countries pursued "bad" policy. If international portfolio investment in emerging markets is push driven and patient, host countries will enjoy considerable policy latitude but will also risk sudden, large, one-time capital outflows occurring after the long-time accumulation of policy errors has affected their capacity to meet international obligations. An example is the debt crisis of the early 1980s that was triggered when the Mexican government informed the U.S. government it could not meet its debt service payments in August 1982.

Patient Capital Pulled into the Host Country

National policy makers in emerging market countries will be more constrained by capital inflows if they are pulled rather than pushed, as just discussed. By definition, capital pulled into a country responds to national policy choices that investors believe shape the borrowers' repayment capacity and/or growth potential.

Patient investors drawn by the specific characteristics of a given emerging market are more likely than investors in the other three categories to provide incentives conducive to a happy marriage of debt and development. Over the long run, host countries know poor economic policy and performance will induce capital outflow. But investor patience allows time to correct policy errors before destabilizing capital outflow occurs. Investor patience also affords host country governments time to demonstrate that policies introduced for primarily political reasons, with relative disregard for their economic consequences, may be salutary for the investment environment in the long run.

Investors in this category often have diversification, in addition to price and yield, as a major goal (Brainard and Tobin 1992). Portfolio investors driven by diversification seek to mitigate exposure to risk from any asset class, country, or region over the long term. Pension funds and insurance companies fall into this category (Reisen 1996).[1]

The constraint on emerging market government policy choices varies according to the frameworks of different types of investors. For those who remember dependency theory, the distinction between arguments that assume that flows are motivated by international (push) rather than domestic (pull) conditions is akin to the difference between early *dependistas* or world systems theorists and the later *dependistas* such as Cardoso and Falleto (Dos Santos 1970; Cardoso and Faletto 1979; Wallerstein 1974). Early dependency theorists argued about the impact of the international economy on developing countries without looking at the filtering role of domestic political institutions or economic circumstances. Later dependency theorists traced the interaction of international economic conditions with

---

1. To my knowledge there has been no systematic research on the correlation between volatility and types of investors in emerging markets. A recent study examined the correlation between U.S. stock price volatility and the extent of institutional investor holdings of those stocks (Sias 1996).

the domestic political economy. If capital flows correspond to international conditions and are pushed into emerging markets by low OECD yields, national policy choices of developing country governments are more and less constrained, depending on events in the global financial market. This argument is similar to one in the early versions of dependency theory. When OECD liquidity dries up, there is little room for policy autonomy, and local interest rates must rise to preserve international capital inflows and the economic conditions they support. When international interest rates are low, borrowing governments have much greater policy leeway.

Investor time horizons also shape the nature of the policy constraint emanating from capital flows. Borrowers' economic goals are often relatively long term; if they require external finance, goals can be compromised if that capital is invested too impatiently. Keeping in mind that these categories are ideal types and that investor motives are often mixed, the constraint on emerging market governments' policy choice should be greatest where short-term, yield-oriented investors dominate. The most salutary flows are long-term flows pulled into emerging markets. The other two are also constraining, in slightly different but equally problematic ways.

This hypothesis places a premium on detailed knowledge about the composition of the emerging markets' investor base. Among portfolio investors what percentage are value versus yield oriented? Mutual fund managers must be yield oriented in order to maintain growth of their funds. "Pension funds are like a supertanker—it takes a long time to change direction," says the director of an investment research firm (Weeks 1996, 20). A manager of pension funds for General Motors remarks, "We look at foreign investment as an asset class and we stay in for the long term" (Weeks 1996, 20). Because it is hard to measure investor frameworks and to identify the breakdown of flows into and from emerging market countries, another strategy is to evaluate the overall behavior of flows and impute the dominance of investor groups whose motivations are consistent with the aggregate patterns. Evaluating the extent to which aggregate flows appear to be "pulled" or "pushed," "patient" or "impatient" is the primary purpose of the next section.

Survey of Existing Econometric Data on Determinants of Portfolio Investment in Emerging Markets

Which of these four categories best captures the behavior of portfolio investment in emerging markets? Data limitations are severe. For example, it is difficult to know whether a flow recorded in balance of payments accounts under a particular label actually behaves as the label would imply. The distinction between long term and short term, for example, is very difficult to capture accurately (Claessens, Dooley, and Warner 1993). It is difficult to know whether econometric tests are inconclusive because of poor data and measurement or because of the complexity of the causal process, or both.

Studies evaluating the impact of different factors on capital flows to developing countries are designed in many different ways. The most obvious design is to try to predict actual flows as measured by the International Monetary Fund (IMF) or other sources. But a variety of other indicators should be associated with flows, including the ratio of the balance of payments to gross domestic product (GDP), exchange rates, the current account balance, and the prices of emerging market financial assets. The logic is simple. Outflows should be reflected in a lower ratio of balance of payments to GDP. Local currency will be more valuable relative to foreign currencies as capital flows in. The current account balance should move inversely with capital inflows, which typically help finance current account deficits. Capital inflows should also correlate with rising prices of emerging market assets other than currencies, namely equities, loans, and bonds. The empirical results summarized in following paragraphs are from studies that use a variety of proxies for capital flows. Although the sum of conclusions of studies of portfolio investment is ambiguous about time horizons, evidence points more strongly toward the dominance of "pull" rather than "push" factors.

The coincidence of rising U.S. interest rates and decline in capital inflows to Mexico, culminating in the Mexican liquidity crisis in late 1994 and the emergency IMF and U.S. loans to that country, stimulated research on the correlation between international interest rates and capital flows to developing countries. Eichengreen and Fishlow (this volume) explore large-scale waves of capital inflows in this century and note that during all three (1920, 1970s, and 1990s), global interest rates were trending down. More quantitative studies include an analysis by Calvo, Leiderman, and Reinhart (1994) of the impact of foreign variables on international reserves and exchange rates. They found that factors external to the developing, recipient or "host" country play a significant role, at least for the larger countries. Calvo and Reinhart (1995) used a more comprehensive measure: balance on the capital account as a percentage of GDP. For a study of eleven countries based on annual observations from 1970 to 1993 these authors found that a 1.00 percent decline in U.S. real interest rates yields a 0.77 percent rise in the proxy for capital inflows, with a one-period lag for smaller developing countries. Frankel and Rose (1996) examined the causes of currency crashes, an indirect measure of capital flows, using panel data for 100 countries between 1971 and 1992. They found that currency crashes are more likely with higher U.S. interest rates.

An exhaustive study by Fernandez-Arias (1996) focused on determinants of portfolio flows (equity and bond purchases). He used quarterly data on portfolio flows from 1988 to 1995 for thirteen developing countries and the annualized nominal yield on ten-year U.S. bonds as a proxy for the alternative return to the developing country investment. He calculated the impact of alternative returns and country creditworthiness on both portfolio flows and stock adjustments and found that international interest rates have a larger impact than country creditworthiness.

Looking at a subset of the flows Fernandez-Arias evaluated, U.S. equity investments, Tesar and Werner (1995) found contradictory evidence. They found only a weak correlation between quarterly data on net equity flows and the return on thirty-day U.S. Treasury bills at the end of the quarter, and between quarterly equity flows and the predicted treasury bill return for the next quarter. One possible reason for the inconsistency between these findings and those of Fernandez-Arias is that quarterly equity flows can be especially lumpy due to the size of new issues and relatively small secondary markets.

Harvey (1994) studied risk and returns for developing country equity markets by looking at month-to-month price variations. Exchange rates, lagged equity returns, local short-term interest rates, and dividends are the four significant variables in his regression analysis. For our purposes the interesting result is the importance of exchange rates and local interest rates. These variables suggest that the investor is concerned primarily with relative returns, in other words, with how the emerging country return holds up against returns on alternative investments involving less foreign country risk.

Another study focusing attention on push rather than pull factors shows that, in the short run (several months), the prices of closed-end country funds in New York trading are more closely related to U.S. securities prices in general than to the net asset value of the individual foreign securities in the country funds (Hardouvelis, La Porta, and Wizman 1995).

An essay by Ul Haque, Mathieson, and Sharma (1997) suggests an innovative way to evaluate whether flows are motivated by external factors, an increase in the productivity of domestic capital, or an upward shift in the domestic money demand curve. They theorized about the expected impact of these differently motivated capital inflows on the country's relative financial asset prices and monetary and credit aggregates. Assuming *im*perfect substitutability between domestic and foreign assets and *im*perfect capital mobility, if local interest rates decrease while equity prices and real estate prices rise with inflows, it is likely that external factors are motivating them. Capital inflows driven by external factors will first raise real money balances, but then higher inflation will lower them. Whereas the evidence suggests that international forces have played a predominant role in explaining capital flows to developing countries to date, an empirical application of Ul Haque's analysis, as yet to be done, could shed further light on the issue.

Turning from the return on alternative investments to the role of country risk or creditworthiness, we find even clearer support for the supposition that international factors dominate strictly domestic variables in determining capital flows into emerging market countries. Country risk or creditworthiness measures the expectation of borrowers' abilities to honor their international financial contracts. It is sometimes called sovereign risk or sovereign default risk. Fernandez-Arias (1996), in the study mentioned above, not only found that international factors weigh more heavily in shaping capital flows to developing countries than country creditworthiness, but he disaggregated country creditworthiness into domestic and international components. He created a creditworthiness index based on the secondary market prices for the countries' bonds. Not surprisingly he found that international interest rates have a substantial indirect impact on country creditworthiness. Combining the direct and indirect impact of international interest rates Fernandez-Arias concluded that they explain 86 percent of the increase in capital inflows for the typical developing country in his sample. In only three of the thirteen countries in his sample did the domestic investment climate have a substantially positive impact on capital inflows.

The importance of pull and push factors is highly sensitive to the time span assumed. Most of the studies cited above focus on variation in flows from week to week, month to month, or quarter to quarter. McCulloch and Petri's (this volume) econometric analysis of portfolio flows focuses on long term (year-to-year) flows. It reveals a correlation between liberal trade policy and portfolio equity investment in emerging stock markets that suggests investors are guided, over the longer term (years), by country, if not firm-specific, "fundamentals." Their data analysis suggests that portfolio investors in emerging markets are both patient and driven by long-term tracking (quarter-to-quarter or year-to-year) of domestic conditions and policies. These assumptions about the behavior of portfolio investment in emerging markets allow the authors to be optimistic about the implications of this form of capital flow for investors and borrowers.

Impatient capital, which refers to capital from investors with extremely short time horizons, is a notion that underlies much discussion of the negative impact of financial integration in developing countries. Patient investors will not flee at the first policy measure that might augur poorly for creditworthiness. The assumption is that the constraint on developing country policy makers emanating from international financial markets varies with the time horizons of investors. Whatever the other determinants of investor decisions, if the investors' time horizons are short, the constraint is greater (Armijo 1995).

In ascending order of volatility, or impatience, analysts typically list flows of long-term bank lending, foreign direct investment, portfolio investment and short-term bank lending (Turner 1994). According to several empirical studies, the problem with this assumption is that the different categories of flows do not exhibit the expected volatility variation. One study looks at time series data on the balance of payments of ten industrialized countries. The study used different measures of persistence of flows, such as autocorrelation and half-life impulses, and in each case found a poor correlation between the time horizon ascribed to different categories of flows and their persistence (Claessens, Dooley, and Warner 1993).

In another study Mushkat (1996) looked at coefficients of variation in flows across the different categories and found that for Argentina, Brazil, Indonesia, Mexico, and Korea, short-term flows have lowest variation whereas equity portfolio, and foreign direct investment flows are most variable. These studies substantiate Fielecke's (1996, 52) conclusion that "the customary characterization of short term capital as the most recidivist villain of the capital shock drama may be somewhat exaggerated."

There are several possible explanations for these findings. One is that the categories are meaningless because capital is so fungible that nothing is really long term. One example illustrates this. An investor making a longer-term investment (e.g., building a factory or buying equity in a local enterprise planning significant long-term domestic expansion) will hedge his or her longer-term risk exposure to that market through a compensating financial transaction. Another possible explanation is that our data are so poor that we cannot accurately distinguish between flows associated with "buy and hold" investors versus short-term investors.

Data problems and the complexity of factors shaping portfolio investment flows confound econometric studies. Existing literature suggests that push factors predominate. Another way to try to identify the predominant investor framework driving north-to-south capital flows is to examine the extent to which flows suggest herding behavior based on partial information or market signals, on the one hand, or behavior governed by use of extensive information, on the other hand. The later is more consistent with the long-term, pull-oriented framework most typical of pension funds and insurance companies. The next sections present results of two modest empirical exercises designed to test the extent to which information informs north-south capital flows.

American Depository Receipt Price Determination and Investor Information Use

The efficient markets hypothesis implies that there is a single "correct" corporate valuation in the equity market. Historical conceptions of equity markets help illuminate this claim. In 1934 Graham and Dodd claimed that "the market is not a weighing machine, on which the value of each issue is recorded by an exact and impersonal mechanism, in accordance with specific qualities. Rather should we say that the market is a voting machine, whereon countless individuals register choices which are the product partly of reason and partly of emotion" (Graham and Dodd 1934, 27). This debate between the market as weighing machine versus the market as voting machine has continued for the better part of the last twenty-five years and does not appear close to resolution (Lehmann 1991). The efficient market hypothesis sees the market as a weighing machine that would never undervalue a company.

One of the historical bases for current high-tech models that assume efficient markets is the simple present value model

$$V = \sum_{t=1}^{\infty} \frac{D_t}{(1+k)^t} \tag{1}$$

where V is the value of the asset, D_t is the future cash flow, rent, or dividend paid by the asset, and k is the applicable discount rate. The discount rate is defined as the interest rate used to convert future payments into present values and is usually represented by some basic market interest rate, such as the U.S. Federal Funds rate. Although this model may have great normative strengths, it does not serve well as a positive model. That is, this model is a good explanation for how assets *should* be priced, but does not always do a good job explaining how assets *are* priced. One means of increasing the positive value of this model is to embed this pricing equation in a rational expectations framework (Shiller 1989; Fama 1976; Scott 1990). The future price of a financial asset is equal to our rational expectation of how price will change based on all available information today. In simplified form, the present value equation becomes

$$p_t = E_t p_t^* + u_t \tag{2}$$

where p_t is the observed price, p_t^* is the ex post, rational price, and u_t is a forecast error.[2] This forecast error is important because otherwise the model would simply claim that $p_t = p_t^*$, that is, observed prices must equal

---

2. It is worth noting that this model assumes the investor holds the asset until $t = \infty$. Because this is clearly not a realistic assumption, another way of writing this model is

$$E(p_{t+n}) = E(\Delta p) + \sum_{k=0}^{\infty} E_t D_{t+n} \prod_{j=0}^{n} \gamma^{j+1}, \ n \geq 0.$$

What this states is that the expected price in the future can be decomposed into the expected capital gains over the holding period and the expected present value of the accrued dividends over the holding period.

expected prices. All changes in price must, according to this condition, be unexpected, resulting in a forecast error. If the market is efficiently using information, the value of u_t, the forecast error, must not be correlated with p_t, the observed price. Such a correlation indicates there is unused and valuable information. This could be information about international conditions (push factors) or host country circumstances (pull factors). In studies of OECD country financial assets, the forecast error is not typically correlated with the observed price. The extent of such a correlation for emerging market country financial assets would suggest the extent to which investors are using full or partial information.

There are some serious methodological problems along the way, however. The most important and daunting obstacle is that p_t^* is not particularly amenable to observation because we cannot know price for infinity. Analysts can, however, approximate p_t^* if they are willing to argue that the discounting of the future dividends expressed in equation 2 is small enough at some time (T) after time t in the future. Even with very long series of data, this still requires assumptions about the present value of dividends at the end of the data series.

This problem is magnified in dealing with emerging markets data because few emerging market financial assets have been trading for extended periods of time. Any conclusions must be viewed as tentative and exploratory. The data employed for the test reported here are American Depository Receipts (ADRs) of companies in developing countries that are listed on the New York Stock Exchange (NYSE) or on the American Stock Exchange (AMEX). Depository receipts are proxies of stocks traded on some foreign exchange that are available for sale on a domestic exchange. As an example, Morgan Guarantee Trust purchases and holds several million shares of Telefonos de Mexico on the Mexican stock market. Morgan then issues Depository Receipts equal to the value of one share of the underlying company and claiming the same dividend.

ADRs have long been seen as a means by which international companies might have access to global capital markets, and a means by which investors might diversify their portfolio without actually purchasing foreign equities. The data series also contains closed-end country funds, which are a much more obvious proxy for investment in an emerging market. The data covers ADRs and closed-end country funds traded on the NYSE and AMEX from 1983 to 1994. It is important that the equities be traded on developed exchanges, both because the SEC disclosure rules guarantee a certain minimum threshold of informational transparency and because the test is whether developed markets make good use of information concerning developing countries and companies from such countries.

The series includes six companies that Latin America, the Middle East, and the Pacific Rim. These companies were chosen, based on availability of data, specifically to maximize the time series. Although there has been a glut of companies and closed-end funds listed on U.S. exchanges in the last five to six years, it was paramount, for the methodological reasons explained above, to have a longer rather than broader data series.

The relationship between the forecast error and observed price is summarized in figure 3.1.[3] Unlike many of the series for developed financial markets, the forecast error in this case is correlated. The strength of the correlation indicated in figure 3.1 implies that ADR markets are not incorporating all available information.

There are some other possible explanations for these results. Some are methodological and some are more substantive. The most important of the methodological issues is the shortness of the series previously mentioned. The frequency of sampling may not only weaken the results but may also skew them.

Another problem is the thinness and illiquidity of the markets for these issues. If trading levels fall below a certain minimum threshold, the continuous change over time implied by the rational expectations discount model may not apply. If the results partially capture illiquid or thin markets, the conclusions are not fundamentally altered. Limited trading suggests poor use of information.

Figure 3.1 Observed price and the forecast error for selected emerging market ADRs and closed-end country funds.

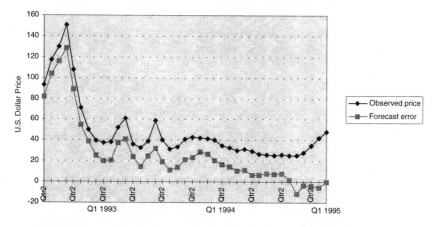

3. We constructed our p_t^* by the recursive substitution Shiller uses. We deflated our series by a moving average of earnings and we used the U.S. Federal Funds rate as a discount factor. Shiller deflated p_t^* by a producer price index to control for inflation, but it seemed to us that, given the comparative nature of the study, controlling for inflation at the aggregate level could skew the result.

The basic result of this limited empirical exercise is the relationship between u_t and p_t summarized in figure 3.1. This graph shows quite dramatically that there is strong correlation between observed price and forecast error. To some extent this dramatic correlation is a function of the short series, but the strong correlation does suggest informational inefficiencies. Moreover, this finding of informational inefficiency is consistent with results of Cashin and McDermott's (1995) study of equity markets in Jordan, Turkey, and Pakistan. Both sets of findings are consistent with investors (such as the short-term, yield-oriented mutual fund managers) who are prone to follow the herd rather than make independent judgments based on all available information. Mutual fund managers follow the herd because their incentive compensation depends on not falling below the industry average.

Local News and Stock Market Indexes

A second empirical exercise designed to test aggregate trends for evidence of the dominant investor framework is based on evaluation of market responses to "bad" news in emerging markets. This test is also plagued by methodological problems, particularly those associated with event analysis. Furthermore it is not a direct test of international portfolio investment because emerging market data does not differentiate by owner nationality. Although inconclusive, this qualitative data also suggests that international portfolio investment is not pulled into the host country based on evaluation of the domestic political economy.

For example, six Latin American countries, examined for the periods beginning when significant stock market activity ensued, witnessed a total of sixty-one instances of either inflationary policy pronouncements or news of political instability, as reported in international information services available to international investors. Daily stock market indexes were available for periods surrounding only twenty of these episodes. As table 3.2 shows, a "sustained" stock market decline followed in only six of the twenty cases. A sustained decline is defined as a decline of more than 0.1 percent, evident more than one day after that news.

In Mexico, for example, the stock market index was higher on January 5, 1994, than it had been the day before the January 1 Chiapas uprising. After a one-day closure the market recovered similarly quickly from the assassination of PRI presidential candidate, Luis Donoldo Colossio, on March 23, 1994. Of course, the principal Mexican stock market index did fall 11.9 percent overall between January and April 1994, bringing the value of foreign investment down with it. As reflected in equity prices, investors in other Latin American countries, albeit somewhat less liquid, also

Table 3.2 "Bad" news and market reaction in Latin America

	Episode	Time 1 (2 days before)	Time 2 (1 week after)	Time 3 (1 month after)
Mexico	1/1/94 Chiapas uprising	2,602.63 (12/30)	2,657.31 (1/5)	2,569.52 (3/4)
	3/23/94 Colosio assassinated	2,383.01 (3/18)	2,410.38 (4/1)	2,485.05 (5/27)
Argentina	12/24/93 Employer contributions to social security cut to decrease labor costs	19,685.8 (12/22)	20,267.30 (12/28)	24,403.10 (2/21)
	3/23/94 United States gives $100 million credit to small and medium producers	20,13.98 (3/23)	19,210.43 (4/1)	n/a[a]
	4/10/94 Leftist Frente Grande gains in constituent assembly	545.57 (4.9)	535.87 (4/15)	601.04 (6/3)
	5/30/94 National employment fund created	597.91 (5/27)	601.04 (6/3)	525.15 (7/25)
	7/18/94 Politically-motivated car bombing kills 100	546.48 (7/15)	525.15 (7/22)	613.10 (9/16)
Brazil	10/2/92 "Mediocre and unknown" minister of finance appointed	43,664 (10/1)	38,291 (10/4)	46,323 (12/2)
	9/15/93 Budget deficit expected to widen as tax on financial transactions ruled unconstitutional	12,084 (9/14)	13,805 (9/20)	28,219 (11/26)
	6/6/94 Poll shows Lula leading	26,959 (6/3)	30,204 (6/10)	44,695 (8/5)
	3/23/94 General strike	1,037.9 (3/21)	1,053.39 (3/28)	1,030.79 (5/23)
	3/29/94 Cardoso announces presidential candidacy	1,053.39 (3/28)	1,052.34 (4/4)	1,016.03 (5/30)
Chile	3/31/94 Former Carabineros sentenced for 1985 murders	4,233.83 (3/28)	4,029.56 (4/4)	4,412.66 (5/27)
	5/18/94 100,000 teachers strike	4,161.04 (5/13)	4,320.09 (5/20)	4,323.44 (7/8)
	8/29/94 Education spending increase announced	4,757.84 (8/26)	4,821.04 (9/2)	5,257.70 (10/10)
Colombia	1/1/94 State of "internal commotion" declared to prevent release of suspected guerrillas and drug dealers	1,021.39 (4/29)	1,045.16 (5/16)	1,001.97 (7/1)
Venezuela	2/27/94 VAT suspended and suspended right	27,193.3 (2/26)	28,418.9 (3/4)	23,600.12 (4/22)
	6/8/94 Government announced bail-out of five financial institutions	145.67 (6/3)	146.82 (6/17)	125.82 (8/5)
	6/26/94 Individual constitutional guarantees suspended	145.70 (6/24)	133.23 (7/1)	144.1 (8/19)

[a] n/a, not available.

appear to have been unconcerned, concerned but patient, or simply ignorant about "bad" policy or political news.

In Asia, markets appear to react negatively to announcements of potentially inflationary social or economic policies and signs of rising political uncertainty, but more frequently and less severely than in Latin America. Declines in response to bad news were fewer in Latin America than Asia, but averaged 6 percent compared with the average 2.7 percent decline in the Asian markets examined. The market for cross-border purchase of Asian equities may be more informationally efficient than the comparable market in Latin American equities. This suggests that the constraints imposed on local policy and politics by international portfolio flows may vary by region.

The trade-off between political and macroeconomic stability is arguably worse in eastern Europe than in Asia or Latin America. The countries in these regions are undergoing economic transitions that involve considerable social dislocation and cost. It is becoming clearer and clearer that simultaneous construction of democracy and capitalism in this region requires policies that will provide a "social safety net." Therefore, market reaction to social and economic policies designed to cushion the effects of economic liberalization and preserve a minimum of government popularity is crucial.

The evidence from a very limited set of eastern European market observations is mixed. In the Polish case, markets supported government wage and pension increases on the two occasions they were observed (January and May 1992). Nor did announcement of government subsidy of farm credits and procurement prices in March 1992 bring the Warsaw stock exchange down. In Hungary, however, the January 1993 government proposal of a national housing policy brought the market down 3.3 percent. Elections that made the Hungarian socialist party the largest parliamentary party brought the market down 1.9 percent. Of five episodes of "bad" news observed in the Polish case, the only market decline came after Solidarity launched a series of nationwide strikes in April 1994, shutting down a portion of the power industry.

A similar study confirms the suggestion of informational efficiency in these results. Loviscek and Crowley (1996) confined their study to four Latin American countries and to events that reflected political shocks but were not linked to potentially expansionary fiscal policy. Other than noting the exclusion of elections, they did not describe the events that they culled from the *Latin American Weekly,* the *Wall Street Journal,* the *New York Times,* and the *Washington Post.* Their results suggest that markets for financial assets in developing countries are not as informationally efficient as those in developed countries. In OECD countries the likelihood of bad news is priced into assets *before* the news is public. The forecast error and

Table 3.3 "Bad" news and market reaction in Asia

	Episode	Time 1	Time 2	Time 3
Korea	9/30/91 Cabinet endorses most expansionary budget since 1981	685.21 (9/27)	720.53 (10/4)	652.47 (11/29)
	6/20/93 60,000 strike at Hyundai, sparking rumors of resurgent political unrest	762.09 (6/18)	760.01 (6/25)	729.86 (8/20)
	3/21/94 Pyongyang refuses to grant international inspectors full access to nuclear facilities	893.07 (3/18)	868.03 (3/25)	950.45 (5/13)
Philippines	6/30/89 Increase in legislated minimum wage	1,069.31 (6/23)	1,005.5 (7/7)	1,157.93 (8/25)
	12/1/89 Major coup attempt against Aquino government	1,369.41 (11/24)	1,317.86 (12/1)	1,016.02 (2/2)
	3/6/90 Amidst rumors of pending declaration of martial law, rift reported within government on monetary policy	1,028.32 (3/2)	1,035.32 (3/9)	924.26 (5/18)
	10/24–5/90 Major strike by KMU rebels in Manila	540.45 (10/19)	599.74 (11/2)	664.10 (12/21)
	10/25/93 Ethnic violence kills 13 in Mindanao	2,260.99 (10/22)	2,372.77 (10/29)	2,997.46 (12/23)
	11/1/93 Labor unions threaten nationwide strike	2,372.77 (10/29)	2,411.32 (11/5)	2,997.46 (12/23)
	Labor unrest leads to suspension of oil product price increase, with negative revenue implications for government	3,013.76 (2/11)	3,051.71 (2/18)	2,639.47 (4/8)
Malaysia	1/18/92 Mahatir suffers heart attack	1,898.80 (1/13)	1,892.05 (1/20)	1,953.49 (3/3)
	12/1/92 Reports ruling party might split	640.48 (11/27)	636.40 (12/4)	624.49 (1/29)
	6/20/94 Mahatir declares war on corruption warning of political instability	1,038.04 (6/17)	1,015.03 (6/24)	1,140.70 (8/19)
	7/20/94 Public sector union demands 53% wage increase	1,012.11 (7/15)	1,000.46 (7/22)	1,185.27 (9/16)

continued

Table 3.3 Continued

	Episode	Time 1	Time 2	Time 3
Pakistan	11/18/92 Benazir Bhutto leads a "long march" as political instability escalates	1,236.29 (11/17)	1,231.76 (11/24)	1,265.34 (1/18)
	4/18/93 Sharif government sacked	1,111.70 (4/15)	1,088.26 (4/21)	1,187.92 (6/15)
	10/9/93 Bhutto wins elections	1,362.86 (10/5)	1,378.83 (10/11)	1,791.40 (12/3)
Sri Lanka	4/24/93 Opposition leader assassinated	764.05 (4/22)	755.24 (4/28)	859.93 (6/21)
	1/1/93 President Premadasa assassinated	755.24 (4/28)	745.33 (5/3)	839.96 (6/25)
	3/20/94 Important electoral victory for opposition, threatening defeat of party ruling for 17 years	1,878.90 (3/17)	1,854.76 (3/23)	1,481.17 (5/17)
	1/1/94 100,000 opposition party members rally	1,555.88 (4/29)	1,489.60 (5/4)	1,462.11 (6/28)
India	12/7/92 Hindu extremists destroy mosque	2,619.90 (12/6)	2,550.22 (12/12)	
	3/31/93 Tension flares in Kashmir	1,021.40 (3/30)	1,070.75 (4/4)	
	7/26/93 Government guarantees continuation of food subsidies	1,027.23 (7/25)	1,087.34 (7/31)	
	8/31/93 Government guarantees continuation of agricultural producer subsidies	1,242.69 (10/1)	1,296.21 (10/6)	
	10/93 Tension again in Kashmir	1,284.73 (10/1)	1,296.21 (10/6)	
	2/28/94 Budget announced, includes 20% defense hike	2,043.56 (2/27)	1,803.63 (3/4)	
Indonesia	11/15/91 Violence in East Timor	248.88 (10/15)	237.24 (11/20)	
	12/24/93 Minimum wage increase	560.598 (12/23)	598.646 (12/31)	
	7/15/94 Resumption of hostilities in East Timor	460.293 (7/14)	462.539 (7/20)	
Thailand	5/31/90 Minimum wage increase	987.31 (5/30)	1,018.86 (6/4)	
	2/23/91 Bloodless coup	776.56 (2/22)	769.13 (2/28)	
	5/9/92 100,000 rally against government	717.62 (5/7)	742.42 (5/24)	
	3/15/94 Minimum wage increase	1,296.55 (3/14)	1,246.84 (3/20)	

observed price correlation exercise reported above, the original event study reported here, and Loviscek and Crowley's (1996) event study do not reveal evidence of informational efficiency. Host countries should be wary of investors whose actions do not consistently follow choice of policy, as reflected in information from or about their country.

Serious evaluation of the claim that international portfolio investment in emerging markets constrains policy autonomy should begin with discussion of the factors that motivate portfolio investment flows. Investor frameworks vary, and alternative frameworks constrain policy choices differently. The empirical literature surveyed here and the two original empirical exercises attempted suggest that the average investor is not responding to careful evaluation of how the domestic political economy is shapes the long-run value of his or her investment. The predominance of push factors in the existing literature to explain north-to-south capital flows suggests most investors are yield oriented. In this case the only direct policy constraint is on borrowing country interest and exchange rates, but not fiscal policy, as some financial integration critics might claim (Page 1997). The predominance of a push or yield-oriented investor framework is consistent with evidence of informational inefficiency in the pricing of emerging market stocks. These informational inefficiencies may be rational for the investor who chooses to act only on the basis of signals about short-term relative yields.

The claim that recent trends in international capital flows to developing and transitional economies directly constrain national policy choices and may even heighten the trade-off between economic and political liberalization must be qualified. There is little empirical support for the assumption implicit in this claim that portfolio investors will react predictably to policy changes by host country governments. Investors appear to follow the herd and the signals about the direction of relatively risk-free yields in OECD markets. Direct constraints run through interest and exchange rate policy but not fiscal policy.

The disaggregation of decision frameworks of portfolio investors suggests that concern about constraints on national economic policy choice is most valid to the extent investors are yield oriented. This hypothesis places a premium on detailed knowledge about the composition of the emerging markets' investor base. Among portfolio investors, what percentage are value versus yield oriented? As evident in figure 3.2, the emerging market allocations of pension funds and insurance companies have been rising since before the Mexican peso collapse (Culpepper 1995). Given the large sums of money managed in pension funds—over $5 trillion—a small increase in portfolio allocation to emerging markets can have a large impact on the relative distribution among different categories of emerging mar-

Figure 3.2. U.S. pension fund investments in emerging markets.

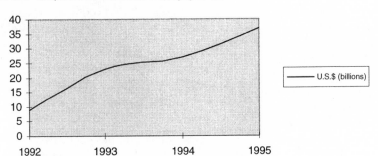

ket investors. Most of these fund managers plan to continue increasing the relative weight of emerging market investments in their portfolios. To the extent that long-term, value-oriented investors increasingly dominate north-to-south flows, the constraints of financial internationalization on host country policy may become more predictable and salutary.

If the hypothesis is correct—that yield-oriented investors are most threatening to emerging market borrowers and to the extent they continue to dominate north-to-south flows—several regulatory/policy conclusions follow. Regulation of the mutual fund industry whether by itself or by public authorities might help reduce the competitive pressure to follow yields. This could be healthy both for fund managers and emerging market borrowers. Borrowers can try to shield themselves from yield-oriented investors by avoiding portfolio investors entirely, or choosing to structure their borrowing to fit the needs of pension funds and insurance companies. Those investors, for example, generally prefer longer-duration bonds. Borrowers can also seek financial advisers who will deliver relatively more value-oriented than yield-oriented investors. Even if types of capital flows cannot be encouraged or discouraged through host country policy, the predominant form of capital inflow should alert emerging market governments to the intensity of need for market-based risk management strategies.[4]

References

Armijo, Leslie. 1995. "Mixed Blessings: Foreign Capital Inflows and Democracy in 'Emerging Markets.'" Paper prepared for Workshop on Financial Globalization and Emerging Markets: Policy Autonomy, De-

---

4. The most direct strategies would involve futures, options, or swaps, but I would also include promotion of national savings pools, through pension funds, for example, in the risk-management menu. On the former see Claessens 1992.

mocratization, and the Lessons from Mexico, Watson Institute of International Studies, Brown University, November 18–19.

Brainard, William, and James Tobin. 1992. "On the Internationalization of Portfolios." *Oxford Economic Papers* 44 (4):533–546.

Calvo, Guillermo A., Leonardo Leiderman, and Carmen Reinhart. 1994. "Capital Inflows to Latin America." In *Economics in a Changing World,* edited by Edman L. Bacha. New York: St. Martin's.

Calvo, Sara, and Carmen M. Reinhart. 1995. "Capital Flows to Latin America: Is There Evidence of Contagion Effects?" In *Private Capital Flows to Emerging Markets,* edited by Morris Goldstein. Washington, D.C.: Institute for International Economics.

Cardoso, Fernando Enrique, and Enzo Faletto. 1979. *Dependency and Development.* Berkeley: University of California Press.

Cashin, Paul, and C. John McDermott. 1995. "Informational Efficiency in Developing Equity Markets." Working paper, WP/95/58, International Monetary Fund, Research and Middle Eastern Departments, Washington, D.C.

Claessens, Stijn. 1992. "How Can Developing Countries Hedge Their Bets?" *Finance and Development* (September):13–15.

Claessens, Stijn, Micheal P. Dooley, and Andrew Warner. 1993. "Portfolio Capital Flows: Hot or Cool?" In *Portfolio Investment in Developing Countries,* edited by S. Claessens and S. Gooptu. Washington, D.C.: World Bank.

Culpeper, Roy. 1995. "Resurgence of Private Flows to Latin America: The Role of North American Investors." In *Coping with Capital Surges,* edited by Ricardo Ffrench-Davis and Stephany Griffith-Jones. Boulder, Colo.: Lynne Reiner.

Dos Santos, Teodoro. 1970. "The Structure of Dependence." *American Economic Review* (May):321–336.

Eaton, Leslie. 1994. "Exits Pose Danger in Emerging Markets." *New York Times,* February 12, sec. 1, p. 35.

Erdman, Peter B., and Michael Brandmeyer. 1994. Editors' Introduction. *Columbia Journal of World Business,* summer, p. 5.

Fama, Eugene. 1976. *Foundations of Finance.* New York: Basic Books.

Fernandez-Arias, Eduardo. 1996. "The New Wave of Private Capital Inflows: Push or Pull?" *Journal of Development Economics* 48:389–418.

Fielecke, Norman. 1996. "International Capital Movements." *New England Economic Review,* March/April, pp. 41–60.

Frankel, Jeffrey A., and Andrew K. Rose. 1996. Discussion paper 1349, Centre for Economic Policy Research, London.

Graham, Benjamin, and David Dodd. 1934. *Security Analysis.* New York: McGraw-Hill.

Hale, David D. 1994. "Stock Markets in the New World Order." *Columbia Journal of World Business,* Summer, p. 21.

Hardouvelis, Gikas, Rafael La Porta, and Thierry Wizman. 1995. "What Moves the Discount on Country Equity Funds?" In *Internationalization of Equity Markets*. Cambridge, Mass.: NBER.

Harvey, Campbell R. 1994. "Predictable Risk in Emerging Markets." Working paper no. 4631, NBER, Cambridge, Mass.

Lehmann, Bruce. 1991. "Asset Pricing and Intrinsic Values: A Review Essay." Working paper no. 3873, NBER, Cambridge, Mass.

Loviscek, Anthony L., and Frederick D. Crowley. 1996. "The Impact of Political Shocks on Market Efficiency." Economics Department, Seton Hall Unversity, South Orange, N.J. Photocopy.

McMurdy, Dierdre. 1994. "The Global Gamble." *Maclean's*, June 13, 107:24, 43.

Mushkat, Miron. 1996. *Taking Other People's Money at Short Notice Is Not Necessarily a Bad Idea*. New York: Lehman Brothers, Global Economics.

Page, Benjamin I. 1997. "Trouble for Workers and the Poor: Economic Globalization and the Reshaping of American Politics." Paper prepared for the annual meetings of the Midwest Political Science Association, Chicago, April 10–12.

Reisen, Helmut. 1996. "Managing Volatile Capital Inflows: The Experience of the 1990s." *Asian Development Review* 14:7.

Rohatyn, Felix. 1994. "World Capital: The Need and the Risks." *New York Times Review of Books*, July 14, p. 51.

Scott, Louis. 1990. "Financial Markets Volatility and the Implication for Market Regulation: A Survey." Working paper, International Monetary Fund, Washington, D.C.

Shiller, Robert. 1989. *Market Volatility*. Cambridge: MIT Press.

Sias, Brian. 1996. "Volatility and the Institutional Investor." *Financial Analysts Journal*, March/April, pp. 13–20.

Tesar, Linda L., and Ingrid M. Werner. 1995. "U.S. Equity Investment in Emerging Stock Markets." In *Portfolio Investment in Developing Countries*, World Bank Discussion Papers 228, edited by Stijn Claessens and Sudarshan Gooptu. Washington, D.C.: World Bank.

Turner, Peter. 1994. "Capital Flows in the 1980s." *BIS Economic Papers* 30:36–49.

Ul Haque, Naddem, Donald Mathieson, and Sunil Sharma. 1997. "Causes of Capital Inflows and Policy Responses to Them." *Finance and Development*, March, pp. 3–5.

Wallerstein, Immanuel. 1974. *The Modern World System*. New York: Academic Press.

Weeks, Scott. 1996. "Earning Dedication." *LatinFinance* 88:20.

Woolley, John. 1994. "Review of *Monetary Sovereignty*, by John B. Goodman and *Business and Banking*, by Paulette Kurzer." *Comparative Political Studies* 27 (2):302.

4

Some Lessons for Policy Makers Who Deal with the Mixed Blessing of Capital Inflows

Carmen M. Reinhart and Vincent Raymond Reinhart

I do not dare state that they are simple; there isn't anywhere on earth a single page or single word that is, since each thing implies the universe, whose most obvious trait is complexity.

—Jorge Luis Borgés
Preface to *Doctor Brodie's Report*

The experience of the past decade attests that international investors have considerable resources at their command in the search for high returns. While they are willing to commit capital to any national market in large volume, they are also capable of withdrawing that capital quickly. Movements of such funds—whether in or out—can have significant macroeconomic consequences, the latest reminders of which are the events in Mexico in 1994 and 1995 and in Asia in 1997. The richness of this experience—shared by highly heterogeneous developing countries and economies in transition in Asia, eastern Europe, the former Soviet Union, Latin America, and parts of Africa and the Middle East—provides us with the opportunity to draw tentative lessons for policy makers coping with a world of increasingly integrated capital markets.

Our first lesson is that attracting global investors' attention is a mixed blessing. Capital inflows provide important support for building infrastructure and harnessing natural and human resources. At the same time, surges in capital inflows may distort relative prices, exacerbate weakness in a nation's financial sector, and feed asset-price bubbles. Our review of the

The authors wish to thank Guillermo Calvo, Jeffrey Frankel, Peter Montiel, and Michael Spencer for helpful comments and suggestions. An earlier version of this chapter was presented at the Study Group Meeting on Private Capital Flows to Developing and Transitional Economies held at the Council of Foreign Relations, New York, on April 10, 1995. The views expressed are our own and are not necessarily shared by the Board of Governors of the Federal Reserve System or any of its staff.

record of policy responses to capital inflows suggests that policy makers recognize these tensions. A *capital inflow* represents an increase in the demand for a country's assets. Hence, in the absence of policy intervention, the currency tends to appreciate on foreign exchange markets. Yet, most of the developing countries that received sizable capital inflows during the first half of 1990s actively resisted the nominal exchange rate appreciation, albeit to varying degrees. This reluctance to allow market forces to take their course has had various rationales, including the authorities' explicit commitment (or the less explicit desire) to maintain a fixed exchange rate, a general perception that the inflows are a temporary phenomenon, or an attempt to prevent or delay a real exchange rate appreciation (so as to maintain international competitiveness). Often voiced among policy circles has been the view that an important share of these cross-border financial flows has been short term and volatile. From that perspective, a flood of "hot money" could add to the vulnerability of the financial sector, particularly if the domestic banking system were playing a dominant role in intermediating these flows.

The recent record also shows that these multiple concerns have produced multiple responses to capital inflows (Calvo, Leiderman, and Reinhart 1993, 1994; Schadler et al. 1993; Montiel 1996). Often, policy makers have resorted to some combination of these policies. In this chapter we catalogue nine such policy responses:

- The policy of first recourse across countries and over time has been *sterilized intervention*.[1] To avoid some (or all) of the nominal exchange rate appreciation that would have resulted from the capital inflow, monetary authorities have tended to intervene in the foreign exchange market. The result of that intervention was an accumulation of foreign exchange reserves. To offset some or all of the monetary expansion associated with the purchase of foreign exchange, central banks have most often opted to sell treasury bills (or central bank paper). But in many cases these open market operations were complemented by increases in reserve requirements (Reinhart and Reinhart n.d.) and shifts of government deposits (or other such funds) from the banking system to the central bank.
- *Fiscal austerity measures*, particularly on the spending side, have been used to attempt to alleviate some of the pressures on the real exchange rate and to cool down overheating in the economy, the effectiveness of which has been magnified when expenditures fall heavily on nontraded goods. Furthermore, fiscal surpluses de-

---

1. To our knowledge, Argentina is the only country in the recent inflow episode that did not attempt to sterilize any part of its foreign exchange market intervention.

posited at the central bank have helped "sterilize" the expansive monetary effects of foreign exchange purchases.

- *Trade liberalization* has been accelerated in some cases, in the hope that productivity gains in the nontraded sector could dampen pressures on the real exchange rate. Moreover, the reduction of distortions associated with controls on trade may temporarily widen the current account deficit, effectively absorbing some of the inflows without boosting domestic demand.

- *Liberalization of capital outflows* has also been a popular response to rising capital inflows. By permitting domestic residents to hold foreign assets, the conventional wisdom holds, gross outflows would increase, thereby reducing net inflows (Labán and Larraín 1994).

- Various forms of *controls on capital inflows*—whether in the form of taxes, quantitative restrictions, or in the guise of prudential measures—usually imposed on the financial sector have also been implemented; most of these have been aimed at deterring short-term inflows. In addition, as argued by Budnevich and Cifuentes (1993), by introducing these capital controls, some measures of short-run monetary independence may be gained, even within a relatively rigid exchange rate regime.

- *Revaluation of the nominal exchange rate* has also been resorted to, particularly as inflows became persistent and the curtailment of the monetary expansion associated with the accumulation of foreign exchange reserves became increasingly difficult and costly. In some cases, the authorities reached the conclusion that, if an appreciation of the real exchange rate was inevitable, it was better that it occur through a change in the nominal exchange rate than through an increase in domestic inflation.

- *Greater exchange rate flexibility,* as in the case of a revaluation, has allowed adjustment to take place through the nominal exchange rate rather than through domestic prices. However, unlike discrete revaluations in the context of an exchange rate peg or a crawl, greater flexibility increases the independence of the domestic monetary authorities and introduces or increases short-run exchange rate risk. The presence of (or increase in) such risk, it is argued, acts as a deterrent to short-term speculative inflows.

- Less conventional measures that have aimed to *curb customer credit and consumption* have been imposed as countercyclical policies in a number of countries. In most cases, these policies targeted consumption of durable goods.

- In the last leg of the inflow episode, some countries, particularly in East Asia, enacted *prudential measures* to curb the exposure of the domestic banking sector to the vagaries of real estate prices and equity markets. Judging from the scope and depth of the banking crises in several Asian countries, these measures may have been implemented too late.

Another lesson that we present in this chapter is that the law of unintended consequences has not been repealed. Multiple policy responses to capital inflows have tended to interact in ways that were probably not anticipated by the framers of such policies. Three examples make this point clear:

- The Mexican mix observed from 1990 to 1993 kept the value of the peso very stable in the short run, sterilized foreign exchange intervention, and allowed international investors free reign in the home market. Unfortunately, these policies combined to attract an even larger volume of short-term inflows, as international investors were lured by short-term dollar returns that were made more attractive by the predictability of the near-term value of the peso and the effect of sterilization operations that boosted domestic rates.
- Brazilians brought together sterilized intervention and controls on inflows in 1994 and 1995. However, the comparatively high interest rate differentials that usually accompany sterilization probably acted as an inducement to circumvent the capital controls.
- East Asians altered the effectiveness of liberalizing controls on outflows to reduce net capital inflows by engaging in sizable sterilized intervention at the same time. The high domestic interest rates kept capital at home and may have attracted more inflows because they were interpreted as a positive signal of the future economic environment (which was also the experience in Malaysia and Thailand).

The evidence is not just anecdotal. Examining the impact of sterilization policies and capital controls on the volume and composition of capital inflows for a panel of fifteen capital-importing countries, Montiel and Reinhart (1997) found systematic evidence that sterilization policies increased the overall volume of capital inflows and skewed their composition toward short maturities.

Because sterilized intervention is the most universal policy response, we review the varied forms this policy has taken. Then we discuss its impact on interest rates, spreads, and the level and composition of capital flows.. After that we focus on two exchange rate policies: a realignment of the exchange rate while maintaining the prevailing exchange rate regime and a change in the exchange rate regime altogether. The fiscal policy response to rising capital flows, as well as the implications it has for the conduct of monetary policy, are covered next. Then we examine policies that affect the capital account, such as the liberalization of capital outflows and policies to discourage inflows. We address issues related to the interaction of these policies in the final section.

Sterilized Intervention

The aims of sterilized intervention are twofold. Intervention in the foreign exchange market is designed to prevent or at least damp nominal exchange rate appreciation. Meanwhile, an accompanying sale of securities in the domestic open market drains domestic reserves so as to offset the effects on total reserves—and hence the money supply—that would otherwise ensue from the central bank's accumulation of foreign exchange reserves.

Although the mechanics are clear, the motive for this policy is less so. Among Robert Mundell's the many contributions is the observation that, when capital is perfectly mobile internationally and assets completely substitutable, sterilized intervention can have no impact on the exchange rate (Mundell 1963). Subsequent research has uncovered some mechanisms through which sterilized intervention can have real consequences. Mussa (1981) suggests a role for signaling. Whereas the intervention per se is inconsequential, it may be the harbinger of a policy action that will have more weight, such as future changes in domestic reserve market conditions. Reinhart and Reinhart (n.d.) point out that, often, injections of reserves acquired in foreign exchange operations are offset by changes in reserve requirements, not open market operations. In that case, there may be real effects because reserve requirements are a tax that distorts deposit or lending rates.

In general, the empirical evidence of the effectiveness of sterilized intervention in industrial countries is mixed. Some researchers (Obstfeld 1990) argue that intervention has not played an important role in currency realignments in recent years, while others (Dominguez and Frankel 1993, for instance) conclude that it has.[2] Studies of developing countries have more often concluded that sterilization has a short-run effect (i.e., changes in domestic credit are not instantaneously offset by changes in net foreign assets) (Schadler et al. 1993). However, other studies have found evidence of high capital mobility in the developing countries that have experienced heavy capital inflows, thus casting greater doubts on the ability of sterilization efforts to have any effect (Frankel 1994a). In any case, there appears to be little room for sterilization policies to have a sustained consequence.

2. Taylor (1993) provides a review of this literature.

Frankel (1994b) analyzed the conditions under which sterilization of capital inflows raises domestic interest rates or simply prevents them from converging to international levels. For instance, domestic interest rates would rise if the domestic-currency assets that investors want to hold (i.e., bank certificates of deposit [CDs], stocks, and bonds) are poor substitutes for short-term central bank paper or treasury bills supplied by the central bank. To induce investors to hold the increased supply of short-term paper, the price of this paper has to decline and yields have to increase. Also, interest rates could rise if the demand for money rose, due, for example, to a successful reduction in inflation or to higher income. By sterilizing, the monetary authorities are not accommodating the increased demand for money and, hence, force the money market to clear at a higher interest rate. Calvo (1991) stresses the potential quasi-fiscal losses associated with sterilization, because the central bank acquires relatively low-yield foreign exchange reserves and issues high-yield sterilization bonds. Focusing on the experience of Colombia in 1991, a recent study cautioned that large-scale sterilization policies could lead to higher domestic short-term interest rates and wider differentials vis-à-vis international interest rates, promoting further inflows of short-term capital (Calvo, Leiderman, and Reinhart 1993).

In the remainder of this section we analyze the recent experience of several countries in which sterilization intervention was a central policy response to the surge in capital inflows. The focus is on episodes with relatively well-defined timing of policy changes (Folkerts-Landau et al. 1995). However, because sterilization policies have taken a variety of forms, it is necessary first to catalogue sterilization's possible manifestations. Specifically, we consider three types of sterilization policies: open market operations, reserve requirement changes, and the management of government deposits.

Open Market Operations

Sterilization through open market operations has usually meant that the central bank sells either government securities, such as treasury bills, or its own paper to offset the effect on domestic reserves of the purchase in the foreign currency market—usually U.S. dollars. Mexico, for instance, sterilized by means of central bank sales of government debt (*cetes* and *tesobonos*). In many countries, including Chile, Colombia, Indonesia, Korea, and the Philippines, the central bank issued its own debt for the purposes of draining domestic reserves from the banking system. In some instances (Malaysia and Sri Lanka), open market operations were initially conducted by selling public sector debt until the central bank depleted its holdings of government debt (either because of the large scale of the sterilization effort or because new issuance dwindled as public finances were consolidated),at which point the central bank began to auction its own debt (table 4.1).

Some analysts have argued that the main advantage of sterilization through open market operations is that it offers a viable way of curtailing monetary and credit expansion without levying a heavier tax burden on the banking system and inducing financial disintermediation, as occurs when reserve requirements are increased (Calvo, Leiderman, and Reinhart 1994). The main disadvantages are that it may entail sizable central bank costs, even in a relatively short period of time.[3] Moreover, sterilization may sufficiently increase the spread of domestic over international interest rates so as to attract *more* short-term capital. Despite these drawbacks, sterilization may be warranted if there are concerns that the banking system is not capable of adequately intermediating capital inflows, or the inflows are perceived to be temporary.

The intensity with which these policies have been applied has varied considerably across countries and over time (see table 4.1). Central banks in Chile during the first half of 1990, Colombia in most of 1991, the Czech Republic during the latter half of 1994 and early 1995, Indonesia during 1991–1992, Malaysia from mid-1991 through early 1993, and Sri Lanka in 1991–1992 conducted open market operations on a scale that sterilized their capital inflows almost fully.[4] Other central banks, including those of Chile (mid-1991 to the present), Korea, Mexico, the Philippines, and Thailand sterilized a portion of the inflows they experienced. For example, when capital inflows peaked in 1993, Mexico sterilized about one-quarter of them (Banco de Mexico 1993).

Reserve Requirements

Reserve requirements can be manipulated to reduce the money multiplier and curtail the monetary expansion associated with central bank intervention in the foreign exchange market (Reinhart and Reinhart n.d.). Some countries have opted simply to increase the statutory reserve requirement on all domestic currency deposits. Leading examples of this policy are Costa Rica, the Czech Republic, Malaysia, and Sri Lanka. At the start of the

3. Rodriguez (1992) suggests that the central bank losses associated with Colombia's sterilization efforts during 1991 amounted to between 0.5 percent and 0.7 percent of GDP. Kiguel and Leiderman (1994) indicate that from 1990 to mid-1992 Chile's central bank losses due to sterilization policies were about 1.4 percent of GDP. Gurria (1993) estimates that the quasi-fiscal losses for Mexico were in the range of 0.2 percent to 0.4 percent per year during 1990–1992. Central bank losses in Indonesia, Malaysia, and Sri Lanka have also been nontrivial.

4. In the cases of Indonesia and Malaysia, forms of sterilization other than open market operations were also being used during those periods. These will be discussed later.

Table 4.1a Sterilization through open market operations: Africa and Asia[a]

Egypt (1991)	
February 1991–1994	Sterilization through open market sales of treasury bills.

Indonesia (1990)	
February 1991	Significant monetary tightening. Sales of SBIs increase sharply.
March 1991	State enterprises are instructed to convert Rp 10 trillion in bank deposits to Bank Indonesia certificates (SBIs).
May 1993	Monetary policy begins to ease and sterilization efforts diminish.

Kenya (1993)	
October 1993–March 1994	Large-scale sterilization through increased sales by the Central Bank of Kenya of treasury bills.

Korea (1992) ·	
April 1993	Korea begins to sterilize through auctions of monetary stabilization bonds (MSBs). Previously, open market operations consisted of a mandatory allocation scheme whereby the Bank of Korea allocated securities at controlled, below-market interest rates.

Malaysia (1989)	
1990	Central bank begins to borrow in interbank market.
1992	Heavy open market operations begin as the central bank steps up sales of treasury bills and borrows heavily in the interbank market.
February 10, 1993	Bank Negara begins ti issue Bank Negara bills (BNBs), which are similar to Malaysian government treasury bills. This move was prompted by the need to have an instrument through which to conduct open market operations, because Treasuries issuance was dwindling in line with the shrinking government deficit. During the first half of 1993 issuance is RM 9,300 billion; during the second half issuance tapers off to RM 4,300 billion.
February 16, 1993	The central bank sells the first issues of the Malaysia Savings Bond (MSB), RM 1 billion.

Philippines (1992)	
1992	Sterilization efforts intensify through issuance of central bank bills and borrowings under the central bank reverse repurchase facility. Further, in view of the central bank's lack of holding of treasury bills, the government is called to issue government securities and deposit the proceeds with the central bank.
Mid-1993	Sterilization efforts diminish and the government shifts its deposits out of the central bank to commercial banks. More adjustment comes through allowing the nominal exchange rate to appreciate.

continued

Table 4.1a Continued

Philippines (1992)	
1991–1992	Intense sterilization efforts through open market operations of treasury bills.
Mid-1993	After depleting its holdings of treasury bills, the central bank begins to issue paper to conduct open market operations. Sterilization efforts moderate.

Thailand (1988)	
1989–91	Heavy sterilization period. The Bank of Thailand increases its rediscount rate from 8 percent at the end of 1989 to 12 percent at the end of 1990.
Late 1989	The central bank reduces commercial banks' access to refinancing facilities. The amount of refinancing is reduced from 100 percent to 50 percent of the face value of qualifying notes.
Mid-1993	Sterilization efforts cease.

Uganda (1993)	
1993–April 1994	Sterilization takes place through central bank sales of Treasury bills. Due to insufficient new issues and the lack of a well-developed secondary market, it becomes increasingly difficult for the central bank to pursue sterilization policies for an extended period of time.

Sources: Alfiler 1994, Asea and Reinhart (1995), Aziz 1994, Banco de Mexico 1993, Bank Negara Annual Report, various issues, Hettiarachi and Herat 1994, and Nijathaworn and Dejthamrong 1994.
[a] The date next to the country name denotes the first year of the surge in inflows.

inflow episode in 1989, Malaysia's statutory reserve requirement was 3.5 percent, but by early 1994 it had been raised to 11.5 percent (table 4.2). Other countries (Colombia in 1991) imposed high marginal reserve requirements. In several countries in which banks receive foreign currency deposits (Chile, Peru, and Sri Lanka), reserve requirements on these accounts were imposed either for the first time or hiked. Whereas this latter measure does not affect the narrow-money multiplier, it does reduce expansion in the broader aggregates relative to domestic reserves.

Not all countries, however, fit this mold. In some, financial-sector reform and liberalization had the effect of reducing reserve requirements during or shortly before the large influx of capital. For example, in April 1989 Mexico replaced reserve requirements with a 30 percent liquidity ratio that could be satisfied by holding interest-bearing government paper (Coorey 1992). Argentina also reduced reserve requirements during the inflow period. In the Philippines in 1994 the Bangko Central reduced reserve requirements with the express objective of inducing a decline in domestic interest rates and a narrowing of the domestic-to-international interest rate spread to reduce capital inflows (Alfiler 1994). In this case, the

Table 4.1b Sterilization through open market operations: eastern Europe and Latin America[a]

Chile (1990)	
January 5, 1990	Large-scale sterilization efforts begin as the central bank increases its long-term real interest rate on bonds from 6.9 percent to 9.7 percent and its interest rate on 90-day paper from 6.8 percent to 8.7 percent.
August 17, 1990	Short term rates begin a moderate decline (from 8.7 percent to 8.2 percent).
March 18, 1991	Further easing of policy, with 90-day paper reaching 5.7 percent and 360-day paper declining from 9.2 percent to 5.9 percent.
April 2, 1992	Further easing with bond rate reduced from 9.7 percent to 6.6 percent.
August 20, 1992	Policy begins to tighten with short-term rate rising to 5.7 percent.
November 2, 1992	Further tightening with short-term rate rising to 6.5 percent and long-term rate rising to 7.7 percent.
September 1993	Yield curve becomes inverted, with 10-year bond rate at 6.4 percent and short rates remaining at 6.5 percent.
November 2, 1992	Further tightening.
Colombia (1991)	
January 1991	Heavy sterilization of inflows begins.
October 1991	Sterilization policies are abandoned.
Czech Republic (1992)	
August 1994–March 1995	Sterilization policies are conducted through heavy sales of government securities and central bank paper.
Mexico (1990)	
1990–1993	Partial sterilization of inflows through sales of government paper, mostly domestic currency–denominated *cetes*.

Sources: Aziz 1994, Banco Central de Chile Memoria Anual, various issues, Banco Central de Chile, Evolucion de la Economica, various issues, Bank Negara Annual Report, various issues, Harinowo and Belchere 1994, Kan 1994, Laporan Mingguan Weekly Report, various issues.
[a] The date next to the country name denotes the first year of the surge in inflows.

reduction in reserve requirements was not offset by changes in reserves, thus the domestic money stock rose.

Reserve requirements are a tax on the banking system that will be passed in whole or in part to customers—either or depositors or borrowers or both.[5] If it is the former, an increase in the reserve tax lowers domestic deposit rates and acts a disincentive to capital inflows. If it increases lending rates, in contrast, it may induce firms to borrow abroad, stimulating further inflows. Applying Dornbush's overshooting model, Reinhart and Reinhart (n.d.) considered the impact on economic activity and relative prices of a

---

5. This assumes, as is the case almost worldwide, that reserves that commercial banks hold at the central banks do not earn interest.

Table 4.2a Changes in reserve requirements: Africa and Asia[a]

Kenya (1992)	
October 1993–March 1994	Statutory cash ratio is increased in three steps from 12 percent to 20 percent.

Indonesia (1990)	
December 14, 1995	Commercial bank reserve requirement is raised from 2 percent to 3 percent.

Malaysia (1989)	
May 2, 1989	Reserve requirement is increased to 4.5 percent from 3.5 percent for commercial banks and 3.0 percent for finance companies.
October 16, 1989	Reserve requirement is increased from 4.5 percent to 5.5 percent.
January 16, 1990	Reserve requirement is increased from 5.5 percent to 6.5 percent.
August 16, 1990	Reserve requirement is increased from 6.5 percent to 7.5 percent.
September 16, 1991	All outstanding ringgit received through swap transactions with nonresidents including offshore banks would be included in the eligible liabilities base and be subject to the statutory reserve requirement.s
May 2, 1992	Reserve requirement increased from 7.5 percent to 8.5 percent.
January 3, 1994	Reserve requirement increased from 8.5 percent to 9.5 percent. The reserve requirement is extended to cover foreign currency deposits and transactions (such as foreign currency borrowing from foreign banking institutions and interbank borrowing). Previously it had applied only to ringgit-denominated transactions.
1994	Reserve requirement increased in two steps to 11.5 percent.
February 1, 1996	Reserve requirement raised to 12.5 percent.

Philippines (1992)	
August 15, 1994	The reserve requirement is reduced from 20 percent to 17 percent, with the objective of inducing a decline in domestic interest rates.

Sri Lanka (1991)	
November 1, 1991	Reserve requirement raised to 13 percent.
January 2, 1992	Reserve requirement raised to 14 percent.
September 4, 1992	Reserve requirement extended to include foreign currency deposits.
September 24, 1992	Reserve requirement lowered to 13 percent.
January 29, 1993	Reserve requirement raised to 13.5 percent.
April 16, 1993	Reserve requirement raised to 14 percent.
May 21, 1993	Reserve requirement raised to 15 percent.

Source: Hettiarachi and Herat 1994.
[a] The date next to the country name denotes the first year of the surge in inflows.

Table 4.2b Changes in reserve requirements: Eastern Europe and Latin America[a]

	Argentina (1991)
August 15, 1993	Reserve requirements on domestic and foreign currency demand deposits are raised from 40 percent to 43 percent. A 3 percent reserve requirement on domestic and foreign currency 30- to 89-day time deposits is introduced.

	Brazil (1992)
July 1, 1994	A 100 percent marginal reserve requirement on demand deposits and a 20 percent reserve requirement on time deposits is introduced. Reserve requirements on saving deposits are raised from 10–15 percent to 20 percent.
August 31, 1994	Reserve requirement on time and saving deposits are raised to 30 percent.
December 6, 1994	A 15 percent reserve requirement is introduced on loans for the purchase of goods.
April 28, 1995	Reserve requirement on time deposits is raised again from 27 percent to 30 percent. The marginal reserve requirement on certificates of deposit is raised to 60 percent. The reserve requirement on loans is raised from 6 percent to 18 percent.

	Chile (1990)
January 1992	Nonremunerated 20 percent reserve requirement is introduced on deposits and loans in foreign currency held by commercial banks. The reserve requirement must be maintained for 1 year.
May 1992	Reserve requirement on foreign currency deposits and loans held by commercial banks is increased to 30 percent. The requirement was designed to make the tax rate fall as the maturity increases. A 30 percent marginal reserve requirement is introduced on interbank deposits.

	Colombia (1991)
January 1991	Marginal reserve requirements of 100 percent are imposed on all new deposits. These reserves are held as interest-bearing central bank bonds.
September 1991	The marginal reserve requirement is replaced by an increase in reserve requirements on most deposits.

	Costa Rica (1991)
October 1992	Reserve requirement on domestic currency demand deposits is raised from 30 percent to 34 percent, and on time deposits from 10 percent to 14 percent.

	Czech Republic (1992)
August 1994	Reserve requirements are raised from 9 percent to 12 percent.

	Mexico (1990)
April 1992	A compulsory liquidity coefficient for dollar liabilities is set at 15 percent. This coefficient must be invested in liquid securities denominated in the same currency

Sources: Aziz 1994, Banco Central de Chile Memoria Anual, various issues, Banco Central de Chile, Evolucion de la Economia, various issues, Bank Negara Annual Report, various issues, Gurria 1993, Hettiarachi and Herat 1994, and Rodriques 1991.
[a] The date next to the country name denotes the first year of the surge in inflows.

rise in reserve requirements paired with an increase in domestic reserves that keeps the domestic money stock fixed. If borrowers have limited access to international capital markets (as is the case in most of these countries), raising reserve requirements tends to depreciate the real exchange rate and improve the current account.

In the majority of cases studied by Reinhart and Reinhart (n.d.), both deposit and lending rates adjusted. Hence, as with open market operations, the impact on of reserve requirement policy capital flows need not be what was intended. Further, if disintermediation occurs and transactions increasingly take place in other financial institutions that are not subject to the requirements, a reserve requirement increase may have the unappealing feature of shifting activities toward entities that are more difficult to supervise and regulate (Calvo, Leiderman, and Reinhart 1994; Folkerts-Landau et al. 1995).

Management of Funds and Government Deposits

Indonesia, Malaysia, Taiwan Province of China, and Thailand have, at various times, shifted deposits of the public sector or pension funds from the banking system to the central bank (table 4.3) (Reisen 1993; Folkerts-Landau 1995). In the case of Mexico, the government also placed its privatization proceeds in the central bank during 1991.

If these funds are counted as part of the money stock, then the transfer to the central bank works to increase reserve requirements (in that the reserve requirement on those deposits is increased to 100 percent). If the deposits are not counted as part of the money stock, then the shift is more akin to a liquidity-draining open market operation, with the difference that the central bank may not have to pay a market rate of interest on its deposits as it would on its sterilization bonds. In this event, this mode of sterilization does not constitute a tax on the banking system, nor does it appear to increase short-term interest rates as much as sales of sterilization bonds. If the deposits are not remunerated, there is no quasi-fiscal cost; if they are remunerated at below-market interest rates, there is a quasi-fiscal cost, but it is below the cost of open market operations.[6] However, these deposit withdrawals, if volatile and unpredictable, could complicate banks' cash management. Moreover, to the extent that some of the funds are not public sector deposits but rather insurance funds—along the lines of Malaysia's Employee Provident Fund or Singapore's Central Provident Fund, with their costs paid by those who contribute to the fund—it is a form of financial repression. Lastly, such policies may be limited in scope

---

6. Quasi-fiscal costs are reduced or eliminated by transferring these costs to the government (i.e., by making them explicit fiscal costs).

Table 4.3 Sterilization through management of government funds[a]

	Czech Republic (1992)
December 1994–February 1995	Commercial bank deposits of the National Property Fund, amounting to about Kc 16 billion (or 10 percent of reserve money), are transferred to the Czech National Bank.
May 1995	An additional Kc 6 billion is transferred.
	Malaysia (1989)
April 1990	The money market operations (MMO) account on the accountant general maintained at the central bank is reactivated. Government deposits that were placed with the banking system maturing that year (about $3.7 billion) are withdrawn from the system and deposited in the MMO account.
1992–1994	Transfer of government and Employee Provident Fund (EPF) deposits to the central bank.
	Philippines (1992)
	The national government issues securities and deposits proceeds with the central bank.
	Singapore
	Savings of Central Provident Fund (CPF) are heavily invested in government bonds.
	Taiwan, Province of China
	Postal savings are transferred from the domestic banks to the central bank
	Thailand (1988)
1989 to mid-1992	Government deposits held at the Bank of Thailand increases from 25 percent of total deposits at the end of 1987 to 82 percent in mid-1992.

Sources: Aziz 1994, Bank Negara Annual Report, various issues, and Folkerts-Landau et al. 1995.
[a] The date next to the country name denotes the first year of the surge in inflows.

by the availability of the eligible funds. For instance, government deposits held at the Bank of Thailand increased from 25 percent of total government deposits at the end of 1987 to 82 percent in mid-1992.

Effects on Interest Rates, Spreads and Capital Flows

Several distinct episodes of intensive sterilization offer an opportunity to gauge the macroeconomic effects of these policies. The main episodes we examine include Chile during the first half of 1990, Colombia through most of 1991, Indonesia during 1991–1992, and Malaysia from mid-1991 through early 1993. Six empirical regularities characterize these episodes.

First, in all cases, considerable international reserves accumulated, suggesting that the central bank had intervened to avoid or mitigate an exchange rate appreciation.

Second, in all cases, despite heavy foreign exchange intervention by the central banks, either the rate of devaluation slowed or there was a revaluation (Malaysia). These two observations jointly attest to the large size of the inflows.

Third, reflecting the heavy open market operations, issuance of central bank notes increased dramatically (in both absolute terms and relative to the monetary base) and in a relatively short period of time. In the case of Colombia, the ratio of open market paper to the monetary base rose from less than 30 percent in late 1990 to more than 80 percent by October 1991. In Chile, that ratio gained more than 100 percentage points in a period of six months. In Indonesia, there was a similar surge in outstanding Bank Indonesia Certificates. In Malaysia, where the central bank was selling treasury bills and Bank Negara bills, as well as borrowing heavily in the interbank market, a more comprehensive indicator of the sterilization effort is required. In 1990, during the first year of heavy inflows, Bank Negara increased liquidity by $6.5 billion; by 1993, the last year of the heavy sterilization effort (capital controls were imposed at the beginning of 1994), Bank Negara was draining liquidity at a rate of $40 billion a year.

Fourth, in all four episodes, domestic short-term interest rose when sterilization began. Short-term rates increased in Korea (1988–1989), Sri Lanka (1992–1993), and the Philippines (1992–1993:first half).[7] On the surface, this rise in domestic rates may appear inexplicable in that the inflows of capital witness to greater demand for domestic assets. Moreover, in several of these countries (including Chile and Colombia), country risk premiums declined, which should also have put downward pressure on domestic interest rates.[8] Table 4.4 summarizes the evolution of interest rates before, during, and after the sterilization period. The evidence in this table shows that the rise in interest rates was often quite pronounced and, given the reduced rate of devaluation (or in the case of Malaysia, an appreciation), the rise in ex post dollar interest rates was even greater.

This pattern may support Frankel's (1994b) contention that imperfect asset substitutability plays a role. If increased investor demand falls on corporate bonds and equities, and they are poor substitutes for the short-term

7. See Hettiarachchi and Herat (1994) for Sri Lanka and Alfiler (1994) for the Philippines. The Colombian experience is detailed by Rodriguez (1992). For a comprehensive study of the Indonesian case see Harinowo and Belchere (1994); for the Malaysian experience see Aziz (1994).
8. An indication of the evolution of country risk is given by the behavior of secondary-market prices for loans, which increased sharply during these episodes (Calvo, Leiderman, and Reinhart 1993).

Table 4.4 Interest rates and sterilization policies (in percent, annual rates)

	In domestic currency		Converted dollars	
CHILE				
	Interest rate on			
	30–89 days		30–89 days	
	Loans	Deposits	Loans	Deposits
Pre-inflow 1988:1–1989:12	28.54	21.41	16.83	10.39
Capital inflows and heavy sterilization 1990:1–1990:7	46.58	37.80	35.16	27.01
Capital inflows and heavy sterilization 1990:7–1994:5	27.93	21.76	18.91	13.17
INDONESIA				
	Prime loans	90-day deposits	Prime loans	90-day deposits
Early inflow period 1989–1990:12	22.54	17.99	17.03	13.24
Capital inflows and heavy sterilization 1991–1992:12	25.27	21.88	20.84	17.58
Capital inflows and moderate sterilization 1993:1–1994:6	19.22	13.66	15.30	9.93
COLOMBIA				
	Prime loans	Central bank paper	Prime loans	Central bank paper
Pre-inflow 1989–1990:12	22.54	17.99	17.03	13.24
Capital inflows and heavy sterilization 1991:1–1991:11	47.16	42.08	10.31	18.85
Capital inflows and moderate sterilization 1991:12–1993:12	36.95	24.31	11.08	20.53
MALAYSIA				
		Deposits		Deposits
Early inflow 1989:1–1991:6		6.21		5.52
Capital inflows and heavy sterilization 1991:7–1993:6		7.92		13.07
Capital inflows, moderate sterilization, and heavy foreign exchange intervention 1993:7–1993:12		6.74		−4.87
Capital controls and currency appreciation 1994:1–1994:6		5.30		18.19

Source: Various central bank bulletins and Bloomberg.

paper (or short-term treasuries) being supplied in increasing quantities by the central bank, domestic short-term rates would rise. In addition, given that capital inflows usually coincided with a period of stronger economic activity (and, in some instances, declining inflation), it is not implausible to suppose that money demand increased. In that circumstance, monetary policy was inadvertently tight in that the central bank was not accommodating an increase in money demand. In any case, interest rates fell when sterilization policies were abandoned.

Fifth, and following from the previous observation, ex post interest rate spreads (in dollars) were kept high by the sterilization policies, suggesting that policy has an impact, at least in the short-run, in determining how quickly domestic interest rates converge to international levels.[9] In all these cases, domestic short-term interest rate spreads remained relatively high compared with those of, say, Argentina, which did not undertake any form of sterilization. However, the monetary authorities' ability to affect domestic interest rates and effectively control the money supply appears to have eroded over time.[10] Indeed, this conclusion runs through many case studies (Alfiler 1994; Aziz 1994; Harinowo and Belchere 1994; Hettiarachchi and Herat 1994; Rodriguez 1992). In all four cases considered, sterilization policies were either abandoned altogether, scaled back, or complemented by capital controls, as it became evident that the high domestic interest rates were attracting more inflows.

Sixth, in addition to attracting further short-term flows, the rise in short-term interest rates (and interest rate differentials) associated with sterilized intervention dampened investment demand when sustained for a sufficient period. That is, as a result of the intervention—holding all else equal—the cost of capital rose with the returns on less risky assets (such as government paper). As a consequence, investment in financial assets increased relative to investment in plants and equipment. Thus, sterilized intervention could have encouraged a shift in the composition of capital inflows away from long-term flows toward short-term flows. In all of these countries, short-term flows as a share of total capital inflows rose, at least initially, in response to sterilization of intervention.[11] There does not appear, however, to have been any pronounced or sustained shift in the composition of capital inflows as a result of such intervention, owing possibly to the briefness of the episodes or mitigating factors (principally those influencing foreign direct investment behavior).

9. Frankel (1994b), for instance, has suggested that expected devaluation can fully account for observed interest differentials. However, his result would not be inconsistent with a steady-state offset coefficient of unity.

10. This is consistent with the findings of Schadler et al. (1993).

11. A more detailed description of changes in the composition of capital flows is provided by Montiel and Reinhart (1997).

Exchange Rate Policy

As a general rule, rising capital inflows have tended to induce an appreciation of the nominal exchange rate. In the short-run, monetary authorities have often opted to limit or avoid the nominal appreciation, but as the inflows persisted and reserves accumulated, these policies became more costly. As a result, several countries allowed their currencies to respond more to market forces by either revaluing or increasing exchange rate flexibility, or as in the cases of Chile and Colombia, allowing both. In the remainder of this section we discuss the relative merits of greater exchange rate flexibility and review the experiences that several capital-importing countries have had with these policies.

Revaluation

In a floating exchange rate regime, an appreciation of the nominal exchange rate in response to an increased demand for domestic assets need not prompt policy action because the exchange rate is free to appreciate. However, if the prevailing arrangement involves an official commitment to a peg, crawling peg, or narrow band, then at some point a decision to realign may be necessary. There are several advantages of allowing the nominal exchange rate to appreciate during periods of heavy capital inflows (Calvo, Leiderman, and Reinhart 1994). First, such appreciation insulates the money supply, domestic credit, and the banking system from the inflows, which is particularly desirable if the inflows are perceived to be highly reversible. If banking supervision is poor and there are inefficiencies in pricing risk, there may be additional reasons to limit banks' role in intermediating the capital inflows. Second, if economic fundamentals warrant a real exchange rate appreciation, the adjustment comes via the exchange rate and not via higher inflation. Third, and related to the previous point, because of the pass-through from the exchange rate to domestic prices, an appreciation may help reduce inflation.

Despite the advantages of allowing the exchange rate to adjust to changing market conditions, revaluations have been a relatively uncommon response to surging capital inflows (hence the prevalence of sterilized intervention policies). In Chile and Colombia, the realignment was sought only after it became evident that the inflows and the exchange rate pressures were more persistent than initially believed. Between April 1991 and June 1991, Chile's band was revalued by a cumulative 3.4 percent (table 4.5). Larger revaluations followed in January 1992 (5 percent) and November 1994 (9.5 percent), as the exchange rate became persistently stuck on the floor of the band (Budnevich and Cifuentes 1993). A similar pattern emerged in Colombia, where a crawling peg system had been in place for

Table 4.5 Revaluations of the exchange rate[a]

Chile (1990)	
April 1991	The band is revalued by 0.7 percent.
May 1991	The band is revalued by 0.7 percent.
June 1991	The band is revalued by 2 percent.
January 23, 1992	The band is revalued by 5 percent.
November 30, 1994	The band is revalued by 9.5 percent.
Colombia (1991)	
June 1991	Nominal revaluation of 2.6 percent.
January 1994	The band is revalued by 5 percent.
December 1994	The band is revalued by 7 percent.

Sources: Banco Central de Chile Memoria Anual. various issues, Banco Central de Chile, Evolucion de la Economia, various issues, Carrasquilla 1995, and Schadler et al. 1993.
[a] The date next to the country name denotes the first year of the surge in inflows.

about 25 years (Carrasquilla 1995). Still within the context of a peg, the exchange rate was revalued by 2.6 percent in June 1991. More substantial realignments occurred much later in 1994 (5 percent and 7 percent in January and November, respectively) in the context of the newly established exchange rate band.

Greater Exchange Rate Flexibility

Allowing the exchange rate to fluctuate more freely in the presence of large capital inflows introduces uncertainty that may well discourage some of the purely speculative (and highly reversible) inflows. Bacchetta and van Wincoop (1994) argue, in the context of a two-country model, that an increase in exchange rate uncertainty creates a bias toward the domestic asset (because the rate of return on the foreign asset is made more uncertain), dampens the sensitivity of the current account to most types of shocks, and reduces net capital flows. Indeed, the higher uncertainty acts like a Tobin tax. In the event of capital outflows, the greater flexibility takes some of the pressure off foreign exchange reserves. In addition, it grants the monetary authorities a greater degree of independence and permits them to exercise more control over the monetary aggregates.

The main disadvantage of a pure float is that massive capital flows may induce steep and abrupt movements in the real exchange rate, which, in turn, may impose a substantial adjustment burden on the economy. In particular, the concern in many countries has been that real appreciation will harm strategic sectors of the economy, for example, the nontraditional export sector. If the inflows are temporary and if there are hysteresis effects—or permanent damage—to exports from the real exchange rate appreciation, there may be reasons for avoiding or dampening the real exchange rate adjustment (Krugman 1987).[12] Some empirical evidence (see, for instance, Grobar 1993) suggests that greater real exchange rate volatility may have negative effects on tradable goods sectors. This result may be due to the existence of incomplete markets, to the extent that financial markets do not provide enough instruments to hedge against such uncertainty.

There is wide cross-country variation in the degree of exchange rate flexibility among the capital-importing countries. Whereas some countries such as Peru and the Philippines have a float, the common ground appears to be that all central banks intervene in the foreign exchange market to some degree. Among the Asian countries, Indonesia widened its intervention band twice (table 4.6), and Malaysia and the Philippines have allowed greater variability in the exchange rate, particularly since 1992 (table 4.7). Among the Latin American countries, Chile, Mexico, and more recently Colombia have allowed some degree of exchange rate flexibility in the context of their exchange rate bands. Both Chile and Mexico widened their bands (see table 4.6 for details), and especially in Chile the exchange rate has been allowed to fluctuate extensively within the band.[13]

However, as table 4.7 highlights, despite announcements of wider bands, the variance of monthly exchange rates in some of these countries has shown little change. The variance of monthly exchange rates in Indonesia, for example, did not change after the band was widened twice in 1994. Similarly, during 1992 and 1993 and most of 1994 the variance of the Mexican peso remained about the same as it was when the exchange rate was fixed (i.e., nil), and about the same as Argentina's exchange rate under the convertibility plan. By contrast, there was a marked jump in the variance of the exchange rate in Colombia after the introduction of the band in January 1994, and in Maylasia there was a more moderate but nonetheless noticeable increase in exchange rate variance.

To date, the historical record is inconclusive as to how much sand is thrown into the gears of international finance by exchange rate variability. But this is because there is too much, not too little, variation in the sample. In the case of Chile, where short-term flows as a proportion of total flows have declined, there were other impediments to short-term inflows (i.e., capital controls) (Reinhart and Smith 1998). In the case of Colombia,

12. Hysteresis effects may arise because of, say, a permanent (or very persistent) loss of market share for a country's exports.
13. Helpman, Leiderman, and Bufman (1995) provide more information about the various aspects of exchange rate bands in Chile and Mexico.

Table 4.6 Increasing exchange rate flexibility[a]

Chile (1990)	
January 1992	The central parity is revalued by 5 percent, and the exchange rate band is widened from 10 percent to 20 percent, 10 percent on each side.
July 1992	The exchange rate ceases to be pegged exclusively to the dollar, and a peg to a basket of currencies (50 percent dollar, 30 percent deutsche mark, and 20 percent yen) is introduced.
November 30, 1994	The central parity is revalued by 9.5 percent. The weights in the currency basket are changed to 40 percent dollar, 35 percent deutsche mark, and 25 percent yen.
Colombia (1991)	
January 25, 1994	An exchange rate band is introduced. the width of the band is 15 percent, and the rate at which the band is to be devalued is equal to 11 percent per year.
Czech Republic (1992)	
February 28, 1996	An exchange rate band is introduced. the width of the band is 15 percent.
Indonesia (1990)	
January 1994	Intervention band widened from 10 to 20 rupiah.
August 1994	Intervention band widened from 20 to 30 rupiah.
January 1, 1996	Intervention band widened from 2 percent to 3 percent.
June 13, 1996	Intervention band widened.
Malaysia (1989)	
Mid-1991	Greater degree of flotation allowed.
Mexico (1990)	
November 11, 1991	An exchange rate band is introduced. The upper limit of the band is depreciated at the rate of 20 cents per day, and the floor remans fixed. Its total width increases from 1.2 percent in November 1991 to 4.3 percent in December 1992.
October 1992	The rate of crawl of the upper limit is increased to 40 cents per day. The band width reaches 8.7 percent by the end of 1993.
Philippines (1992)	
Mid-1992	Reduced foreign exchange intervention allows for a nominal appreciation of the peso.
Thailand (1988)	
January 17, 1997	Central bank board members approve doubling the width of the baht's fluctuation band against the dollar; the move was expected later in the year.

Sources: Aziz 1994, Alfiler 1994, Carrasquilla 1995, Harinowo and Belchere 1994, Gurria 1993, Helpman, Leiderman, and Bufman 1995, and Schadler et al. 1993.
[a] The date next to the country name denotes the first year of the surge in inflows.

Table 4.7 Exchange rate variability (variance of monthly exchange rate changes, in percent)[a]

	Argentina (1991)	Chile (1990)	Colombia (1991)	Mexico (1990)	Indonesia (1990)	Malaysia (1989)	Philippines (1992)	Thailand (1988)
1988	54.18	0.91	0.05	0.56	0.07	0.65	0.21	0.40
1989	12788.58	2.66	0.01	0.01	0.07	0.80	0.16	0.41
1990	3768.23	2.22	0.07	0.07	0.03	0.17	6.16	0.27
1991	358.61[b]	1.22	0.05	0.02	0.02	0.76	0.58	0.37
1992	0.06	5.21	0.01	0.40	0.03	2.69	12.38	2.43
1993	0.07	0.76	0.01	0.09	0.02	2.95	6.43	0.15
1994	0.01	0.75	13.95	3.61	0.02	2.63	2.69	0.14

Source: International Financial Statistics, IFS.
[a] The dates in parentheses indicate the year in which capital inflows began.
[b] Convertibility plan begins in April 1991.

where the composition of flows show a pattern similar to Chile's, the introduction of the band coincided with the imposition of a tax on short-term borrowing, which makes it difficult to isolate the effects of individual policies. For Malaysia, the effects of increased exchange rate variability may have been offset by tight money policies that kept short-term domestic interest rates above world levels.

Fiscal Policies

Another policy reaction to capital inflows has been to tighten fiscal policy by reducing expenditures or increasing taxes, or both (table 4.8). The logic was that fiscal restraint can lower aggregate demand. However, the devil is in the details of how the fiscal gap is closed. For instance, if government expenditure is more heavily weighted toward nontraded goods than is private expenditure, then a cut in government spending may be more effective than heavier taxation of the private sector for alleviating pressures on the real exchange rate. The use of tax policy is even less desirable if consumer credit is readily available, as it usually is during periods of heavy capital inflows. In that circumstance, the greater availability of financing may compensate for the reduction in disposable income owing to the increase in taxes, a tendency that would be particularly pronounced if the tax is perceived as temporary. However, a contraction of government expenditure is always a sensitive political issue that cannot be undertaken on short notice. Such delays increase the risk that, ex post, the policy is procyclical. Further, fiscal policy is usually set on the basis of medium- or long-term considerations such as infrastructure and social spending needs rather than in response to potentially short-term fluctuations in international capital movements (Bercuson and Koenig 1993).

The clearest example of the use of fiscal restraint as a key policy response to capital inflows is Thailand, particularly from 1988 through 1991 (see also Schadler et al. 1993 and Nijathaworn and Dejthamrong 1994). Moderation of government expenditure and a strong cyclical improvement in revenues swung the government budgetary balance from a deficit of 1.4 percent of nominal gross domestic product (GDP) to a surplus of 4.9 percent in 1991.[14] Thailand also provides an example of the conflict between near-term expediency and longer-run ambitions. In the years that followed, the booming growth of the economy generated a need to improve the country's infrastructure, but the pressures on the real exchange

---

14. Public consumption as a share of GDP, which averaged 13.6 percent during 1984–1988 declined to 9.9 percent during 1989–1993, which were the early years of the surge in capital inflows (Calvo, Leiderman, and Reinhart 1994).

Table 4.8 Fiscal austerity measures[a]

Chile (1990)	
1990–1994	Moderation of expenditure. Nonfinancial public sector surplus averages 2.5 percent during this period.
Mid-1990	An increase in the value-added tax rate to 18 percent, an increase in the corporate tax to 15 percent, and an increase in the progressiveness of the personal income tax.
Malaysia (1989)	
1992–1993	Fiscal consolidation. Real public consumption growth is reduced significantly (0.4 percent in 1992). Public sector deficit is reduced to about 1.5 percent of the GDP.
Thailand (1988)	
1988–1991	Moderation of government expenditure. Government budgetary balance (as a percent of the GEDP) swings from a deficit of 1.4 percent to a surplus of 4.9 percent in 1991.
1992	Introduction of a value-added tax.

Sources: Gonzalez 1995, Nijathaworn and Dejthamrong 1994, and Schadler et al. 1993.
[a] The date next to the country name denotes the first year of the surge in inflows.

rate that accompanied the surge in inflows warranted fiscal restraint. Such infrastructure bottlenecks were not exclusive to Thailand. Malaysia, which averaged an annual growth rate of more than 8 percent for seven consecutive years, faced similar constraints. By substantially limiting public consumption, Malaysia began to downsize its public sector during 1992. In that year the overall public sector deficit shrank by about 1 percent of GDP to around 1.5 percent of GDP. Since mid-1990, Chile has also sought fiscal restraint through an increase in the value-added and corporate taxes and by moderating expenditures.

Most other capital-importing countries have not resorted to fiscal restraint in respond to rising capital inflows. Indeed, many of the fiscal austerity measures that were undertaken in the early 1990s were part of domestic inflation stabilization plans, privatization efforts, or adjustments associated with fund programs that were begun at that time or already underway. Examples of such consolidation efforts include Argentina, Mexico, and Sri Lanka. Hence, because of lags and difficulties in initiating a policy change and because of its medium-term focus, fiscal policy is not a particularly effective means of dealing with capital inflows, particularly if the flows are temporary and subject to abrupt changes. There are also important asymmetries in fiscal policy when dealing with fluctuations in international capital inflows. In particular, although fiscal tightening has sometimes been suggested as a means of dealing with inflows, loosening of fiscal policy would not likely stem outflows.

Capital Account Measures

Perhaps frustrated by the indirect and unpredictable means by which traditional stabilization tools influence capital inflows, several countries have adopted direct policies to alter their volume or composition. These policies naturally fall into two groups: those that discourage inflows and those that encourage outflows.

Taxing Short-Term Flows and Prudential Regulation

Government intervention takes its starkest form in the taxation of gross inflows, often as a tax that falls more heavily on short-term inflows. The father of such policy advice, of course, is James Tobin, who has for many years advocated imposing a transactions tax to shift investors' focus to longer-term and presumably more stable outlets for their funds. The theory and practice of a Tobin tax have been explored in Haq, Kaul, and Grunberg (1996) and Reinhart (n.d.). This is one area, though, where practitioners have probably moved more rapidly than theoreticians, in that the policies adopted by Chile in 1991, Colombia in 1993, and more recently, in Thailand in 1996 all could be described as Tobin taxes. In these cases, nonremunerated reserve requirements must be deposited at the central bank on liabilities in foreign currency from direct borrowing by firms. In the case of Colombia, the reserve requirement must be maintained for the duration of the loan and applies to all loans with a maturity of five years or less, except for trade credit with a maturity of four months or less. The percentage of the requirement declines as the maturity lengthens; from 140 percent for funds that have a maturity of thirty days or less to 42.8 percent for five-year funds. Chile's tax is in the form of a nonremunerated 30 percent reserve requirement to be deposited at the central bank for a period of one year on liabilities in foreign currency from direct borrowing by firms. In principle, because of their breadth, these measures affect the household sector, nonfinancial business, and the banking system's ability to borrow offshore.

Brazil has implemented a variety of taxes on inflows, with greater variation across assets as well as across maturities. As with Chile and Colombia, the tax on foreign issuance bonds falls on the borrower. However, some other taxes are paid by foreign lenders. Notably, foreigners investing in the stock market have to pay a 1 percent tax up front.[15] Hence, the tax falls more heavily on active investors that trade more often and hold stock for only relatively short periods of time. The tax paid by foreigners on fixed-income investments has similar characteristics.

15. This was eliminated on March 10, 1995, to encourage inflows in the wake of the Mexican crisis.

The main disadvantage with these measures is that flows are likely to be rerouted through other channels, for example, through over- or underinvoicing of imports and exports because trade credits are exempt from the tax. Others have argued that, in the case of Chile, overinvoicing of imports is not likely to be an attractive alternative because imports are taxed at a comparable rate (Labán and Larraín 1994).[16] Indeed, inflows to Chile in 1991 were below those observed in 1990, possibly attesting to the success of this policy. Whereas net inflows increased, once again in 1992 and beyond, the increases were primarily in foreign direct investment and other long-term flows. A similar pattern emerged in Colombia during 1994, with short-term flows accounting for a declining share of total flows; however, *total* inflows to Colombia continued to increase in 1994.

In other instances, capital controls have been quantitative in nature. Measures implemented have included prudential limits or prohibition on non-trade-related swap activities, offshore borrowing, and banks' net open market foreign exchange positions (Indonesia, Malaysia, Philippines, and Thailand); caps on banks' foreign currency liabilities (Mexico); or more blanket measures that prohibited domestic residents from selling short-term money-market instruments to foreigners (Malaysia).

In Malaysia, a combination of sizable domestic and foreign interest rate differentials and widespread expectation of an appreciation of the ringgit during late 1993 led to a surge in short-term capital inflows that culminated in January 1994 with the imposition of measures to restrict inflows. The inflows came in the form of a marked rise in short-term bank deposits and were seen as speculative in nature. Consequently, most of the measures were directed toward the control of the activities of the financial sector, and most were announced to be temporary (Aziz 1994; Reinhart and Smith 1998). It appears that the most successful of these measures in reducing short-term inflows was that which prohibited domestic residents from selling short-term money-market instruments to foreigners; as the CDs matured and could not be rolled over, short-term inflows (and the monetary aggregates) began to shrink. However, as with taxation of inflows, if such policies are maintained indefinitely they will likely reduce competitiveness and retard the development of the financial sector.[17]

In April 1992, Mexico passed a regulation that limited foreign currency liabilities of commercial banks to 10 percent of their total loan portfolio. However, it is not clear to what extent this measure acted to reduce the size of the capital inflows, because banks' total loan portfolios had been expanding rapidly throughout that period, and the initial share of loans in

16. However, some circumvention of the tax is effected by reclassifying loans as trade related.
17. Malaysia removed most capital controls during the second half of 1994.

foreign currency was well below the 10 percent limit. For example, bank assets grew 41 percent in 1992 while foreign currency loans grew 88 percent; a similar pattern emerged in 1993, with foreign currency loans increasing 50 percent while total loans rose 25 percent. Indeed, the constraint appears to have become binding only in 1994 when total and foreign currency loans both rose by 27 percent.

Based on the recent experiences of these selected countries with policies directed toward curbing short-term capital inflow, two observations stand out. First, the Chilean and Malaysian experience attests that, at least in the short-run, their distinctly different policies were successful in reducing the *volume* of inflows in a relatively brief period of time. Hence, if the inflows are seen as a largely temporary phenomenon, such policies could be effective; the longer the inflows persist or the longer the policies remain in place, however, the greater the chances that the controls will become less binding. Second, it could be argued that, as desired, these policies stretched out the maturity of capital inflows (as was also the case in Colombia).

Liberalizing Capital Inflows

A different approach to tempering the impact of large gross capital inflows has been to remove controls on capital outflows, thereby increasing outflows and lowering net inflows. These policies have usually allowed domestic investors (notably pension funds) to acquire foreign assets. Chile, Colombia, Malaysia, Mexico, Philippines, Sri Lanka, and Thailand are among those that have liberalized capital outflows (table 4.9). This approach assumes that the existing controls on outflows were binding, a proposition that has been questioned by several researchers. It also assumes that gross inflows will *not* be affected in a *positive* manner by the liberalization announcement, which is potentially problematic. On theoretical grounds and based on the evidence from many country cases, it appears that liberalization of outflows has actually induced heavier inflows (Labán and Larraín 1994). Examples include Italy and New Zealand in 1984, Spain in 1986, Yugoslavia in 1990, and Chile in the 1990s. Lifting restrictions on capital outflows sends a positive signal, increasing the confidence of the foreign investors and further stimulating capital inflows.

Lastly, a policy that liberalizes capital outflows presumes that a greater ability by domestic residents to invest abroad will translate into greater investment abroad. In that regard, the effectiveness in inducing outflows may be undermined if domestic interest rates are kept high relative to international levels (say by sterilization policies), because domestic residents would lack sufficient inducement to make the shift into foreign assets

Table 4.9a Liberalization of outflows: Asia[a]

	Malaysia (1989)
August 1993	The minimum amount of equity that must be held by an indigenous Malay group, company, or institution is lowered from 51 percent to 35 percent.
	Philippines (1992)
July 1994	Bangko Central raises the limit on outward investments sources from the banking system from $1 million to $3 million. Restrictions on repatriation of investments (and earnings accruing therefrom) funded by debt-to-equity conversions under the old debt restructuring program are lifted.
	Sri Lanka (1990)
1993	Removal of limits on foreign currency working balances of commercial banks and a lower reserve ratio on foreign currency deposits to the extent that the funds were invested abroad.
	Thailand (1988)
April 1991	Foreign exchange earners are allowed to open foreign exchange accounts with commercial banks in Thailand for amounts up to $500,000 for individuals and $2 million for corporations. Thai investors can freely transfer up to $5 million abroad for direct investment. Bank of Thailand approval requirement of repatriation of investment funds is eliminated.
February 1994	The amount of Thai baht that can be taken out of Vietnam and bordering countries is raised to B 500,000.

Sources: Hettiarachchi and Herat 1994, Nijathaworn and Dejthamrong 1994, and Schadler et al. 1993.
[a] The date next to the country name denotes the first year of the surge in inflows.

(even though it is now permissible). Certainly, stock market returns in dollars during 1990–1993 for several of the countries that liberalized (including Chile, Colombia, Malaysia, Mexico, and Thailand) far exceeded the returns available in major industrial countries.

Banking Regulation and Supervision

A major concern about the intermediation of international capital flows through the domestic banking system is that individual banks are subject to free or subsidized deposit insurance. In other words, there is an implicit commitment by the authorities that banks—especially those of large size—will not be allowed to fail. Made complacent by the assurance of such a safety net, banks may take on more risk in the search for higher return and pay little attention to matching deposit maturities against loan maturities (the former typically being shorter than the latter). Similarly, there could be a mismatch between the currency denomination of bank loans and the currency denomination of profits and incomes of the borrowing sector; for example, consider the producer of a nontradable commodity who borrows

Table 4.9b Liberalization of outflows: Latin America[a]

	Chile (1990)
April 1990	New regulations liberalize foreign exchange market operations. Previously, all foreign exchange market operations were prohibited unless under the central bank's specific authorization. Now, all transactions are permitted unless specifically restricted by the central bank.
1991	In a number of steps (February, April, May, and October), commercial banks are permitted to increase external trade financing and use up to 25 percent of foreign exchange time deposits for foreign trade financing. Joint venture rules are simplified, and the waiting period for remitting capital invested in Chile under the debt conversion program is shortened. Procedures for enterprises to directly invest abroad are modified and made easier. (These types of transactions were already being done through the legal informal market.)
March 1992	Pension funds are allowed to hold a portion of their portfolio in foreign assets (government bonds, certificates of deposit, and bankers' acceptances). Limit on these investments is increased gradually to 10 percent of investment portfolio. Limit on net foreign exchange holdings of commercial banks is doubled. Share of export receipts exempt from surrender requirements is increased. Allocations of foreign exchange for a variety of payments abroad (including travel) are raised. Period for advance purchase of foreign exchange for debt service is extended.

	Colombia (1990)
June 1990	Ceiling applicable to foreign currency deposits held by domestic commercial banks increases to 15 percent (from 8 percent).
October 22, 1991	Liberalization of foreign investment regime (under Resolution 51) to expand existing guarantees and ease the way to new investment. Foreign firms allowed to remit up to 100 percent of net annual profits.
December 1991	Investors permitted to buy up to 100 percent locally listed companies. Abolition of restrictions on capital and income repatriation.
February 1992	Export surrender requirement proceeds are eased: all exporters are allowed to retain part of export proceeds abroad. Previously, this was granted only to coffee growers and state enterprises exporting oil and minerals. Residents are allowed to hold up to $500,000 of foreign stocks and other foreign portfolio investments abroad. Higher amounts require approval of the National Planning Department.
February 1992	Minimum maturity on foreign loans is reduced from five years, with two years' grace, to one year. Such loans are permitted only to finance working capital or fixed investment. Limit on contractual interest rate (London interbank offered rate [LIBOR] + 2.5 percent) eliminated for the private sector.
April 1994	Limits on foreign investments of domestic pension funds, insurance companies, and mutual funds are raised from 3 percent to 4 percent. The share of export proceeds subject to surrender requirements is reduced from 90 percent to 85 percent, and the period of surrender of foreign exchange is extended from 150 days to 180 days.
October 1994	The share of export proceeds subject to surrender requirements is further reduced from 85 percent to 80 percent.

	Mexico (1990)
November 1991	Abolished foreign exchange surrender requirements and related exchange control measures permitting unification of controlled and free-market exchange rates.

Sources: Conzalez 1995, Labán and Larraín 1994, and Schadler et al. 1993.
Sources: Alfiler 1994, Banco de la Republica, Annual Report, various issues, Bank Negara, Annual Report, various issues, and Schadler et al. 1993.
[a] The date next to the country name denotes the first year of the surge in inflows.

in U.S. dollars to finance his activity. All these factors increase the vulnerability of the financial system to reversals in capital flows—reversals that have the potential to end in financial crises.

It is the role of bank regulation and supervision to diminish these risks. As discussed earlier, attempting to insulate the banking system from short-term capital flows is a particularly important goal when a substantial portion of the inflows is in the form of short-term bank deposits. Regulation that limits the exposure of banks to the volatility in equity and real estate markets could help insulate the banking system from the potential bubbles associated with sizable capital inflows. In this vein, risk-based capital requirements in conjunction with adequate banking supervision to insure such requirements are complied with could help insulate the domestic banking system from the vagaries of capital flows.

Policy: Some Lessons

All of the countries we have discussed in this chapter have had experiences that have one theme in ocmmon: individual policies interact either to produce unintended effects on the composition of capital inflows or to undercut the policies' individual effectiveness.

The Mexican experience from 1990 to 1993 provides an example of the former (table 4.9). A combination of little or no short-term exchange rate uncertainty (as is the case when there is an implicit or explicit peg), sterilized intervention (which tends to prevent domestic short-term interest rates from converging toward international levels), and no binding impediments to capital inflows (through either taxation or quantitative constraints) likely maximizes the volume of short-term capital inflows a country receives. Thailand in the period leading up to its July 1997 financial crisis also had this policy mix. This is the case because the pairing of little or no short-term exchange rate risk and relatively high domestic interest rates favors the short-term investor; for the long-term investor there is always exchange rate risk because, over longer horizons, the probability of a realignment of the peg or a change in the exchange rate regime increases. Further, long-term investments (such as foreign direct investment) tend to be less interest sensitive.

In contrast, the mix of sterilized intervention and controls on inflows may undermine the individual effectiveness of these policies. The comparatively high interest rate differentials that usually accompany sterilization may act as an inducement to circumvent the capital controls (i.e., firms and banks may find ways of borrowing offshore). To the extent that they are successful in dodging the controls, some of the contractionary effects of the sterilization efforts will tend to be offset. Along the same lines, the

Table 4.10 Policy mix in response to capital inflows

Country	Fiscal Restraint	Revaluation	Increased Exchange Rate Variability	Sterilized Intervention	Controls on Capital Inflows	Liberalization of Capital Outflows	Trade Liberalization Accelerated
Argentina	No[a]	No	No	No	No	No	No
Chile	Yes	Yes	Yes	Yes	Yes	Yes	No
Colombia	No	Yes	Yes	Yes	Yes	Yes	Yes
Indonesia	No	No	No[b]	Yes	Yes	No	No
Malaysia	Yes	No	Yes	Yes	Yes	Yes	Yes
Mexico	No[a]	No	No[b]	Yes	No[c]	Yes	Yes
Philippines	No	No	Yes[d]	Yes	No	Yes	No
Sri Lanka	No[a]	No	No[d]	Yes	No	No	Yes
Thailand	Yes	No	No	Yes	Yes	Yes	Yes

[a] Fiscal consolidation (including privatization efforts) are part of the inflation stabilization programs and no a response to the rise in capital inflows perse. The convertibility plan in Argentina begins in April 1991, whereas the Mexican plan predates the surge in inflows and begins in December 1987.
[b] Despite announcements of broader intervention bands, exchange rate variability does not change appreciably (see the "Exchange Rate Policy" section in this chapter).
[c] Caps on foreign currency liabilities of banks were not binding until 1994 (see Reinhart and Smith 1995).
[d] The Philippines and Sri Lanka already had a relatively flexible exchange rate system at the start of the inflow episode.

policy of liberalizing controls on outflows to reduce net capital inflows may backfire if domestic interest rates are high relative to international levels, or if the liberalization is interpreted as a positive signal about the future economic environment. Indeed, several countries (Chile, Malaysia, and Thailand, see table 4.10) liberalized outflows while at the same time engaging in substantial sterilization efforts.

It is now 1998, about nine years after the initial surge in capital inflows. We have witnessed the abrupt reversal of flows in Mexico and Argentina in 1994 and 1995 and in the Czech Republic and East Asia in 1997, and the apparently far-reaching contagion associated with those episodes. This sorry record should remind policy makers that capital inflows are not always a reward for good behavior. All too often, capital inflows fed the mistaken belief that rapid economic growth and booming asset prices would be a permanent feature of a new era. Policy makers who fell into that trap were more likely to be insufficiently guarded in their fiscal spending—relying on the rapid revenue growth of the boom years—and leave the banking sector's regulation and supervision grossly unattended. If the boom during the inflow years is overly exuberant, the investors' retrenchment, and the punishment it will cause, may be equally exuberant.

It may be the case that even the best policy mix cannot altogether avoid the eventual reversal of capital flows. However, the appropriate policy mix may dampen the amplitude of the swings in capital flows, thus delivering a softer landing when international investors pull back. In this regard, the strongest policy lesson that emerges is the need for conservative fiscal policies, a zealous supervision of the domestic financial sector at all times, and a strengthening of this commitment during the boom phase of the cycle, when expectations are buoyant. Unfortunately, in most cases, policy makers have focussed their attention on the financial sector only when problems started to emerge. With regard to monetary and exchange rate policy, greater exchange rate flexibility may stem the cycle of foreign exchange intervention and sterilization that appears to act as a magnet for capital flows and leaves countries with "too much of a good thing."

References

Alfiler, F. Enrico. 1994. "Monetary and Exchange Rate Policy Responses to Surges in Capital Flows: The Case of the Philippines." Paper prepared for the Eleventh Pacific Basin Central Bank Conference, October 31–November 2, 1994, Hong Kong.

Asea, Patrick, and Carmen M. Reinhart. 1996. "Le Prix de l'Argent: How (Not) to Deal with Capital Inflows." *Journal of African Economics,* Vol. 5, no. 3, p. 6.

Aziz, Zeti Akhtar. 1994, "Capital Flows and Monetary Management: The Malaysian Experience." Paper prepared for the Eleventh Pacific Basin Central Bank Conference, October 31–November 2, 1994, Hong Kong.

Bacchetta, Philippe, and Eric van Wincoop. 1994. "Net Capital Flows under Exchange Rate and Price Volatility." Working Paper No. 94/03, *Studienzentrum Gerzensee.*

Banco Central de Chile. *Evolucion de la Economia.* Various issues. Santiago: Banco Central de Chile.

Banco Central de Chile. *Memoria Anual.* Various issues. Santiago: Banco Central de Chile.

Banco de la Republica. Colombia, *Annual Report.* Various issues. Bogota: Banco de la Republica.

Banco de Mexico. 1993. *Informe Anual.* Mexico City: Banco de Mexico.

Bank Negara Malaysia. *Annual Report.* Various issues. Kuala Lumpur: Bank Negara Malaysia.

Bercuson, Kenneth, and Linda Koenig. 1993. *The Recent Surge in Capital Inflows to Asia: Cause and Macroeconoic Impact.* Occasional Paper No. 15, South East Asian Central Banks Kuala Lumpur, Malaysia.

Budnevich, Carlos, and Rodrigo Cifuentes. 1993. "Manejo Macroeconomico de los Flujos de Capitales: La Contrastante Experiencia de Chile." Paper presented at the CIEPLAN Conference on Capital Flows, July 29–30, 1993, Cartagena, Colombia.

Calvo, Guillermo. 1991. "The Perils of Sterilization." *IMF Staff Papers* 38 (December):921–926.

Calvo, Guillermo, Leonardo Leiderman, and Carmen R. Reinhart. 1993. "Capital Inflows to Latin America: The Role of External Factors." *IMF Staff Papers* 40 (March):108–151.

Calvo, Guillermo, Leonardo Leiderman, and Carmen R. Reinhart. 1994. "The Capital Inflows Problem: Concepts and Issues." *Contemporary Economic Policy* 12 (July):54–66.

Carrasquilla, Alberto. 1995. "Exchange Rate Bands and Shifts in the Stabilization Policy Regime: Issues Suggested by the Experience of Colombia." Working Paper WP/95/42, International Monetary Fund, Washington, D.C.

Coorey, Sharmini. 1992. "Financial Liberalization and Reform in Mexico." In *Mexico: The Strategy to Achieve Sustained Economic Growth, IMF Occasional Paper 99,* edited by Claudio Loser. Washington, D.C.: International Monetary Fund.

Dominguez, Kathryn M., and Jeffrey A. Frankel. 1993. "Does Foreign Exchange Intervention Matter? The Portfolio Effect." *American Economic Review* 83(December): 1356–1369.

Folkerts-Landau, David, Garry J. Schinasi, Marcel Cassard, Victor K. Ng, Carmen M. Reinhart, and Michael G. Spencer. 1995. "Effects of Capital

Flows on Domestic Financial Sectors in APEC Developing Countries." In *Capital Flows in the APEC Region, IMF Occasional Paper 122*, edited by M. S. Khan and C.M. Reinhart, Washington, D.C.: International Monetary Fund.

Frankel, Jeffrey A. 1994a. "Have Latin American and Asian Countries So Liberalized Portfolio Capital Inflows That Sterilization is Now Impossible?" Institute for International Economics, Washington, D.C. Photocopy.

———. 1994b. "Sterilization of Money Inflows: Difficult (Calvo) or Easy (Reisen)?" Working Paper WP/94/159, International Monetary Fund, Washington, D.C.

Grobar, Lisa M. 1993 "The Effects of Real Exchange Rate Uncertainty on LDC Manufactured Exports." *Journal of Development Economics* 41:367–376.

Gurria, Jose Angel. 1993. "Capital Flows: The Mexican Case." Paper prepared for the ECLAC-IDRC workshop, "New Private Flows into Latin America," December 6–7, 1993, Santiago, Chile.

Haq, Mahbub ul, Inge Kaul, and Isabelle Grunberg. 1996. *The Tobin Tax: Coping with Financial Volatility.* New York: Oxford University Press.

Harinowo, C., and William C. Belchere. 1994. "Monetary and Exchange Rate Management with International Capital Mobility: The Indonesian Experience." Paper prepared for the Eleventh Pacific Basin Central Bank Conference. October 31–November 2, 1994, Hong Kong.

Helpman, Elhanan, Leonardo Leiderman, and Gil Bufman. 1995. "A New Breed of Exchange Rate Bands: Chile, Israel, and Mexico." *Economic Policy: A European Forum* 9:260–306.

Hettiarachchi, W., and U. Herat. 1994. "Coping with Capital Inflows: The Case of Sri Lanka." Paper prepared for the Eleventh Pacific Basin Central Bank Conference, October 31–November 2, 1994, Hong Kong.

IMF (International Monetary Fund). *International Financial Statistics.* Various issues. Washington, D.C.: International Monetary Fund.

Kang, Joong-Hong. 1994. "Monetary and Exchange Rate Policies in a Newly Industralizing Economy: The Korean Experience." Paper prepared for the Eleventh Pacific Basin Central Bank Conference, October 31–November 2, 1994, Hong Kong.

Kiguel, Miguel, and Leonardo Leiderman. 1994. "On the Consequences of Sterilized Intervention in Latin America: The Case of Colombia and Chile." Tel Aviv University, Tel Aviv). Photocopy.

Krugman, Paul. 1987. "The Narrow Moving Band, the Dutch Disease, and the Competitive Consequences of Mrs. Thatcher: Notes on Trade in the Presence of Economies Scale Economies." *Journal of Development Economics* 27:41–55.

Labán, Raul, and Felipe Larraín. 1994. "Can a Liberalization of Capital Outflows Increase Net Capital Inflows?" Pontificia Univeridad Catolica de Chile, Santiago, Chile. Photocopy.

Laporan Mingguan Weekly Report. Various issues. Djakarta: Bank Indonesia.

Montiel, Peter J. 1996. "Managing Economic Policy in the Face of Large Capital Inflows: What Have We Learned?" In *Private Capital Flows to Emerging Markets after the Mexican Crisis,* edited by G. Galvo, M. Goldstein, and E. Hochreiter. Washington, D.C.: Institute for International Economics.

Montiel, Peter J., and Carmen M. Reinhart. 1997. "The Dynamics of Capital Movements to Emerging Economies during the 1990s." UNU/ WIDER Project on Short-Term Capital Movements and Balance of Payments Crises, Helsinki.

Mundell, Robert A. 1963. "Capital Mobility and Stabilization Policy under Fixed and Flexible Exchange Rates." *Canadian Journal of Economics and Political Science* 29:475–485.

Mussa, Michael L. 1981. "The Role of Intervention." Occasional Paper No. 6, Group of Thirty, New York.

Nijathaworn, Bandid, and Thanisorn Dejthamrong. 1994. "Thailand: Monetary and Exchange Rate Management with International Capital Mobility." Paper prepared for the Eleventh Pacific Basin Central Bank Conference, October 31–November 2, 1994, Hong Kong.

Obstfeld, Maurice. 1990. "The Effectiveness of Foreign Exchange Intervention: Recent Experience." In *International Policy Coordination and Exchange Rate Determination,* edited by W. Branson, J. Frenkel, and M. Goldstein. Chicago: University of Chicago Press.

Reinhart, Vincent R. N.d. "How the Machinery of International Finance Works with Sand in Its Wheels." *Review of International Economics,* forthcoming.

Reinhart, Carmen M., and Vincent R. Reinhart. N.d. "On the Use of Reserve Requirements to Deal with the Capital Flow Problem." *International Journal of Finance and Economics,* forthcoming.

Reinhart, Carmen M., and R. Todd Smith. 1998. "Too Much of a Good Thing: The Macroeconomic Effects of Taxing Capital Inflows." In *Managing Capital Flows and Exchange Rates: Perspectives from the Pacific Basin,* edited by R. Glick. Cambridge: Cambridge University Press.

Reisen, Helmut. 1993. "The 'Impossible Trinity' in Southeast Asia." *International Economic Insights,* March/April,.

Rodriguez, Carlos A. 1992. "Situacion Monetaria y Cambiaria en Colombia." Centro de Estudies Monetarios entas Americas, Buenos Aires, Argentina. Photocopy.

Schadler, Susan, Maria Carkovic, Adam Bennett, and Robert Khan. 1993. "Recent Experiences with Surges in Capital Inflows." IMF Occasional Paper No. 108, International Monetary Fund, Washington, D.C.

Taylor, Mark P. 1995. "Exchange Rate Behavior." *Journal of Economic Literature* 33:13–47.

5

Alternative Responses to Capital Inflows: A Tale of Two Countries

Andrés Velasco and Pablo Cabezas

The recent financial meltdown in Asia has reminded the world—and emerging market pundits in particular—that foreign capital can leave just as quickly as it arrived, and debt-led economic expansion can easily turn into financial panic. Countries that once seemed the star performers of development are suddenly saddled with depreciated currencies, bankrupt banks, slower growth, and surging fiscal deficits.

The lesson, of course, is not new. Most of Latin America learned it in the 1980s, and Mexico and other countries in the region relearned the hard way in 1994. Indeed, in the early 1990s Latin America experienced an upswing that, in its financial aspects at least, was quite similar to that experienced by the emerging markets of Southeast Asia in the mid-1990s. Capital began pouring into Mexico, Argentina, Brazil, and several of the other larger Latin American nations early in the decade, in response to both the fall in interest rates in industrialized economies and wide-ranging economic reforms in the recipient countries. Policy makers in Latin America welcomed this—at first. Foreign capital could finance much needed imports and investment, reigniting growth. In the local financial markets the money was also welcomed because it quickly yielded stronger prices for most assets including domestic currency and real estate.

But the capital inflow soon created problems. The incoming money tended to strengthen Latin American currencies to the point where many new exporting firms (an important creation of the trade reforms of the 1970s and 1980s) found it difficult to compete abroad. External deficits, not a bad thing in themselves, tended to grow beyond what prudence dictated. Banks had to recycle the funds domestically, sometimes overextend-

Support from the C. V. Starr Center for Applied Economics at NYU and the Harvard Institute for International Development is gratefully acknowledged.

ing themselves into risky areas such as commercial property finance and consumer credit.

Optimists minimized the extent of such dangers. With reformed governments running fiscal surpluses, they stressed, it was private firms doing the borrowing. Capital arrived to finance productive investment, not government-owned white elephants. Currency appreciation was simply a sign of growing productivity and economic strength. Nothing could possibly be wrong with this.

But in late 1994 the combination of higher interest rates abroad, political uncertainty at home, and lax macroeconomic management all around caused a run on the Mexican peso and on Mexican government debt. The peso plunged, interest rates shot up, and the Mexican economy entered a deep recession that was to last six quarters. The so-called tequila effect spread far and wide, causing a bank panic and a recession in Argentina, and currency turmoil in places as far away as the Philippines. The pessimists had clearly won the day.

Latin America's recent boom-and-bust cycle had its peculiarities, but many of its features have reappeared in a number of other episodes, including those that occured recently in Asia: large capital inflows, real appreciation, a bubble in asset prices, a domestic lending boom, weakening financial institutions, a sudden reversal of expectations, and intertwined bank and currency collapses.[1] It is likely, then, that the Latin American experience holds policy lessons that are applicable beyond the confines of the region. We attempt to extract these lessons by reviewing the consequences of capital inflows and the policy response to them in two countries: Chile and Mexico.

These countries are interesting for three reasons. The first is that, much like Malaysia or Thailand, these countries have often been singled out as examples of countries with successful reforming economies. As such, they provide (in Mexico's case) an example of how things can go wrong even if the policy makers do most things right.

The second reason is that, thanks to their strong record of economic reforms, both countries were the most successful in the region in earning the confidence of foreign investors. In table 5.1 we can see that, relative to the size of the economy, capital inflows were especially high for Chile and Mexico. For Chile (table 5.1a) during the period 1990–1994 capital inflows averaged more than 6.7 percent of its gross domestic product (GDP). In Mexico (table 5.1b) net capital inflows averaged 6.2 percent of

1. The similarities should not be exaggerated, however: Southeast Asian nations such as Indonesia, Malaysia, and Thailand (let alone Hong-Kong and Singapore) have consistently enjoyed much stronger investment-savings performances than any economy in the Western Hemisphere, with the resulting faster growth and greater export diversification.

Table 5.1a Chile (shares of GDP)

	Trade balance	Current account	Capital account	Reserves Flow	Reserves Stock
1987	6.4	−4.2	4.5	0.3	12.5
1988	9.7	−1.0	3.9	2.9	13.8
1989	5.9	−2.5	4.3	1.8	13.6
1990	4.4	−1.8	9.6	7.8	21.2
1991	4.9	0.3	3.3	3.6	22.0
1992	1.9	−1.7	7.5	5.8	23.7
1993	−2.2	−4.6	5.9	1.3	22.0
1994	1.4	0.0	7.6	7.6	29.1

Source: International Monetary Fund (IMF), various issues, Balance of Payments Statistics Yearbook.

Table 5.1b Mexico (shares of GDP)

	Trade balance	Current account	Capital account	Reserves Flow	Reserves Stock
1987	5.7	2.7	−0.1	2.5	7.3
1988	1.6	−1.7	−2.0	−3.7	3.3
1989	0.2	−2.8	2.7	−0.1	3.5
1990	−0.4	−3.0	3.9	0.9	4.5
1991	−2.8	−5.1	7.9	2.8	6.9
1992	−5.3	−7.3	7.8	0.5	6.3
1993	−4.1	−6.4	8.3	1.9	7.7
1994	−5.5	−8.6	2.9	−5.7	1.9

Source: IMF, various issues, Balance of Payments Statistics Yearbook.

its GDP during the same period. Other Latin American economies also experienced some capital inflows, but not of this same magnitude. As an example, for the period 1990–1994 Argentina received inflows that averaged 1.2 percent of its GDP, whereas Brazil's capital inflows averaged 1.8 percent of its GDP.

The third reason is that both countries differed substantially in their policy response to the capital inflows. As is well known, Mexico embraced foreign capital warmly (skeptics will say that, given the size of external deficits, it had no choice), whereas Chile endeavored to keep it at arm's length. But neither country was run by wild-eyed populists taking advantage of the inflows to embark on an unsustainable fiscal expansion, nor by grim-faced bureaucrats denouncing the evils of foreign investment and closing the door to all inflows. Insofar as the two countries' policy stances have differed, they have differed in respects about which "reasonable people can disagree." That is why Mexico and Chile provide especially fertile ground for extracting useful policy lessons.

What do (or should) policy makers worry about when contemplating the possible effects of large-scale capital inflows? Any shopping list—influenced not only by recent events, but also by the experience of Latin America in the early 1980s—must include the following:

- Real exchange rate appreciation, which might be especially costly if it has to be reversed under conditions of hysteresis
- Loss of control over monetary aggregates in cases where a fixed exchange rate policy is pursued
- Volatility of flows, which may cause unexpected and sharp required swings in the current account
- Intermediation of the flows through the domestic banking system, which might give rise to a spurt of high-risk lending and sow the seeds of an eventual banking crisis

Of course, many well-known caveats are applicable. Real exchange rate appreciation may well be an equilibrium phenomenon (a response to reform-induced productivity changes, for instance) and not something for policy makers to agonize over; loss of control of the money supply may be a good thing, in that it brings with it monetary discipline; some of the consequences of volatility are hedged in today's financial markets; potential banking instability may be the result of poor regulation or outright fraud, not the capital inflows themselves. Nonetheless, the recent experience—not just of Mexico, but of countries such as Argentina, Brazil, the Czech Republic, Thailand, and the Philippines—suggests that these concerns may be real indeed.

Policy makers' worries can be tackled by an array of possible measures. Choices made in the following areas are particularly important in determining how the capital inflows will affect the macroeconomy:

- The exchange rate regime, and the choice among fixing, flexing, crawling, or some combination of these
- The extent of sterilization, and the effects sterilization has both on the exchange rate and on fiscal accounts
- Other supporting measures—especially fiscal policy, which can be especially important in limiting real appreciation and moderating the external deficit
- Capital controls of one kind or another
- Regulation to ensure the soundness of the banking system

In what follows we review the Chilean and Mexican experience in the light of these policy issues and the policy responses they elicited. The next section is largely descriptive in that it summarizes the macroeconomic environment in each country and the size and nature of the capital inflows it received. The next five sections deal in a more analytical vein with policy options in the areas of exchange rates, money, debt management, capital controls, and bank regulation. A final section concludes and offers some policy suggestions.

Chile and Mexico: Two Star Performers?

Chile and Mexico are often seen from the outside as "twin" economies: two highly market-oriented economies that liberalized internal and external markets; both went through successful stabilization, deregulation, and privatization of state-owned enterprises. These similarities, however, can obscure other very fundamental differences. Some of these differences became extremely important when the countries had to confront the capital inflow—and later outflow—of the 1990s.

A first contrast has to do with the timing and maturity of the reforms. Whereas Chile implemented a first wave of structural reforms (trade and fiscal) in the mid-1970s and a second one (further privatization and deregulation) in the mid-1980s, Mexico had only started its reforms by 1983, and some of the most important ones (deregulation and trade) were in fact delayed until after 1987. This meant that by the 1990s most of the initial costs of the reforms were for Chile a thing of the past, and the country was poised to begin enjoying its growth and efficiency benefits. In Mexico the painful part of the process is still under way, and growth has been very slow in coming. The numbers are telling: Chile enjoyed an average yearly rate of growth of 7.1 percent from 1988 to 1994 (table 5.2), but Mexico displayed a barely acceptable average of 2.8 percent per year for the same period (table 5.2). Chilean economic growth was also reflected in an enormous increase in employment. Unemployment rates came down from an average of 22 percent for 1980–1985 to a comfortable 4 percent during 1993, and 6.2 percent during 1994. Mexico's unemployment figures are notoriously unreliable, but there is evidence of substantial unemployment and especially underemployment during the period. There was greater similarity between the two countries in the trajectory of wages. Together with the decrease in the unemployment rate, Chile's real wages showed a steady recovery, increasing 24 percent between 1988 and 1994 (table 5.3); real wages in Mexico increased by slightly more than 25 percent between 1988 and 1994 (table 5.3).

A second difference is that in Chile inflation stabilization was achieved in the late 1970s, whereas in the early 1990s Mexico was still undergoing

Table 5.2 Gross Domestic Product (annual growth rates)

	Chile	Mexico
1988	7.3	1.2
1989	9.9	3.3
1990	3.3	4.5
1991	7.3	3.6
1992	11.0	2.8
1993	6.3	0.7
1994	4.3	3.5

Source: IMF, International Financial Statistics (IFS), various issues. Chilean 1992–1994 figures come from new revisions made by Chilean Central Bank.

Table 5.3 Real wages (annual growth rates)

	Chile	Mexico
1986	2.1	−13.1
1987	−0.2	4.0
1988	6.6	−2.1
1989	2.0	13.6
1990	1.9	4.0
1991	5.0	6.4
1992	4.6	2.0
1993	3.4	−1.2
1994	4.7	−0.9

Source: IMF, IFS, various issues, and Banco Central de Chile, Monthly Bulletin, various issues.

the effects of the stabilization program undertaken late in 1987. As a result, it is hard to decide whether some of the problems of the period—exchange rate overvaluation and a current account deficit, most importantly—were caused by the exchange rate–based stabilization, the capital inflows, or some combination of both. But regardless of timing, both countries' success at fighting inflation was impressive. Mexico curbed its inflation from a high of 130.8 percent in 1987 to 6.9 percent in 1994 (table 5.4). Chile lowered its inflation rate from 26.6% in 1990 to 12% in 1994 (table 5.4), its control of hyperinflation having been achieved one and one-half decades earlier.[2]

2. Annual averages. If we compute December-to-December rates, Chile's inflation also achieved single digits in 1994.

Table 5.4 Inflation (annual averages)

	Chile	Mexico
1986	19.5%	87.3%
1987	20.4%	130.8%
1988	15.3%	114.3%
1989	16.2%	20.1%
1990	26.6%	26.6%
1991	22.0%	22.7%
1992	15.6%	15.5%
1993	12.1%	9.7%
1994	12.0%	6.9%

Source: IMF, *IFS,* various issues

In terms of fiscal policy, through the 1990s both Chile and Mexico have engaged in rather conservative management of government expenditures. As part of the stabilization process, Mexican authorities made important efforts to bring their big deficit down. The overall Mexican fiscal deficit (including the inflationary component of interest payments) accounted for 10.3 percent of the GDP in 1988; by 1990 and after the fiscal adjustment, the budget was almost balanced. The Chilean experience has been similar. The participation of government consumption over GDP has been stable at about 10 percent since 1988. The Chilean government has shown a steady surplus on its accounts, even though as a share of GDP this surplus has decreased slightly in recent years (table 5.5).

Even greater differences between the two countries emerge from an analysis of the external sector. Even though real exchange rates appreciated in both countries, the magnitudes of the appreciation differed. Use of the exchange rate as a nominal anchor produced a real appreciation of 22.2 percent for the Mexican peso (table 5.6) from 1989 to 1994. In

Table 5.5 Fiscal deficit and public consumption (shares of GDP)

	1988	1989	1990	1991	1992	1993	1994
Chile							
Fiscal deficit[a]	−0.2	4.8	3.5	2.5	3.0	2.2	2.2
Public Consumption	10.4	9.9	9.8	9.5	9.4	9.7	9.3
Mexico							
Fiscal deficit[a]	−10.3	−5.0	−2.8	−0.2	1.5	0.4	−0.9
Public Consumption	8.6	8.5	8.4	9.0	10.1	10.8	NA

Source: IMF, *IFS,* various issues.
[a] Negative numbers reflect deficit.

Table 5.6 Real effective exchange rate (annual average)

	Chile		Mexico	
	Index	% Change	Index	% Change
1987	93.7	7.2%	135.2	3.7%
1988	99.8	6.5%	110.0	−18.6%
1989	97.4	−2.4%	103.2	−6.2%
1990	100.0	2.7%	100.0	−3.1%
1991	96.8	−3.2%	91.1	−8.9%
1992	91.4	−5.6%	83.8	−8.0%
1993	90.7	−0.8%	78.8	−6.0%
1994	88.8	−2.0%	80.3	1.9%

Source: IMF, *IFS*, various issues, and author's calculations.

Chile, partially as the result of a deliberate government policy to limit real revaluation, the Chilean peso appreciated by only 8.8 percent from 1989 to 1994 (table 5.6).

In terms of the balance of payments, the two countries presented quite different results. In the 1990–1994 Chilean case, current account deficits showed a stable and decreasing trend, averaging 1.6 percent of the GDP per year. That, coupled with a big capital account surplus averaging 6.8 percent of the GDP, implied a massive increase of international reserves held at the central bank: almost $8 billion in 1990–1994, which amounted to 5.2 percent of the GDP annually (able 5.1a). This increase in reserves posed a big problem for the conduct of monetary policy, as we will see later. The Mexican experience was rather different. As a response to the appreciated peso, and boosted by inflated expectations about future growth fueled by entry into the North American Free Trade Agreement (NAFTA), the current account began to worsen in the late 1980s, reaching an annual average of 6.1 percent of the GDP in 1990–1994 and peaking at 8.6 percent of the GDP in 1994. Capital inflows therefore largely went to finance this deficit, and the impact on international reserves was moderate: between 1987 and the reserve peak of December 1993, reserves grew by an annual average of 0.7 percent of the GDP (table 5.1b).

In terms of the composition of net capital inflows, Chile and Mexico show yet another important difference. For Mexico (table 5.7b), the principal component of the capital inflow was short term: in the strong capital inflow period of 1990–1993 short-term flows—portfolio investment and loans under a year of maturity—account for approximately 55 percent of the total, with the remaining 45 percent long term (foreign direct investment [FDI] and long-term loans). For Chile, the equivalent breakdown is 45 percent short-term loans and 55 percent long-term loans (table 5.7a).

Table 5.7a Chile: Net capital inflows as a percentage of total flow

	1990	1991	1992	1993	1994
Foreign direct investment	63.5	103.3	33.3	57.1	57.5
Medium and long run credit	9.4	23.3	22.2	25.0	31.5
Portfolio investment	12.5	26.7	20.4	41.1	27.4
Short run credit	30.2	63.3	44.4	30.4	9.6
Others	−16.7	−113.3	−18.5	−53.6	−26.0
Total	100.0	100.0	100.0	100.0	100.0

Source: Banco Central de Chile, *Monthly Bulletin,* various issues.

Table 5.7b Mexico: Net capital inflows as a percentage of total flow

	1990	1991	1992	1993	1994
Foreign direct investment	11.5	56.7	29.6	25.0	32.9
Medium and long run credit	28.1	90.0	35.2	41.1	30.5
Portfolio investment	−22.9	106.7	79.6	94.6	8.2
Short run credit	12.5	40.0	33.3	3.6	1.4
Others	7.3	−10.0	−27.8	−5.4	−2.7
Total	100.0	100.0	100.0	100.0	100.0

Source: Banco de Mexico, *Monthly Report,* various issues.

Finally, Chile also outperformed Mexico in terms of indicators of long-term growth potential. Throughout the period 1989–1994, Chile's investment rate surpassed Mexico's by an average of more than 3 percent of the GDP per year. Differences in savings were even more dramatic: Chilean savings rates were higher by an average of 7 percent of the GDP per year (table 5.8). Even under perfect capital flows a temporarily low savings rate need not be a problem for economic growth, as long as the country can

Table 5.8 Shares of GDP

	1989	1990	1991	1992	1993	1994
Chile						
Current account	−2.5	−1.8	0.3	01.7	−4.6	0.0
Investment	25.5	26.3	24.5	26.8	28.8	26.8
Savings	23.0	24.5	24.8	25.1	24.2	26.8
Mexico						
Current account	−2.8	−3.0	−5.1	−7.3	−6.4	−8.6
Investment	22.2	22.8	23.4	24.4	23.2	23.5
Savings	19.4	19.8	18.3	17.1	16.8	14.9

Source: IMF, *IFS,* various issues.

finance its desired increase in capital stock in the international credit market. A different story arises once international capital dries up. In an environment with no external funding, high domestic savings rates are crucial to maintain the pace of investment, and in that sense they represent a key requirement for a stable growth path.

Exchange Rate Policies: Fix, Flex, or Crawl?

Policy makers in Chile and in Mexico have faced some standard trade-offs in the design of an optimal exchange rate regime.[3] A fixed or semifixed rate is effective in bringing down inflation and (almost by definition) minimizing short-term nominal fluctuations; as a result, both countries relied on rate fixing in the early stages of their stabilization processes. Over the longer haul, however, greater degrees of flexibility may be desirable in dealing with capital movements and in achieving some small degree of monetary independence. As a consequence, in the late 1980s and early 1990s both moved toward comparable mixed regimes of crawling pegs plus bands. The similarities were sufficient to lead observers to hail Chile and Mexico (along with Israel) has having devised a novel and successful exchange rate regime (Helpman, Leiderman, and Bufman 1994). But again, these apparent similarities were offset by seldom-stressed but nonetheless important differences. After describing the regime policies implemented by each country, we speculate on how these differences may have determined macroperformances in each country.

Since 1983 Chilean exchange rate policy has explicitly attempted to target the real exchange rate. For this purpose, the "reference" nominal exchange rate is adjusted periodically by the central bank to reflect the difference between domestic and international inflation. In addition, in the early days the exchange rate was allowed to float in a band of plus or minus 5 percent with respect to the reference level. Such a system was adopted after an important real devaluation and worked well for the remainder of the decade in terms of offering the export sector a competitive and reasonably predictable rate of exchange.

Two things changed in 1990. First, capital began flowing in as a result of events in the United States and elsewhere in the industrialized world. Second, the newly independent central bank undertook a drastic anti-inflation effort based on tighter money. Spreads between domestic and international interest rates increased sharply, and short-term speculative capital flew massively to Chile. During the first half of 1990 the nominal exchange rate went from ceiling to floor of its band and remained there

3. This section draws on Sachs, Tornell, and Velasco 1996a.

for the rest of the year. The central bank had to intervene massively at the bottom of the band, accumulating $2.4 billion in reserves during 1990 alone.

Such a situation posed a thorny dilemma for Chilean policy makers. High interest rates were deemed essential to curb inflation, but the real exchange rate appreciation that followed could potentially threaten the export performance on which much of Chile's success was predicated. The central bank could not also be sure whether the capital inflows were permanent or transitory. If the latter was true, the case for letting the exchange rate appreciate strengthened considerably. A fiscal contraction could have helped absorb the capital inflow while minimizing the effect on relative prices, but there was limited room for making fiscal policy even more austere than it already was. Furthermore, public finance officials felt that fiscal policy should be targeted at medium-term objectives and that it could not attempt to respond to every tremor in world interest rates.

During 1991, and with the intention of discouraging short-term inflows, the economic authorities tried to introduce some noise to the exchange rate market by pursuing a policy of unexpected but small revaluations followed by compensating devaluations. Dirty floating within the band was also attempted. Despite the interventions, pressures to revalue mounted further, and in January 1992 the central bank allowed a revaluation of the peso of 5 percent and an increase of the width of the flotation band to plus or minus 10 percent.

An additional change was introduced in July of 1992, also in order to discourage speculation by making the peso-dollar parity less predictable: the peg to the dollar was replaced by a peg to a baskets of currencies that included the mark and the yen. The weights in the basket—40 percent dollar, 30 percent yen, and 10 percent mark—reflect current trade patterns and attest to the growing diversification of Chile's export sector. This policy had the additional advantage of preventing a loss in competitiveness for exports sold to non-U.S. markets whenever the American dollar experienced an appreciation with respect to other currencies. By late 1994 the center of the band had to be revalued again, this time by 10 percent, in order to ease the growing reserve pressure on the central bank. After the Mexican crisis, capital inflows slowed down, but markets soon noticed the differences between Chile and Mexico, and upward pressure on the Chilean exchange rate returned.

During the stabilization process and until 1988, Mexican authorities used the nominal exchange rate as a nominal anchor; the Mexican peso-dollar parity was fixed in an attempt to curb inflation. During January 1989, and in order to defuse the trend toward appreciation, the system was changed to a preannounced peg system; the peso/dollar rate was allowed to depreciate by 1 peso per day in 1989, 80 cents per day in 1990, and 40 cents per day in 1991. Finally, during November 1991 the system evolved to a crawling peg with adjustable bands. The moving band system involved a lower bound fixed at a level of 3.05 new pesos per dollar, whereas the upper band was devalued at a rate of 0.0004 new pesos per day. Hence, the band was designed to widen slowly over time. By September 1994 the band was (plus or minus) 6 percent wide around a central parity of 3.2438 pesos per dollar.

Much as in Chile, Mexican authorities intervened by dirty floating within the band. But unlike in Chile, this was done to minimize fluctuations in the politically delicate period of NAFTA negotiation and ratification. Dirty floating produced an increase in the level of international reserves, from 6.5 billion in 1989 to 25.4 billion by the end of 1993.

Over time, real appreciation became an increasing worry. Between 1990 and 1993 the nominal exchange rate depreciated by 17 percent, but because of the big disparity between domestic and international inflation the real exchange rate appreciated somewhere between 25 percent and 35 percent, depending on the actual index used. But by early 1994 Mexican inflation had declined sufficiently that the extent of overvaluation had stabilized. Moreover, in March 1994 the nominal exchange rate experienced a depreciation of 10 percent, and the U.S. dollar itself was depreciating in real terms against the European currencies and the Japanese yen. Hence, Mexico's multilateral real exchange rate was less appreciated than its bilateral real rate vis-a-vis the U.S. dollar. Regardless of any of this, however, concerns over the unsustainability of the overvalued rate (and the huge external deficits that it had helped create) were to play a major role in making investors skittish and in prompting the December 1994 panic.

The choice of exchange rate regime is often described as a trade-off between flexibility and credibility. The description is particularly revealing in the case of Mexico and Chile. Think of possible regimes as a continuum with totally fixed rates at one end, crawling and adjustable pegs and target zones somewhere in between, and clean floating at the other end. The more fixed the rate, the argument goes, the greater the commitment against inflation and therefore the greater the credibility;[4] the more flexible the rate, on the other hand, the greater the ability of the government to offset shocks.

Chile's crawling peg has emphasized flexibility at the expense of credibility. There is a degree of automatic accommodation of domestic inflation, given that the central parity is readjusted on a daily basis to offset

4. The standard caveat is that credibility could also be attached to a monetary rule under flexible exchange rates. Arguing that credibility is more easily obtained under fixing requires (1) the assumption that there are large political costs attached to the abandonment of a fixed parity or (b) the belief that monetary targets are too costly to be observed by agents.

inflation differentials. Moreover, the authorities have not been shy about moving the central parity (and thereby the edges of the band) in a surprise manner in order to accommodate perceived changes in market conditions. In particular, as evidence has mounted that an important share of the capital inflow is in fact long term (FDI and related categories), real appreciation has been allowed for. Mexico's regime, by contrast, has put the emphasis on credibility. The edges of the band are predetermined rather than being allowed to respond endogenously to inflation differentials. And when facing pressure at one of the bounds—as happened in March 1994 after the assassination of Luis Donaldo Colosio—the Banco de Mexico has been unwilling to move the band to curtail reserve changes.

Mexico's stress on credibility at first seemed to pay off. Inflation rates converged relatively quickly, edging toward dollar inflation in 1994. Chile, by contrast, spent over a decade (from the early 1980s to the early 1990s) with inflation in the 20 percent to 30 percent range, until attaining single-digit inflation for the first time in thirty years in 1994. In addition, there were serious fears that Chile lacked a nominal anchor (monetary policy targeted real interest rates), so an exogenous shock could seriously destabilize the price level.

Yet it was not Chile's lack of monetary and exchange rate discipline, but Mexico's lack of exchange rate flexibility that has proven costly over the longer haul. The real test for Mexico came with the shocks of 1994: first the hike in U.S. interest rates and then the political turmoil caused by peasant uprisings and political assassinations. In the days that followed the March assassination, the exchange rate went all the way to the top of the band, in what constituted a nominal devaluation of about 10 percent.[5] The exchange rate spent the rest of the year at or very near the ceiling. Both marginal and inframarginal intervention led to large reserves losses. The upshot is that between and March and December Mexico operated an essentially pegged exchange rate in that only the top of the band was relevant.[6]

Having allowed the real exchange rate to become overvalued in previous years, Mexico's unwillingness to lift the ceiling of the band in response to the shocks in March and later in the year was to prove costly. Opponents of moving the band ceiling emphasized the possible credibility costs: a devaluation might lead investors not just to doubt the commitment to low inflation, but also to revise their assessments of the reformers in power with regard to their commitment to property rights. In the end the issue

---

5. The fact that in the same period the central bank also lost approximately $9 billion in reserves attests to the magnitude of the shock.
6. Of course, the ceiling itself was gradually depreciating—a total of nearly 5 percent in the period.

was moot. The combination of loose money (in the course of 1994) and a fixed rate allowed reserves to dwindle, making it increasingly likely that the peg could not be sustained regardless of policy makers' wishes. When investors ran on Mexican assets at the end of the year, there was little the government could do but let the exchange rate float.

Sterilization of Capital Flows: How Wise?

At least since David Hume, economists have understood that fixed exchange rates require that the money supply be determined mainly by the balance of payments. Domestic credit expansion must be limited if the pegged rate is to remain intact. The adjustment mechanism under fixed exchange rates, as outlined by Hume two centuries ago, operates in practice by pushing down interest rates when foreign lending increases, thereby increasing domestic absorption and enlarging the external deficit (or increasing it to the level willingly financed at the lower interest rates); the opposite occurs when capital flows out.

But the Humean adjustment mechanism is seldom allowed to operate in practice. Take the recent experience of Mexico as an example. In the upswing (when the capital was flowing in), the central bank sterilized the monetary effects of capital inflows—as did all other countries in the region except for Argentina—fearing that large increases in nominal money would be inflationary. In the downswing (when foreign lending fell sharply) the central bank once again sterilized—this time to keep interest rates from going through the roof. Thus, the automatic correction mechanism was systematically aborted.

In practice, then, under fixed exchange rates, sterilization of inflows is a key component of most policy packages, in spite of what the above theory would advice. Indeed, Calvo, Leiderman, and Reinhart (1993) claim that "sterilized intervention has been the most common policy response to the surge in capital inflows in both Asia and Latin America." The mechanics of sterilization are well known. Sterilized intervention allows the government to control monetary aggregates while defending the fixed exchange rate by mopping up the liquidity resulting from foreign exchange operations. Frankel and Okongwu (1995) helpfully distinguish between narrow sterilization—which leaves the monetary base unchanged through the sale of domestic bonds—and broad sterilization—which leaves the money supply constant even if the base changes, for example by changes in reserve requirements. Both techniques have been widely used in many countries including Chile and Mexico.

Even though both countries received proportionally similar capital inflows (roughly 8 percent of GDP since 1989), Chile had to sterilize a substantially larger share of these inflows than Mexico did. The reason is that, given Chile's remarkable trade results and small current account deficits, the bulk of capital inflows went to reserve accumulation. By contrast, Mexico's large current account deficits, peaking at almost 8 percent of GDP in 1994, absorbed an important portion of the capital inflow, relieving the central bank from the need to sterilize.

In Chile, international reserves held by the central bank increased from a level of 12.5 percent of GDP in 1987 to 29.1 percent of GDP in 1994, creating big pressures for sterilization. Because of this intervention, during 1990–1994 the central bank's internal debt increased by an average of almost $1.9 billion a year. By 1994, total internal debt had more than doubled relative to its 1990 level.

In Mexico the amounts to be sterilized were smaller: between 1989 and the end of 1993, international reserves increased by $6.1 billion. From 1992 to 1993 Mexican authorities intervened in the exchange market with a monthly average of $1.3 billion in total transactions using *cetes,* which are mostly short-term peso bonds. As a result, the ratio of M3 (M2 plus non-bank short-term securities) to GDP grew from 36 percent in 1989 to 41 percent in 1993. At the end of 1993, *Cetes* alone represented close to 100 percent of net international reserves. The impact on overall domestic public debt, however, was different than in Chile. Because of the fall in real interest rates in the early 1990s and the amortization of substantial amounts of debt (often using privatization proceeds), internal public debt as a share of GDP decreased from almost 28 percent in 1988 to 12 percent in 1993.

What about broad sterilization? On this point the policy course of the two countries also diverged. Chile, in keeping with its more activist reputation, increased reserve requirements on foreign currency deposits held by commercial banks by 50 percent, using a structure such that the required reserve decreased as the maturity of the deposit increased. Together with this increase in reserve requirements, the central bank introduced a 30 percent marginal reserve requirement on interbank deposits. Mexico, by contrast, engaged in reverse broad sterilization; a zero legal reserve requirement for banks was instituted, sharply increasing the money multiplier.

Sterilization is not without perils. With broad sterilization, increases in reserve requirements for banks can gradually cause a process of disintermediation, with a consequent loss in efficiency. Matters are more problematic in the case of narrow sterilization, because the list of possible ills is long:

- It may increase interest rates (relative to what they would have been with a capital inflow but without sterilization) and hence perpetuate the inflow.[7]

7. Frankel (1994) has sorted out the conditions under which this is so.

- It may deteriorate fiscal and quasi-fiscal accounts, because the domestic bonds typically used to for sterilization carry interest rates that are highter than those earned by reserve holdings.
- Also in the fiscal realm, it may dangerously increase the stock of domestic debt.

Of these, the most serious problems are the fiscal ones. Calvo (1991), an early voice of concern on the issue, has even claimed that these policies—aimed at curtailing monetization and enhancing the credibility of the anti-inflation stance—may actually increase expected and realized inflation. This increase would occur if a perverse monetarist arithmetic is at work, such that the large increase in debt leads to expectations that it will be eventually monetized. But without going to such an extreme, the adverse fiscal impact of sterilization was clearly felt in Chile and Mexico. In Chile, preliminary estimates suggest that in 1990–1993 the central bank incurred annual losses of about 0.5 percent of GDP because of the interest rate differential between domestic bonds issued by the bank and international reserves. In Mexico during 1990–1993, the same loss averaged to an annual 0.25 percent of GDP.

Internal Debt Management

The management of the internal debt created by sterilization can also be a source of headaches. The experience of both countries is quite dissimilar with respect to their internal debt management. We saw above that the amounts to be sterilized were substantially smaller in Chile. An even greater difference lies in the types of instruments chosen to carry out his sterilization, both in terms of their denomination and maturity.

Mexico used an array of instruments, including the peso-denominated *cetes* and *bondes,* the inflation-indexed *ajustabonos,* and the dollar-indexed *tesobonos.* Until 1993, however, it was the peso assets that predominated, accounting for roughly three-quarters of domestic government interest-earning liabilities. Chile, by contrast, relied heavily on indexed debt. All liabilities over 30 days in maturity were (and are still) denominated in UF, an inflation-linked unit of account.

The structure of maturities was also different. Early in the decade Mexico relied rather heavily on short-term *cetes,* perhaps gambling that as the stabilization process was consolidated, rates would come down—which made it fiscally unadvisable to borrow long. By the end of 1993 the average maturity of Mexican internal public debt was 290 days (table 5.9), and short-term debt (of less than a year of maturity) accounted for 60 percent of total domestic debt (table 5.10).

Table 5.9 Average maturity of new debt suscribed by the central bank (in days)

		Chile	Mexico
1994	January	765	293
	February	848	295
	March	1,376	297
	April	725	306
	May	1,146	291
	June	1,170	281
	July	642	276
	August	974	261
	September	1,246	254
	October	532	254
	November	546	249
	December	998	206

Source: Banco Central de Chile, *Monthly Bulletin,* various issues, and author's calculations.

Table 5.10 Maturity of internal public debt (share of total debt)

	1990	1991	1992	1993	1994
Chile[a]					
Short-term debt[b]	18.0	24.0	53.0	34.0	35.0
Long-term debt	82.0	76.0	47.0	66.0	65.0
Mexico					
Short-term debt[c]	45.3	43.0	45.2	62.6	78.4
Long-term debt	54.7	57.0	54.8	34.7	21.6

Source: Banco Central de Chile, *Monthly Bulletin,* various issues, Banco de Mexico, *Monthly Report,* various issues, and author's calculations.
[a] Debt suscribed by the Central Bank, representing almost all internal public debt.
[b] Debt with maturities of less than one year.
[c] Corresponds to *cetes* and *tesobonos.*

The Chilean experience was quite different. When at the end of 1989 the newly independent central bank launched its tight money policy, it attempted to establish credibility as swiftly as possible. One policy chosen was to offer ten-year indexed bonds with a high real interest rate. Throughout the first year of heavy sterilization (1990) the central bank kept issuing long-term debt. The policy was abandoned at the end of the year. During 1991 short-term bonds (with maturities of less than a year) where used to sterilize, once again reflecting expectations about the future course of interest rates. Between 1992 and 1994, the average maturity of the sterilization bonds was increased steadily, showing an underlying preference to balance the average maturity of the central bank's stock of debt around a

Table 5.11 Short-term internal public debt (share of total reserves)

		Chile	Mexico
1994	January	25%	104%
	February	22%	93%
	March	23%	106%
	April	22%	141%
	May	20%	157%
	June	21%	173%
	July	21%	182%
	August	22%	180%
	September	22%	183%
	October	24%	172%
	November	29%	280%
	December	29%	410%

Source: Banco Central de Chile, *Monthly Bulletin,* various issues, Banco de Mexico, *Monthly Report,* various issues, and author's calculations.

target of about two years (table 5.9). As a consequence of this maturity management, from 1990 to 1994 Chilean short-term stock of domestic debt was kept on average at 33 percent of total liabilities, or equivalently, 31 percent of international reserves (Tables 5.10 and 5.11).

In terms of macroeconomic performance, these differences in debt management were to prove important. It is likely that the presence of a large stock of nonindexed debt kept alive in investors the fear that the Mexican government would eventually return to a high-inflation policy to reduce the value of outstanding liabilities.[8] As a result, ex post real rates of interest were generally higher in Mexico than in Chile in the early 1990s. The shorter maturity of Mexican debt was also to matter. As a growing literature suggests,[9] short-maturity debt can make the government particularly vulnerable to crises of confidence and self-fulfilling runs. Differences were obscured until 1993, that is to say, as long as both countries enjoyed an environment of relative macroeconomic stability, falling country risk premiums, and decreasing world interest rates.

But in the course of 1994 three things happened that were to set Mexico far apart from Chile. First, total Mexican government short-term domestic debt, regardless of currency denomination, grew both in absolute magnitude and as a multiple of reserves. Expressed in dollars, domestic

8. Calvo (1988) offers a model that emphasizes this point, and which shows that non-indexed- indexed debt may open the door to multiple equilibriums.

9. (Calvo and Guidotti 1990; Alesina, Pratti, and Tabellini 1990; Cole and Kehoe 1996).

debt amounted to 1.7 times reserves in December 1993 and 2.6 times reserves in September 1994.

Second, and more important, the average maturity of Mexican domestic debt shrank drastically during 1994. This was the result of a deliberate policy choice. With the increased turmoil in 1994, the yield curve became steeper, and issuing long-term debt became increasingly expensive. Conjecturing that the shock was transitory, the Mexican government followed the correct policy of borrowing short in order to get over the hump (until the end of the year, for example) without wrecking public finances. Ex post facto, we know that this strategy had two weaknesses: (1) the shock could turn out not to be transitory, in which case a real fiscal adjustment would have been needed to compensate for the higher interest payment burden; and (2) the shorter maturities rendered the government largely defenseless against any circumstance in which investors refused to roll over their government bonds.

Third, after the March assassination of leading presidential candidate, Colosio, and the accompanying perceived increase in devaluation risk, the Mexican government began rolling over its short-term peso-denominated debt into short-term dollar-indexed debt. Starting at $1 billion at the beginning of the year, by the end of September (before the last great decline in central bank foreign assets) the stock of *tesobonos* outstanding equaled the amount of reserves. In December the stock of *tesobonos* reached $18 billion. This large stock of short-term public debt created, as Calvo (1994) stressed, an important source of financial fragility.

Such fragility was soon to prove lethal. The December 20 devaluation of the Mexican peso provoked an investor panic. As the *tesobonos* matured, investors were unwilling to roll them over, and several bond auctions found no takers. Mexico was on the brink of default.

Capital Controls: To Be Interventionist or Not?

When confronted with an inflow (and often concerned with a possible future outflow) a number of countries have been tempted to resort to capital controls. In this regard, Chile and Mexico stand as polar opposites in the range of Latin American experience. Chile has resorted to a battery of policies intended to limit short-term inflows. Mexico, by contrast, has been largely opposed to such moves, with the exception of a couple of relatively mild policies intended to discourage interest arbitrage by Mexican banks.

In Chile the major policy initiative was the June 1991 imposition of an implicit tax on capital inflows.[10] The tax took the form of a non-interest-

10. In addition, there was the long-standing requirement that all FDI stay in the country for at least one year. This applies only to capital; profits can be repatriated immediately.

bearing deposit in the central bank equivalent to 20 percent of total investment. This required reserve was to be maintained at the central bank for a period that varied from ninety days to one year, depending on the maturity of the loan. In addition, a stamp tax of 1.2 percent per year, previously applied only to domestic currency loans, was extended to foreign currency loans in operations of up to one year. In July 1991 an alternative to the reserve requirement was created; instead of maintaining a cash reserve, borrowers were permitted pay up front the equivalent of the financial cost of the reserve requirement. In May 1992 the reserve requirement was extended to 30 percent of the foreign loan, and the period it was required to be held in the central bank was fixed at one year no matter the maturity of the loan.

The combination of reserve requirement (whether paid directly or indirectly) and stamp tax imposed no marginal cost on medium- and long-term lending, but it imposed a heavy financial cost on short-term loans (less than one year). Ffrench-Davis and Agosín (1995) calculated that for a foreign loan of one-year maturity the value of the implicit taxes have fluctuated from an annual 2.6 percent in the second semester of 1992 to a high of 3.9 percent in 1994. The percentages are substantially higher for loans of shorter maturities.

In Mexico, by contrast, the monetary authorities have continued to liberalize the capital account. Since 1990, foreign investors heve been allowed to invest in government bonds and in shares in the financial system (not voting shares). Foreign investors can invest in basically any project developed in Mexico. Capital mobility is, in essence, unimpeded.

The only exception to the deregulation trend came in 1992. Concerned over the big exposure to exchange risk that the banking system was undertaking, Mexican authorities imposed a minimum liquidity coefficient to foreign exchange transactions: 15 percent of foreign exchange borrowing must held in liquid securities denominated in the same currency. During 1992 a regulation that limited foreign currency liabilities of commercial banks to 10 percent of their total loan portfolio was approved. Both policies limit the scope and profitability of cross-border interest arbitrage—borrowing abroad in dollars, lending at home in pesos, and earning the differential—by banks, which had been an important source of capital inflows. But they could also be justified on prudential grounds as ways of diminishing the currency risk exposure of deposit-taking institutions at home.

What are controls expected to do and do they do it? It is a commonplace of international economics to assert that capital controls are not very effective because they can, relatively easily. be evaded. It is much less commonplace, regrettably, to be clear about what it is that controls are ineffective at doing. Any evaluation of the usefulness of controls must start by specifying what it is that they are expected to accomplish. At a most basic level, controls of the sort we have described have as a basic aim the discouragement of speculative capital inflows. Somewhat more subtly, however, this can be split into three distinct tasks:

- To partially sever the link between domestic and foreign interest rates, creating a wedge that endows domestic monetary policy with a modicum of independence
- To reduce the total size of the inflow, presumably to reduce the extent of real currency overvaluation
- To change the composition of the inflows while leaving the size of the flow mostly unchanged, encouraging short-term (hot) flows to become longer-term (cooler) flows

How well have capital controls performed these three tasks? Chilean evidence on the first point is mixed. On the one hand, Chile has been able to keep nominal and real rates above the relevant U.S. benchmark to a greater extent than simple risk premium calculations would suggest. Labán and Larraín (1993) present evidence suggesting that the "offset coefficient" has declined since 1991—precisely the year when capital controls were tightened—thereby endowing the Chilean central bank with a greater degree of monetary independence. On the other hand, the scope to exploit this degree of independence is severely limited. There have been numerous episodes since 1990 in which rates of interest that were deemed "excessively high" by agents brought forth a surge in inflows, forcing as a counterpart the relaxation of the domestic monetary stance.

On the other two points (effects on the size of inflows and their composition) the evidence is also controversial, but a consensus view increasingly holds that controls have been quite effective at changing the composition of flows toward longer-term maturities, and relatively ineffective at reducing the overall level of the flow.[11] Econometric evidence from Chile presented by Soto (1995), for instance, suggests that a combination of evasion and substitution toward longer maturities has meant that, after controlling for other determinants of flows, the tax has little discernible impact on overall volumes of funds entering the country. The composition of the flows, however, seems sharply responsive to the tax. Similar evidence is provided for the Colombian case by Cárdenas and Barrera (1995).

Does this mean that controls should be discarded because they are incapable of keeping out capital? Not necessarily. Affecting only the composition of flows may be just what policy makers need. Sachs, Tornell, and Velasco (1996b), in a study of twenty emerging markets in the aftermath of the tequila effect shock, found that the degree of financial and currency

11. See Ffrench-Davis and Agosín 1995 and Soto 1995 for differing views on these issues.

vulnerability is not systematically correlated with the size of the previous capital inflow; many Asian countries, along with Chile and Colombia, absorbed large amounts of foreign capital in 1989–1994 and felt no tequila effects. It is, however, correlated with the composition of such flows; the larger the share of short-term flows, other things being equal, the greater the disarray in the local financial markets in the first half of 1995.[12]

Intermediation of Flows and Bank Lending Booms

The different behavior of local banks in 1989–1994 offers the last—and perhaps most important—piece of evidence as to why Mexico found itself in financial disarray in late 1994 and early 1995, while Chile did not.[13] Banking and currency difficulties often go hand in hand. The link has been present in crises ranging from that of the U.S. in the 1930s to that of Chile in the early 1980s.[14] But the sheer magnitude of both bank and currency crises in the recent case of Mexico—and also in Venezuela and Argentina to cite just two additional examples—-has brought back the issue with a vengeance.[15]

Theoretically, the link between these twin crises is not hard to ascertain. Abrupt changes in the demand for money (caused, for instance, by expectations of devaluation and an incipient speculative attack) can cause a sharp fall in bank deposits. But under a fractional reserve system, banks do not have the cash in hand; in the absence of an injection of liquidity from the outside (typically from the central bank), cessation of payments and a bank panic can readily occur. Even if banks could simply wait until loans mature in order to satisfy depositor's demands (something that would take time, given banks' essential role as maturity transformers), the ensuing adjustment would not be easy or painless. The resulting credit squeeze on borrowing firms would send interest rates sky-high. In emerging markets, banks are the main sources of corporate credit, and most firms cannot simply turn around and borrow from the world market, no matter how dereg-

---

12. Technically, that study measures financial and currency pressures by means of an index that is a weighted average of nominal exchange rate depreciation and reserve losses. The behavior of local stock markets in early 1995, not reported in that paper, also fits this pattern of correlation.

13. This section draws on Sachs, Tornell, and Velasco 1996b.

14. Wigmore (1987) has argued that the failure of the Federal Reserve to protect the U.S. banking system in the winter of 1932–1933 was the result of the Federal Reserve's fears that lender-of-last-resort credit to the banks would undermine the link of the U.S. dollar to gold. In Chile in 1982, high interest rates under a fixed exchange rate helped precipitate a banking collapse; the associated expansion of domestic credit helped precipitate the end of the exchange rate peg. See Velasco 1991 for details.

15. See Kaminsky and Reinhart 1995 for a detailed analysis of a number of such episodes.

ulated the capital account may be.[16] The need to avoid a wave of bankrupt-
cies and serious economic disruption provides yet another rationale for
the authorities to step in.

One upshot is that the monetary base is not the only claim on the central bank that can be called in during times of trouble. The reality is that,
with bank liabilities covered by implicit or explicit government guarantees,
all M2 is potentially a liability of the government, to be redeemed with dollars at the time of a crunch. A second upshot is that links to the financial
system make it even more likely that self-fulfilling runs against a currency
will succeed, as Obstfeld (1994) has stressed. If fears of devaluation
prompt a bank run, which in turn causes an expansion of liquidity with
which central bank reserves can be bought, the circle is fully closed. And,
as the recent experience of Argentina suggests, the problem is not eliminated by the adoption of a rigid peg or currency board system in which the
central bank is prevented from issuing domestic credit. We (Sachs, Tornell, and Velasco 1996a) argue that in fact the problem may be worsened
because the absence of a lender of last resort can magnify fears of bank
illiquidity and turn those fears into problems of insolvency.

The discussion so far implies that such a vicious cycle can affect all banking systems. But banks, like Orwell's animals, are not all equal. The kind of
vulnerability that we have been describing depends crucially on two features of a banking system. One is the size of the liquidity cushion: the
greater the ratios of reserves and bank capital to deposits, the greater the
likelihood a bank can withstand a shock. The second is the quality of
the banks' portfolio: weak borrowers mean weak banks because a small
tremor in interest rates can lead to a large share of nonperforming loans.
Both are of course related: a growing share of doubtful credits eats into
capital and reduces the cushion available to cover additional shocks.

What determines bank weakness? Portfolios can be made suddenly weak
by an exogenous shock—think of oil prices and Texas banks in the mid-
1980s. But bad luck is not the only culprit. Portfolios are more often than
not endogenously made weak by swift expansions of credit, with boom
leading to bust. As Hausmann and Gavin (1995) persuasively argue, the
empirical link between lending booms and financial crises is very strong.
Rapid growth in the ratio of bank credit to GDP preceded financial troubles in Argentina (1981), Chile (1981–1982), Colombia (1982–1983),
Uruguay (1982), Norway (1987), Finland (1991–1992), Japan (1992–
1993), Sweden (1991), Mexico (1994), the Czech Republic (1997), and
Thailand (1997). The rationale for this link is simple. When lending expands very quickly, lenders' ability to screen marginal projects declines,
and they are more likely to end up with a large share of weak borrowers in

16. Calvo (1996) stresses this point.

their portfolios. High-risk debt such as credit cards and consumer and real estate loans, tend to grow more than proportionately. In addition, regulators (particularly in developing countries) soon find their limited oversight capacity overwhelmed. Thus, a bank portfolio that is extremely vulnerable to the vagaries of the business cycle is the most likely product of a lending boom.

Table 5.12 shows the evolution of the claims by the domestic financial system on the domestic private sector (as a share of GDP) for four selected Latin American countries.[17] If there is one single indicator that sets Chile and Mexico dramatically apart, this is it. Between 1989 and 1994, bank credit to the private sector grew by 207 percent in Mexico, while it grew by only 8 percent in Chile.

Two caveats concerning lending booms are in order. First, it is extremely important to distinguish levels from rates of increase. Many countries show very high ratios of private sector credit to output. This is of course nothing but financial deepening, and is not something to be concerned about. What is worrisome is sharp increases in lending to the private sector within a short period of time. Such increases are likely to lower average loan quality. Second, lending activity is likely to be closely related to the stabilization cycle. On the other side of the bank balance sheet are the deposits that finance the loans. Deposits are highly correlated with money demand and, therefore, with expected inflation. When a policy turnaround puts an end to hyperinflation, deposits swell and so do bank loans. This effect, which is nothing but a beneficial payoff (greater financial intermediation) from stabilization, probably explains some of the sharp increase in lending in a country such as Argentina. It does not, however, explain an episode such

Table 5.12 Credit boom

	1994 vs. 1989	1994 vs. average of 1989–1989
Argentina	23%	38%
Brazil	21%	51%
Chile	8%	−12%
Mexico	207%	361%

Source: IMF, *IFS.*

17. This variable was constructed in the following way. For each year we calculated the ratio of claims on the private sector by deposit money banks and monetary authorities (IFS line 32d) to GDP (IFS line 99b). When inflation is high this ratio is biased upward because the available annual figure for claims on the private sector corresponds to the figure for December, whereas nominal GDP reflects the average price level over the entire year. To correct for this bias we multiplied the biased ratio by the ratio of the average price level to December's price level. When inflation is low this factor essentially equals one.

as Mexico's, in which stabilization occurred in 1988–1989 and the increase in credit occurred in 1991–1994.

Why did a lending boom happen in Mexico (and to some extent in Argentina) but not in Chile? A commonly cited culprit is the swift liberalization of the capital account, followed by a surge in inflows that presumably get intermediated by the banking sector. There are two problems with this explanation. The first one is that both countries have had reasonably open capital accounts for a long time. The second is that there is no obvious correlation between the size of the capital inflow and the ensuing behavior of bank credit. As we saw earlier, both countries experienced similarly large capital inflows, and bank lending grew tremendously in Mexico but not in Chile.[18]

But if capital account liberalization does not seem to have mattered, the same is not true of domestic financial liberalization. As early as the late 1970s and early 1980s the cycle from bank privatization and deregulation to lending boom to eventual bust was clearly visible in a number of countries. In Latin America, Argentina, Chile, Colombia, and Uruguay went through this cycle.[19] The point, of course, is not that deregulation is bad per se, but that it can lead to rapid credit expansion. For instance, financial liberalization in 1988–1990 was followed by a lending boom in Indonesia. In Mexico, privatization and deregulation of the banking system in the early 1990s had a similar effect.

A key difference is that in Mexico the capital inflow took place simultaneously with a decrease in banks' required reserve ratios, whereas in Chile such ratios were increased (at least for dollar deposits). As Rodriguez (1993) has stressed, this can set the stage for the inflow to cause a large increase in domestic bank lending. The stance of bank supervisors probably also made a difference. Chile and Colombia experienced a credit boom and a financial crisis in the early 1980s, leading to bank interventions, liquidations, and bailouts—all at a substantial cost to the taxpayer. The lesson was deeply ingrained, and in subsequent years both factors made the enhancement of bank supervision and capitalization a priority for Chilean policy makers. By contrast, in Mexico (and to some extent Argentina) the lending boom was allowed to continue unhindered[20]—even though policy makers routinely vowed to have learned the lessons from earlier banking collapses in the region, and to prove it they implemented Basle accord capital standards and other liquidity tests for suspect institutions.

18. Sachs, Tornell, and Velasco (1996b) also find no such correlation for their sample of twenty developing countries.
19. See Baliño and Sundarajan 1991 for studies from a set of countries, including Argentina, Chile, Uruguay, and the Philippines.
20. See Rojas-Suárez and Weisbrod 1995 for evidence on the recent Argentine and Mexican banking troubles and restructuring packages.

The Mexican lending boom had two dire consequences. One was a deterioration of bank portfolios as macroeconomic conditions changed and interest rates rose in during 1994. This problem was to increase exponentially after the December devaluation and financial meltdown. The second problem was that bank weakness severely curtailed the ability of policy makers to pursue a tough monetary policy in 1994. Interest rates did go up in Mexico in the wake of the March shock, but not enough to entice foreign lenders or reduce the current account deficit. The Banco de México itself recognized that bank troubles were the reason for this situation, as stated in its 1995 monetary program: "[The fall in foreign reserves] made it necessary to carry out compensatory operations in the money market. Had liquidity not recovered through these operations, interest rates would have reached exorbitant levels, which would have affected debtors, including financial intermediaries, in a highly unfavorable way. That fact could have caused additional capital flight and could have required an eventual expansion of primary credit" (Banco de México 1995, 36).[21]

Conclusions and Policy Lessons

Exchange Rate Policy

Although building credibility in monetary and exchange rate policy is clearly important, unrealistic "toughness" on the exchange rate need not increase credibility. Holding on to the peso exchange rate until the bitter end did not serve to build Mexico's long-term stature as a sound-money country. In any event, the idea that a pegged exchange rate is the only linchpin to credibility is misguided. Central bank independence, publicly announced inflation targets, flexible labor markets, and solid fiscal policies are all forms of nominal anchors that can keep inflation low even with a floating exchange rate.

Both the data in this chapter and the broader sample studied by Sachs, Tornell, and Velasco (1996b) suggest that currency overvaluation is almost always associated with eventual turmoil in currency markets. The same is true of the plight of Thailand, Malaysia, and the Philippines (and to a lesser extent Indonesia) in 1997. This suggests that cautious policy makers will want to endeavor to prevent excessive appreciation. Most economists would agree that, if the capital inflow and therefore the change in the fundamental real exchange rate are more or less permanent, then in the long run, real exchange rate targeting cannot succeed; repeated nominal devaluations would simply elicit repeated increases in prices, failing to affect the

---

21. The translation is our own.

real exchange rate. But as usual, definitions of what constitutes the long run vary widely. If there is enough price stickiness over plausibly short periods, and if capital inflows are also short-lived, so that a brief period is all that is at stake, then nominal exchange rate policy may well have some ability to prevent real appreciation. But this policy is not costless.In the 1990s Chile and Colombia (both of which targeted the real rate) had higher inflation than the other Latin American countries, in spite of virtuous fiscal policies. In short, an accommodating nominal exchange rate policy may be able to limit real appreciation over the short-to-medium run, though probably at some expense in terms of inflation.

Sterilization and Debt Management

If a country confronts highly volatile capital movements, then some degree of sterilization is probably both inevitable and desirable. Even in Argentina's currency board the central bank has manipulated bank reserve requirements (for instance, during the capital outflow and bank run of the first quarter of 1995) to insulate the money supply, at least partially, from the whims of Wall Street traders. But just as with real exchange rate targeting, this should be a temporary measure not a permanent one. Sterilization is fiscally costly, and over time such costs build up. A long and heavy sterilization episode can cause quasi-fiscal losses that undermine the credibility of the overall monetary stance.

Regarding domestic debt management, policy makers must recall what corporate financial officers have always known: borrowing short can sometimes save interest charges, but can also leave one hostage to the mood changes of lenders. Moreover, the vulnerability of countries is greater than that of companies because the presence of exchange risk, and the absence of an international lender of last resort and of an international bankruptcy procedure can easily lead to creditor panic; if one lender expects other lenders will not roll over short-term debt, it pays to do exactly the same. A solvent country can become a country in default overnight.

Capital Controls

Most economists are understandably weary of capital controls because the state can easily put up an iron curtain of costly and inefficient regulations. But such skepticism must confront the fact that several of the more successful developing countries—such as Korea, Malaysia and Indonesia in Asia, and Colombia and Chile in Latin America—have on occasion created disincentives to short-term inflows. And, most important, it was precisely these emerging markets that came through the tequila effect shock with the smallest hangovers.

How does one ensure that such controls do more good than harm? The experience of Chile suggests two lessons. First, get the cosmetics right. Liberalize outflows as in inflows are restricted, to make sure that investors do not come to fear a return to the populist policies of yesteryear. Second, do not expect controls to do more than they can. The amount of monetary independence a Tobin tax affords is, almost by definition, limited by the size of the tax wedge. Attempts to fix unrealistically high interest rates (relative to world rates) can only cause, as Chile has occasionally found out, additional large and destabilizing inflows.

Lending Booms and Bank Regulation

The recent experience of Mexico in this regard is unusually revealing, as is the experience of Thailand, which provides the same policy lessons. A lending boom may not only lead to an eventual banking problem. The resulting bank weakness may also severely curtail the ability of the government to carry out a sound monetary and fiscal policy and may therefore endanger the whole stabilization effort. Receiving large amounts of foreign capital need not cause a frenzy in bank lending and a growing stock of bad loans, as the experience of Chile shows. Mexican regulators attempted to deal with the problem by stressing bank capitalization requirements. That they failed to contain an impending banking crisis says less about supervisory incompetence than about the limited usefulness of that kind of policy. During lending booms everyone is liquid, credit is plentiful, and portfolios that will turn out to be weak look good on paper. In Hausmann and Gavin's (1995) words, "It isn't that what you get is what you see; it's what you don't see that gets you." This suggests that additional policies, both microeconomic (loan-by-loan portfolio evaluation) and macroeconomic (sterilization) may be necessary to ensure that a capital inflow does not lead to a financial crisis.

References

Alesina, A., A. Pratti, and G. Tabellini. 1990. "Public Confidence and Debt Management: A Model and a Case Study of Italy." In *Public Debt Management: Theory and History*, edited by R. Dornbusch and M. Draghi. Cambridge: Cambridge University Press.

Baliño, Tomás, and Vasudevan Sundarajan. 1991. *Banking Crises: Cases and Issues*. Washington, D.C.: International Monetary Fund.

Banco Central de Chile. *Monthly Bulletin*. Various issues. Santiago: Banco Central de Chile.

Banco de Mexico. *Monthly Report.* Various issues. Mexico City: Banco de Mexico.

Calvo, Guillermo. 1988. "Servicing the Public Debt: The Role of Expectations." *American Economic Review* 78(4):647–661.

——. 1991. "Temporary Stabilization Policy: The Case of Flexible Prices and Exchange Rates." *Journal of Economic Dynamics and Control* 15 (1):197–213.

——. 1996. "Capital Flows and Macroeconomic Management: Tequila Lessons." Department of Economics, University of Maryland, College Park, Md. Photocopy.

Calvo, Guillermo, and P. Guidotti. 1990. "Indexation and Maturity of Government Bonds: An Exploratory Model." In *Public Debt Management: Theory and History,* edited by R. Dornbusch and M. Draghi. Cambridge: Cambridge University Press.

Calvo, Guillermo, Leonardo Leiderman, and Carmen Reinhart. 1993. "The Capital Inflows Problem: Concepts and Issues." Working Paper PPAA/93/10. International Monetary Fund, Washington, D.C.

Cole, H., and P. Kehoe. 1996. "Reputation Spillover across Relationships: Reviving Reputation Models of Debt." Working Paper 5486, National Bureau of Economic Research, Cambridge, Mass.

Cárdenas, M., and F. Barrera. 1995. "On the Effectiveness of Capital Controls in Colombia." Fedesarrollo, Bopotá, Colombia. Photocopy.

Ffrench-Davis, Ricardo, and Manuel Agosín. 1995. "Managing Capital Inflows in Latin America." Department of Economics, University of Chile, Santiago. Photocopy.

Frankel, J. 1994. "Sterilization of Capital Inflows: Hard (Calvo) or Easy (Reisen)?" Working paper, International Monetary Fund, Washington, D.C.

Frankel, J., and C. Okongwu. 1995. "Have Latin American and Asian Countries So Liberalized Portfolio Capital Inflows That Sterilization Is Now Impossible?" Department of Economics, University of California, Berkeley. Photocopy.

Hausmann, Ricardo, and Michael Gavin. 1995. "The Roots of Banking Crises: The Macroeconomic Context." Paper prepared for the Conference on Banking Crises in Latin America, October 1995, Washington, D.C.

Helpman, E., L. Leiderman, and G. Bufman. 1994. "A New Breed of Exchange Rate Bands: Chile, Israel and Mexico." *Economic Policy* 19.

IMF (International Monetary Fund). *Balance of Payments Statistics Yearbook.* Various issues. Washington, D.C.: International Monetary Fund.

——. *International Financial Statistics.* Various issues. Washington, D.C.: International Monetary Fund.

Kaminsky, Graciela, and Carmen Reinhart. 1995. "The Twin Crises: The Causes of Banking and Balance-of-Payments Problems." Working Paper No. 544, International Finance Paper, Board of Governors of the Federal Reserve System, Washington, D.C.

Labán, R., and F. Larraín. 1993. "The Chilean Experience with Capital Mobility." In *The Chilean Economy, Policy Lessons and Challenges,* edited by B. Bosworth, R. Dornbusch, and R. Labán. Washington, D.C.: Brookings Institution.

Obstfeld, M. 1994. "The Logic of Currency Crises." *Cahiers Economiques et Monetaires* (Bank of France) 43:.

Rodriguez, C. 1993. "Money and Credit under Currency Substitution" *IMF Staff Papers* 40 (2):414–426.

Rojas-Suárez, Liliana, and Steven R. Weisbrod. 1995. "Managing Banking Crises in Latin America: The Do's and Don'ts of Successful Bank Restructuring Programs." Paper prepared for the Conference on Banking Crises in Latin America, October 1995, Washington, D.C.

Sachs, J., A. Tornell, and A. Velasco. 1996a. "The Collapse of the Mexican Peso: What Have We Learned?" *Economic Policy* 22:13–56.

——. 1996b. "Financial Crises in Emerging Markets: The Lessons from 1995." *Brookings Papers on Economic Activity* 1:147–198.

Soto, M. "Encaje a los Créditos Externos: La Evidencia Empírica." 1995. Department of Economics, Catholic University of Chile, Santiago. Photocopy.

Velasco, A. 1991. "The Chilean Financial System: Liberalization, Crisis, Intervention." In *Banking Crises: Cases and Issues,* edited by T. Baliño and V. Sundarajam. Washington, D.C.: International Monetary Fund.

Wigmore, B. 1987. "Was the Banking Holiday of 1933 a Run on the Dollar Rather Than the Banks?" *Journal of Economic History* 47:739–756.

6

Equity Financing of East Asian Development

Rachel McCulloch and Peter A. Petri

By November 1997, shock waves from the financial turmoil in East Asia had reached stock markets in Europe, Latin America, and the United States. Whether investors had come to Asian markets in search of diversification or higher returns, the results were nothing short of disastrous. Not only had Asian share-price indices plummeted by as much as 60 percent in U.S. dollars since the start of the year, but events had revealed substantial linkage between the performance of Asian markets and their counterparts elsewhere. Yet the disillusionment of investors was minor in comparison to the bitterness of East Asian leaders who had opened their financial markets to funds from abroad and now sought to place blame for the debacle on the actions of foreign speculators.

Just a year before, it had seemed that developing East Asia could do no wrong, at least as far as investors were concerned. Per capita incomes in the region were soaring, the growth fueled by massive investment (table 6.1). Although domestic saving had traditionally financed the bulk of East Asia's capital formation, a growing share of the funds for new investments, particularly in Southeast Asia's "tiger economies," now came from abroad (table 6.2). Relative to gross domestic product (GDP), 1995 net private inflows averaged about 5 percent for the region, 6 percent for Thailand and Indonesia, 8 percent for China, and 15 percent for Malaysia, with foreign direct investment accounting for more than half of these flows (World Bank 1996b, 1997b).

Portfolio equity investment, negligible a decade earlier, had become a substantial component of capital inflows to East Asian economies. Notwithstanding 1994's peso crisis, new portfolio equity investments in 1995 stood only modestly below their 1993 peak, constituting 11 percent of total inflows, about the same as in 1990 (World Bank 1996b). Investor interest in Asian shares continued to build in 1996 and the first half of 1997 as the

Table 6.1 Growth rates of GDP and investment, 1970–1995

	GDP			Gross Domestic Investment		
	1970–1980	1980–1990	1990–1995	1970–1980	1980–1990	1990–1995
China	5.5	10.2	12.8	6.3	11.0	15.5
Indonesia	7.2	6.1	7.6	13.1	7.0	16.3
Korea	10.1	9.4	7.2	7.4	11.9	7.2
Malaysia	7.9	5.2	8.7	9.3	2.6	16.0
Philippines	6.0	1.0	2.3	6.8	−2.1	3.2
Singapore	8.3	6.4	8.7	6.2	3.7	6.0
Thailand	7.1	7.6	8.4	9.8	9.4	10.2

Sources: World Bank 1995, World Bank 1997b.

Table 6.2 Foreign financing for gross domestic investment (% GDP)

	Gross domestic investment/GDP		Net resource inflows/GDP		FDI inflows/ GDP
	1980	1995	1980	1995	1995
China	35	42	1	8	5.1
Hong Kong	35	35	4	n.a.[b]	n.a.
Indonesia	24	38	3	7	1.4
Korea	32	37	8	2	0.2
Malaysia	30	41	9	15	6.7
Philippines	29	23	4	5	1.4
Singapore	46	33	13	−18	10.2
Thailand	29	43	7	6	1.9
Average	29	39	3	8	

Sources: World Bank 1997b, IMF 1995b.
[a] For Hong Kong, Korea, Singapore (current account balance/GDP).
[b] n.a., not available.
[c] Low- and middle-income East Asia and Pacific.

American bull market raised U.S. equities to historically high valuations. Emerging-market mutual funds focusing on East Asia grew in size and multiplied in number. But then the rosy scenario abruptly unraveled, beginning with the collapse of the Thai bhat in early July and culminating in October with heart-stopping market swings around the world. Although large losses were later reversed in some markets, East Asian equities remained sharply below their dollar values at the start of 1997, and investors and analysts had no way to gauge whether they were observing the end of a turbulent period, or only the beginning.

Southeast Asia's sudden reversal of fortune has revealed obvious gaps in knowledge concerning emerging markets, with respect both to the role of stock markets in financing the growth of developing countries and to the role of emerging-market equities in optimizing the portfolios of international investors. The question, in short, is whether portfolio investment in emerging-market equities has a future. We begin with an account of the main factors underlying the surge in foreign portfolio investments in emerging markets that began in the late 1980s, with a particular focus on East Asia. We relate these investments to the overall determinants of investors' portfolio choices and evaluate the implications for the choices faced by government and private-sector decision makers in developing nations. We argue that, even in the light of recent events, the long-term potential for attracting portfolio equity into developing countries remains great, with inflows to any specific host country depending mainly on its ability to pursue stable, outward-oriented economic policies. Ultimately, portfolio equity flows could rival direct investment in importance because they can take place even in the absence of the complex enabling factors that are necessary for a successful direct-investment project.[1]

But recent events also underscore that overall market conditions play a key role that neither investors nor policy makers can safely ignore. Aftershocks from the Mexican peso crisis in 1994 and the Thai bhat crisis in 1997 rapidly extended into equity as well as bond markets and produced adverse consequences around the world. For a short time following the peso crisis, new flows even into Asian markets came to an abrupt halt. Likewise, markets in eastern Europe and Latin America soon contracted the 1997 Asian flu. These vivid demonstrations of market contagion establish that host countries, even those such as Hong Kong with an exemplary policy environment, need to exercise caution in their reliance on mobile foreign capital.

To some extent, the crisis of 1997 reflected traditional macroeconomic problems, namely the persistent pegging of East Asian currencies to the U.S. dollar, which had appreciated substantially against most major currencies in previous months. But any special circumstances that might explain Mexico's crisis in 1994 or Thailand's in 1997 must be placed in context. Even prior to 1994, up to half the variation in bond and equity flows from the United States to developing Latin America and Asia was attributable to factors *external* to individual host nations, although the sensitivity to such external influences was much smaller for Asia than for Latin America (Chuhan, Claessens, and Mamingi 1993). Thus, we must also address the overall macroeconomic consequences for host countries of large and potentially volatile portfolio inflows.

---

1. The theory of direct investment suggests that necessary conditions include advantages specific to the investing firm (e.g., technology), advantages specific to the host economy (e.g., low labor costs), and advantages of internalizing the project within a firm rather than implementing it through markets. Because of these complex requirements, relatively few countries participate significantly in either direct investment outflows or inflows.

Although we see a continuing and perhaps even expanded role for portfolio equity financing of economic development in Asia and elsewhere, we
argue that the unusually high rates of return experienced by early investors
in some emerging stock markets are unlikely to be repeated because they
reflected premiums associated with incompletely integrated capital markets. Also, because the increased role of internationally mobile capital in
emerging markets tends to link market conditions there to financial markets elsewhere, the diversification benefits of holding emerging-market equities are likely to be reduced, although not eliminated, as emerging markets mature and become fully integrated into global markets.

Why Foreign Portfolio Equity Investment Grew So Fast

If equity markets in developing countries grew to be as large relative to
GDP as markets in developed countries, then the capitalization of
developing-country stock markets would grow by roughly $2.3 trillion.
Much of the money flowing into growing equity markets represents the
mobilization of domestic saving. However, if just one-fifth of new equities were sold to foreigners, then nearly $500 billion of new capital
inflows would be generated. Even if the sales took place over several
decades, this would radically change the landscape of international
capital markets and dramatically alter the economic policy options
faced by developing-country governments.

Large as the numbers may seem, they are not implausible. Developing
countries as a group have been tapping global equity markets at unprecedented rates. In 1988 portfolio equity flows accounted for only $1 billion,
or about 1 percent of net resource flows (table 6.3). In 1989 these flows
more than tripled. They again doubled by 1991, nearly doubled in 1992,
and tripled in 1993 before dropping back to lower but still important levels. After two years of no growth following 1993's record inflows of $45 bil-
lion, new foreign investments in emerging stock markets reached nearly
$46 billion in 1996, with about $14 billion going to markets in East Asia
and the Pacific (IFC 1997).

Investors' Motives

Why such immense interest? The timing of the rush into emerging markets suggests that early investors were attracted by the prospect of high current yields during a period of temporarily low interest rates and little
growth in equity prices in the United States. However, a completely different and potentially more important motive for longer-term shifts toward
emerging markets involves the international diversification of developed-

Table 6.3a Aggregate net long-term resource flows to developing countries (US$ billions)

	1981	1982	1983	1984	1985	1986	1987	1988	1989	1990	1991	1992	1993	1994	1995	1996
Official finance	33.7	34.6	34.8	33.6	39.7	43.9	43.9	40.8	41.1	56.3	65.6	55.4	55.0	45.7	53.0	40.8
Grants	11.4	10.9	10.43	12.6	15.6	16.0	16.7	18.3	19.0	29.2	37.3	31.6	29.3	32.4	32.6	31.3
Loans	22.3	23.7	24.4	21.0	24.1	27.9	27.2	22.5	22.1	27.1	28.3	23.9	25.7	13.2	20.4	9.5
Private loans	53.3	45.1	30.7	27.4	20.6	9.3	8.6	11.0	10.1	16.6	16.2	35.9	44.9	44.9	56.6	88.6
Banks	44.0	32.9	23.4	23.0	7.8	1.8	1.1	7.9	3.9	3.0	2.8	12.5	-0.3	11.0	26.5	34.2
Bonds	1.3	4.2	1.6	-0.1	5.6	0.8	1.0	2.9	4.2	2.3	10.1	9.9	35.9	29.3	28.5	46.1
Other	8.0	8.0	5.7	4.5	7.2	6.7	6.5	0.2	2.0	11.3	3.3	13.5	9.2	4.6	1.7	8.3
Direct investment	12.9	11.4	8.6	9.4	11.3	10.1	14.5	21.2	24.7	24.5	33.5	43.6	67.2	83.7	95.5	109.5
Portfolio equity	0.0	0.0	0.0	0.2	0.1	0.6	0.8	1.1	3.5	3.2	7.2	11.0	45.0	32.7	32.1	45.7
Total net flows	99.9	91.1	74.0	70.5	71.6	63.8	67.7	74.0	79.3	100.6	122.5	146.0	212.0	207.0	237.2	284.6

Sources: World Bank 1997a, World Bank 1996a, World Bank 1996b. Data for 1996 is preliminary.

Table 6.3b Net long-term resource flows to developing countries (percent of total)

	1965	1981	1987	1996
Official Finance	63	34	65	14
Private Loans	10	53	13	31
Direct Investment	27	13	21	39
Portfolio Equity	0	0	1	16
Total Net Flows (billion $US)	9.3	99.9	67.8	284.6

Source: Table 6.3a.

country portfolios. According to the capital asset pricing model (CAPM), the benefit from adding an additional security to a portfolio depends not only on the distribution of its expected return, but also on the way its performance is correlated with that of other assets in the portfolio. Thus, while many investors in the United States and other industrial countries were initially attracted to emerging markets by high average returns, others sought new opportunities for diversification.

Although stocks in emerging markets are risky (expected returns have high variance), the risk is not highly correlated with the performance of developed-country stock markets (table 6.4). Expanding the set of available securities to include those traded on emerging markets therefore has the effect of transforming some systematic risk into diversifiable risk. In equilibrium, systematic risk requires compensation through a risk premium incorporated into expected returns. The inclusion of emerging market assets in a developed-country portfolio will tend to reduce the

Table 6.4 Total returns in developed and emerging markets, 1989–1994

	5-year average return	5-year standard deviation	Correlation with U.S. market
U.S. market[a]	14.6	8.8	1.00
Other developed[b]	9.1	13.7	0.33
Emerging markets	10.6	16.8	0.19
East Asia (average)	16.8	34.8	0.13
China	19.7	69	0.02
Indonesia	20.8	26.4	0.41
Korea	0.2	26.3	−0.02
Malaysia	22.2	23.4	0.17
Philippines	24.8	28.5	0.08
Taiwan	15.7	37.7	0.07
Thailand	14.0	32.0	0.18

Source: IFC 1997.
[a] S&P 500.
[b] Morgan Stanley EAFE index.

portfolio's systematic risk. On these grounds, it would be attractive to include emerging market assets even if their risk-adjusted expected returns were somewhat *below* those of developed markets.

Because market returns until 1994 were substantially higher in emerging markets than in developed markets, much of the initial flurry of interest reflected the promise of higher yields rather than lower overall portfolio risk. However, current-yield-oriented investors were unprepared for the high variance typical of these markets. Chastened by large losses in some markets and disappointingly small gains in others, these investors reduced or eliminated their holdings of emerging-market issues. Yet following a period of slower overall growth, by 1996 current-yield-oriented investors in the United States and other OECD (Organization for Economic Cooperation and Development) countries were again shopping for Asian equities as the U.S. bull market increasingly appeared poised for a correction.

OECD holders of emerging-market equity issues thus fall into two groups with very different goals: those willing to assume extra risk to earn the highest possible returns, and those willing to accept lower returns in order to reduce portfolio risk. Holdings motivated by the goal of high current yield obviously contribute to the characterization of portfolio equity inflows as highly volatile; holdings based on the desire for broad diversification (e.g., emerging-market index funds) are likely to provide a more stable source of external equity financing. As the diversification benefit becomes better understood by investors, the fraction of equity investment based on desire for broad diversification has the potential to grow substantially.

Issuers' Motives

If emerging-market assets can find buyers among developed-country investors, developing-country firms issuing such securities should experience lower capital costs. Raising capital abroad with securities that promise returns only in the issuer's domestic currency also helps to reduce firms' exposure in foreign exchange markets and thereby saves the cost of alternative hedging strategies. (Other comparisons between equity offerings and alternative forms of finance are discussed later.)

From the viewpoint of the economy's capital markets, the participation of foreign investors provides an impetus to the development of market institutions. Much of the infrastructure required by equity markets, including especially research and information services, has substantial economies of scale, and so the volume of transactions undertaken by foreign investors is likely to contribute to the quality of market-related institutions and services.

Finally, the development of well-functioning stock markets has favorable implications for economic efficiency. An equity market provides continuous monitoring of firms, helps to flag problems in specific industries or enterprises, and may also provide a market for control in cases where a change in management or firm organization is needed to achieve efficiency. In theory, there may be cases in which foreign control is inappropriate or contrary to national interest; for example, a foreign competitor could acquire a controlling interest in a domestic firm simply to shut down its production and monopolize the local market. However, as developing economies open to world markets and their governments adopt pro-competitive policies, the potential for such deleterious action is increasingly seen as remote and the risk negligible in relation to the concrete benefits of an active equity market.

Who Are the Investors?

Although the longer-term internationalization of investment portfolios by institutional investors (insurance companies, pension and retirement funds, and mutual funds) has its roots in the industry trend toward scientific portfolio selection (i.e., selection that reflects asset-return correlations, as guided by CAPM), the initial surge came as U.S. interest rates fell relative to rates available on comparable securities issued in other currencies. Internationalization began primarily with bonds of other industrial countries, later encompassed equities, and later still, included bonds and equities of developing countries. The pattern is consistent with the hypothesis that fund managers begin with alternatives that have modest information costs. However, the move into emerging markets has also been constrained by government-imposed limits on inward equity investment, by the small size of particular markets, and for institutional investors, by government or industry regulations limiting portfolio choices.

Regardless of the underlying motive, interest in emerging market investing has spawned a whole industry of new instruments. First came country funds, typically established as closed-end investment funds listed on the New York or another major stock exchange. These funds were sometimes the only ways of investing in a market—for example Korea and India—where government severely limited foreign access. Open-end U.S. mutual funds soon became a second popular vehicle. By March 1995, no fewer than 960 mutual funds were active in emerging markets, with approximately half of these specializing in East Asian securities. There were 38 percent more emerging market funds in March 1995 than a year earlier, and they controlled assets totaling $120 billion (IMF 1995b).

Larger investors can also purchase securities directly on Asian markets, and an increasing number of issues are also listed in international markets such as London or New York. Consistent with the implications of investment theory, many portfolio managers have increased the weight of emerging markets in a wide range of portfolios. Unfortunately, we have found no estimate of the extent of foreign ownership of emerging-market shares, or of ownership distribution across investing countries. The International Finance Corporation (IFC) of the World Bank has played an active role in promoting investment vehicles for channeling industrial-country savings into emerging markets. The IFC has provided technical assistance in the areas of privatization and initial public offerings and has cosponsored closed-end country funds (IFC 1993). For example, the IFC and the European Bank for Reconstruction and Development invested $8 billion and $16.6 billion, respectively, in a $50 million Russian equity fund.

What Are the Risks?

Dominated by institutional investors, especially from the United States, portfolio equity flows initially generated uncritical enthusiasm on the part of both borrowers and issuers. From the start, some analysts in the financial community did raise warning flags, reminding investors that the impressive equity returns of the early 1990s might indicate nothing more than a speculative bubble, and high interest rates on bonds could reflect merely the market's required compensation for substantial risk of default or currency devaluation. Likewise, specialists in economic development strategy began to worry about the impact on developing countries should the enthusiasm of foreign portfolio investors subside and net inflows slow or even reverse, and about the constraints on national policy therefore implied by heavy reliance on mobile foreign funds.

The crisis that began with Mexico's devaluation of the peso in December 1994 quickly infected the markets for assets of other Latin American countries sharing some of Mexico's characteristics. The contagion produced a scenario uncomfortably similar to the unfolding of the 1980s' debt crisis that began with Mexico's 1982 default.[2] These events in turn stimulated new research on the fundamental causes of the Mexican debacle and, implicitly or explicitly, on the likelihood that other similar-seeming economies are destined to experience similarly disruptive reversals of portfolio investment. Even so, investors were not prepared for the collapse of Thailand's currency less than three years later, soon followed by declines in Malaysia, Indonesia, and the Philippines. Thailand, which enjoyed rapid growth, low inflation, high domestic savings, and a budget surplus, was no Mexico. Yet certain crucial elements were the same: a high interest rate on short-term funds (in Thailand, as deposits in poorly supervised banks) and commitment to a pegged exchange rate.

2. The superficial similarity may be misleading. Cline (1995) diagnoses 1994 as "more in the nature of an Italian exchange-rate collapse than a debt crisis of the Mexico-1982 variety." The crisis originated in investors' recognition that the government's short-term dollar liabilities far exceeded the central bank's reserves.

Although our focus is on portfolio equity rather than debt, many of the same issues are relevant: for investors, risk of devaluation or inconvertibility; for policy makers, consequences for exchange rates and domestic macroeconomic stability of reliance on substantial inflows of highly mobile capital. Moreover, the two markets are closely linked because firms must choose between debt and equity financing, and investors regard debt and equity as alternatives in portfolio selection. Although the problems in Southeast Asia began with Thai banks and finance companies, the impact quickly reached the stock markets.

Alternative Channels for External Finance

A striking feature of capital flows to developing countries is the dramatic change over time in the relative importance of different investment vehicles (table 6.3). From the end of World War II until the mid-1970s, the flow of resources into developing countries was dominated by official development assistance. The one important source of private financing was foreign direct investment, which in 1965, for example, accounted for 27 percent of total net resource flows and 73 percent of total private flows.[3] The recycling of petrodollars that began in 1974 gave rise to a new investment regime. A huge increase in the supply of funds available for international bank lending allowed developing countries the much-desired opportunity to augment or replace direct investment with loans from large international banks.[4] In 1981 more than half of the resource flows to developing countries consisted of private lending.

The option of borrowing from banks abruptly disappeared in 1982 when Mexico declared a moratorium on the payment of interest on foreign debt, ushering in an era of debt crisis. Total private flows to developing nations dropped dramatically. Foreign banks continued to lend only to the extent required in refinancing agreements negotiated by banks and international agencies. By 1987, just 13 percent of resource flows to developing countries consisted of private loans, and banks accounted for less than

---

3. Private bond finance had been an important source of capital for development from the nineteenth century until the massive defaults of the 1930s; like the ill-fated bank loans of the 1970s, these bond issues were dominated by governments seeking budgetary relief as well as capital for infrastructure projects (Eichengreen and Fishlow 1996).

4. The pre-1970's development literature emphasized the concept of *unbundling*, the direct investment package of capital, technology, and managerial know-how. In the 1970s, many countries borrowed in international capital markets to finance new projects and then used arm's-length transactions to obtain technology and know-how. The goal was to capture the high rates of return achieved by multinationals. However, for reasons discussed below, the unbundling approach also entailed assuming risk that had previously been borne by the multinationals.

10 percent of that smaller share. Official finance had expanded to 65 percent of net resource flows. The modest rebound in bank lending that began in 1988 reflected primarily the U.S.-sponsored Brady plan.

With the virtual disappearance of the international banks as major sources of external financing, many countries sought to restore, or in some cases to create for the first time, legal and economic conditions conducive to direct investment. Direct investment rose to 21 percent of net long-term inflows in 1987 and 39 percent in 1996, compared with 13 percent in 1981. For many countries, attracting direct investment became a top policy priority. This renewed interest may have stemmed initially from the need to replace bank loans, but it also reflected an enhanced appreciation of the special characteristics of direct investment. In particular, developing host countries now court multinationals to facilitate the transfer of advanced technology and managerial know-how that often cannot be obtained through arm's-length transactions alone.

The most recent shift in the composition of capital flows to developing countries has been the rapid growth of portfolio investment in bonds and stocks that began in the late 1980s. In 1981, portfolio inflows had accounted for only 1 percent of net resource inflows, almost entirely through sale of sovereign bonds. The growth of portfolio inflows accelerated at the start of the 1990s, increasing more than threefold between 1990 and 1993. Inflows dropped sharply in the wake of the 1994 Mexican financial crisis, but by 1996 the demand for emerging-country issues had again begun to grow. In 1996, 16 percent of net long-term inflows to developing countries was from portfolio equity, with another 16 percent from bonds (table 6.3).[5]

The rapid growth of portfolio investment was driven by two main forces. The first was the generation of profitable new investment opportunities by policy reforms that stressed the role of market forces and outward-oriented development strategies. This new emphasis spawned an important new class of potential borrowers and a new set of attractive lending opportunities, including equity issued in connection with privatization of major companies. In contrast to the earlier surge of bank lending, much of the capital raised through bond and equity issues flowed to the private sector rather than to government agencies. The second force was the discovery by U.S. investment professionals and the investing public of the favorable risk and return characteristics of the newly available stocks and bonds issued by companies in the developing world, particularly East Asia. The initial attraction of the new assets was heightened by the domestic in-

---

5. The cycle was milder and shorter in Asian equities; the IFC's Asian regional index of total dollar returns had returned to its pre-Mexico level by October 1995 ("Resilience of Developing" 1996).

vestment climate in the United States, with bond interest rates extremely low by historic standards and equity prices stagnant. Supported by country-risk analysts' favorable assessment of the future policy environment in these emerging markets, the two forces led to the rethinking of investment strategies and the development of a whole new industry of Asian investment instruments.

Although the initial demand for emerging-market equities was fed in part by unusually low returns on alternative investments in OECD financial markets, the result was nonetheless a permanent change in investor awareness of these new opportunities. To be sure, two major crises in emerging markets should also have produced a permanent change in investor awareness of the potential risks. Yet, the very rapid post-Mexico recovery of investor interest in emerging-market issues suggests that these assets will continue to play a significant role in the diversified portfolios of OECD investors.

The key to ongoing growth is that portfolio flows to developing countries, particularly through equity investment, can benefit both developed-country investors and developing-country issuers. In much the same way that opportunities for trade in goods create gains for all trading partners, so the international exchange of assets creates gains for both investors and issuers. As we discuss in the next section, the risk-return characteristics of portfolio equity investment are very different from those of bank loans or bond issues. Equity inflows allow developing countries to spread the risks related to their domestic industries by shifting some risk to foreign stockholders. The development of active equity markets also establishes valuable services for monitoring firms and creates information to guide the allocation of capital from all sources.[6]

How Channels Differ

Analyses of capital flows to developing nations typically emphasize the total volume of flows and, in light of Mexico and Southeast Asia, the volatility of

6. In light of increased concern about volatility of portfolio capital inflows, it would be instructive to examine the motives and behavior of foreign equity investors versus bond investors, as to how they affect the likelihood of abrupt reversals of inflows, that is, to determine whether in emerging markets there is reason to characterize equity purchases more than bond or bank-deposit investments as "hot money." An interesting aspect of the problem is that the bulk of emerging-market investments is made through mutual funds. In volatile markets, the behavior of fund managers in anticipation of redemptions by fund investors may as important as the behavior of investors themselves. Shares are sold in advance to cover expected redemptions. Moreover, managers are likely to sell shares that have fallen relatively less, thus contributing to the contagion across markets. In the post-Mexico period, managers of open-end funds sought to minimize the cost of meeting expected obligations to shareholders by selling shares in the more buoyant Asian markets (World Bank 1996b).

those flows, rather than the particular channels flows happen to take. Yet the channel can be crucial to the effectiveness of foreign capital in achieving sustained development, as well as to the consequences should lenders' and borrowers' expectations fail to be met. This is because channels differ in the way lenders and borrowers interact both in shaping productive activity and in sharing risks and rewards. A comparison of alternative channels suggests some strong advantages to issuers associated with the equity-based flows over borrowing.

Bank lending. Bank lending entails a contract between lender and borrower that stipulates interest to be paid and a schedule for repayment of principal. Short of default, all risk associated with the activity financed is borne by the borrower, and all resulting economic profit accrues entirely to the borrower.[7] In particular, required payments are not linked to the borrower's ability to pay or to the relative success of the venture.[8]

A bank in one country assessing the creditworthiness of a particular borrower in another faces the complication that a country's *aggregate* fixed commitments entailed by foreign bank loans must meet the test of year-to-year macroeconomic feasibility: total net payments to foreign lenders must be matched by an equal trade surplus, or equivalently, an equal surplus of domestic saving over domestic investment. Thus, even solvent private borrowers may be unable to meet their contractual commitments to make hard-currency payments; default may depend as much, or more, on the country's overall economic fortunes as on those of the borrowing firm. Moreover, because the burden in terms of local currency of contractual hard-currency payments depends on the exchange rate at the time of payment, the solvency of otherwise healthy borrowers may be threatened if the economy as a whole experiences unexpectedly large outflows of portfolio capital, and currency devaluation results.[9]

Because all the risks associated with projects financed by bank lending in the 1970s were contractually assigned to borrowers, the rise in world interest rates, the fall in most commodity prices from their mid-1970s' peaks, and the rise in the international value of the U.S. dollar in the 1980s to-

7. The role of banks in shaping activities that borrowers undertake, as well as banks' participation in management of enterprises thus financed varies markedly across countries. Whereas German and Japanese regulation and custom favor an active role for banks in managing the businesses operated by their borrowers, lending by American and British banks entails little or no influence over borrowers' business operations once loans are made.

8. In reality the sharing of risk is less stark because default is usually counterproductive for both parties. Large borrowers can therefore anticipate some degree of forbearance from lenders when default appears likely in its absence.

9. Intermediation by emerging-market banks and finance companies between offshore depositors and local borrowers has similar features, with the additional possibility of disruptive bank runs if depositors begin to suspect that borrowers will be unable to repay their loans.

gether placed severe adjustment burdens on indebted countries. Because most of the heavily indebted countries attempted to adjust at least partly through fiscal and monetary restraint, throughout the 1980s these countries invested much less and grew much more slowly (if at all) than those with little debt or the rare ability to adjust quickly. The resulting shortfall of output generated a major global loss; the extreme policies adopted by debtor nations in order to make required payments may in the end have left even the lenders with less than they would have earned under a more diversified assignment of risks. Similar concerns were raised in late 1997 as the International Monetary Fund (IMF) began to negotiate the terms of rescue packages with Southeast Asian countries.

Bond sales. Bond sales are similar to bank loans in that the borrower's commitments are locked in at the time of issue, and these terms are altered only in the case of default. An important difference, however, is that a bond issue, in effect, slices the borrower's total financing requirements into smaller, individually tradable pieces. This facilitates risk diversification by lenders and thus reduces the cost of capital to the borrower.[10] The fragmentation of bond ownership (relative to bank loans) may also make it easier for the debtor to default in extreme cases of bad luck and move on with growth-oriented economic policies. Of course, the feasibility of low-cost risk spreading does not ensure that diversification is achieved in practice. In 1994, the positions of U.S. institutional investors in Mexican bonds (and equity) were large enough to turn Mexico's devaluation and threatened default on its dollar-denominated government debt into a political issue in the United States as well as in Mexico.[11]

Another potentially significant difference between bonds and bank loans is that in an active bond market new information concerning the risk of default is assessed continuously and reflected in movements in bond prices. A rise in perceived risk will require a fall in bond prices, that is, a further yield premium over that earned by "safe" alternative assets. Whereas trades at a premium or discount do not alter the borrower's commitments to holders, they do change the yield available to actual or potential holders via variation in the market price and provide information useful in pricing new issues. Trading in developing-country debt similarly generates ongoing arm's-length assessments of creditworthiness. However, the secondary market in bank debt materialized only after the

10. Loan syndications achieve a qualitatively similar effect, but the feasible minimum size of participation is larger due to higher marginal transaction costs.

11. Opinion remains divided as to whether aid to Mexico (extended by the Clinton administration and the International Monetary Fund) constituted a bailout of U.S. investors, thus raising an obvious moral hazard issue, or merely prudent lender-of-last-resort action required to sustain the domestic political viability of Mexico's economic reforms, as suggested by Eichengreen and Fishlow (1996).

shakiness of the loans was well established and new bank lending out of the question.

Like bank loans, bonds still leave risk (short of default) with the borrowing economy. Thus, to the extent that a country's efforts to maintain debt service under adverse economic conditions lead to macroeconomic contraction, bond finance contributes to the amplification of bad luck in the same way as bank borrowing. Also, as with bank borrowing, firms' collective ability to meet their hard-currency contractual obligations to bond holders is subject to an overall macroeconomic constraint.

Equity sales. Equity sales differ from loans and bond sales in that the issuer makes no explicit commitment regarding principal or interest—no debt is incurred.[12] The buyer shares in the fortunes of the enterprise through dividends and/or movements in share prices, and investor returns in the first instance come in the form of local currency. Risk to holders depends on the prospects of the enterprise, but also on the terms on which future returns can be repatriated. Foreign investors will of course commit money to a market only when there is a reasonable expectation of taking out more (in their own currency) at a later date. However, the absence of a contractual schedule allows issuing firms a degree of flexibility with regard to timing and amount of dividend payments. Foreign equity investors likewise enjoy a degree of flexibility with regard to timing and amount of share sales and of repatriation of local-currency proceeds.

As with bonds, the creation of small, homogeneous tradable units lowers the marginal cost of diversification by lenders and thus reduces borrowers' cost of capital. And, as with bonds, the existence of an organized market on which units are traded imposes a discipline on issuing firms because the cost of *new* capital will rise (via a fall in share prices) whenever investors become dissatisfied with current performance. Active trading in securities also provides daily public reinforcement of the government's commitment to outward-oriented policies. While movements in the relative prices of securities issued by different firms in the same country reflect firm- or industry-specific considerations, across-the-board trends can be seen as summarizing investor sentiment regarding a nation's overall economic prospects.

Had members of the Organization of Petroleum Exporting Countries (OPEC) in the 1970s announced an intention to recycle their petrodollar surpluses via equity markets rather than banks, it is possible that developing countries would have shifted much sooner toward market-guided, outward-oriented strategies for growth. Moreover, successful equity investments would have left lenders with a proportionate share in the rewards of

---

12. Foreign-owned equity is nonetheless often included in statistical measures of a country's foreign indebtedness.

that success; failed investments would have produced disappointed lenders and shrunken asset values, but not precipitated a debt crisis.

Foreign direct investment. Even after the investor rush into emerging markets in the 1990s, arm's-length equity trading on organized markets still plays a relatively modest role in marshalling private equity capital from abroad; for most East Asian countries, foreign direct investment continues to dominate private equity financing. For host countries, direct investment carries many of the benefits associated with portfolio equity investments, plus additional benefits unique to this channel. But it depends on a more complex set of enabling conditions and is inherently more limited in scope.

Unlike equity and bond portfolio investment, where flows depend to a significant extent on conditions in global financial markets, direct investments are not mediated by well-developed financial markets and are only modestly affected by prevailing asset-market conditions. Sector-specific investment opportunities, together with a country's overall prospects for economic reform, are the most important determinants. Because foreign direct investment is constrained by sector-specific factors, inflows may not be well correlated with a country's ability to put additional foreign capital to productive use. When investment opportunities are mainly in industries in which foreign firms possess no special competitive advantage, direct investment is unlikely to generate a return high enough to offset the investors' extra costs of operating in a foreign economy.

Policy Determinants of a Strong Equity Market

Whereas portfolio equity flows potentially offer benefits to both investors and issuers, the growth of an active stock market that can support such transactions requires appropriate policies. There must be laws and institutions in place to facilitate the ownership, valuation, and transfer of equities. In addition, governments must foster the development of the equity market through policies that encourage long-term planning, investment, and international linkages. As table 6.5 shows, countries differ significantly in the size of their stock markets, and these differences cannot be attributed entirely to levels of development.

Conducive Economic Environment

An important requirement for a strong equity market is macroeconomic stability. Accelerating inflation, large current-account deficits, and volatile exchange rates are anathema to equity investors. Macroeconomic instability adversely affects equity markets because it diverts attention from long-run investments to short-term arbitrage, and because it carries within it

Table 6.5 Characteristics of developed and emerging markets, 1996

	Number of companies	Market value US$ (billions)	Market value/GDP
Developed markets	20141	17952	1.00
Emerging markets	22263	2226	0.46
East Asia	4010	1705	1.03
China	540	114	0.25
Hong Kong[a]	561	449	6.31
Indonesia	253	91	0.60
Korea	760	139	0.40
Malaysia	621	307	4.52
Philippines	216	81	1.42
Singapore[a]	223	150	2.59
Taiwan	382	274	0.87
Thailand	454	100	0.76

Source: IFC 1997.
[a] Hong Kong and Singapore are here grouped with East Asia; in IFC sources they are grouped with developed markets.

the seeds of future, painful deflationary efforts. The Brazilian stock market, for example, lost roughly two-thirds of its value in dollar terms when Brazil's inflation accelerated between 1986 and 1990.

A second important requirement is openness to international markets. Openness helps to reassure investors that the profits gained from investments can be freely negotiated and repatriated. In addition, outward-looking policies directly enable the economy to generate the foreign exchange necessary for international transactions—including the repatriation of profits—without large changes in the exchange rate. These conditions are most likely to be met if the value of an economy's trade is large relative to its current and potential capital transactions.

The third crucial requirement is predictability, that is, confidence that current favorable economic policies will continue into the future. Such commitments are most credible when an economy has a high stake in maintaining stability, for example, because its current economic status depends on continuing relationships with foreign investors and trade partners. Hong Kong is a case in point: because the external linkages of this economy are so important to its success, investors can take some comfort in the presumption that Chinese administrators will be reluctant to dismantle Hong Kong's free markets, even though elsewhere they interfere extensively in economic management.

Empirical Tests of Environmental Hypotheses

The hypothesis that these aspects of economic policy affect equity investment can be tested by statistically relating market capitalization to alterna-

Table 6.6 Variable definitions and sources

Variable	Definition	Source
Trade	merchandise export plus imports	Worldtables
FDI	balance of payments measure of gross FDI inflows	Balance of Payments Yearbook
Stock	stock market capitalization	IFC Emerging Markets Handbook
Population	millions	Worldtables
Income	US$	Worldtables
Enrollment	primary school enrollment	Worldtables
Fuel Export	ratio of fuel exports to total exports	Worldtables
Tariff	unweighted average of tariff rates	Worldtables
NTB Frequency	percentage of commodity lines covered by NTBs	WDR 1991
FX Premium	1981–90 average black market premium on foreign exchange	WDR 1991
Inflation	1981–90 average inflation in consumer price index	Worldtables
Creditworthiness	Survey index of credit worthiness	Institutional Investor

Worldtables refers to the 1993 diskette version of the World Bank's Worldtables database. WDR 1991 refers to the special database constructed by the World Development Report 1991 team.
Notes: Unless otherwise indicated, data are averaged for 1988–1990.

tive indicators of the environment. The sample used to evaluate these hypotheses consists of 27 low- and middle-income developing countries. The results of a number of regression models are shown in table 6.7. (Definitions of the variables are given in table 6.6.) Each column represents a separate relationship, although in all cases the dependent variable is the market capitalization:GDP ratio in 1990.

The first regression model relates the size of a country's equity market to its population and per capita income. Following Chenery and Syrquin (1975), four variables are used to capture this relationship: log of population, log of income, and the squares of these two variables. A substantial part of the variation in stock-market capitalization can be explained with these determinants alone. The log of income and its square carry the bulk of the explanatory power.

The second model adds endowment and policy factors to the relationship. Endowment factors are included because the industrial structure of an economy may determine, to some extent, its capital structure. For example, an economy consisting of advanced, relatively large manufacturing enterprises is more likely to have highly developed capital markets than a rural economy based on small-scale farms. The variables measuring en-

Table 6.7 Determinants of stock capitalization: GDP ratio, 1990

	1	2	3	4	5
Constant	0.316	0.121	0.417	−0.114	−0.490
	(0.93)	(0.28)	(1.45)	(−0.32)	(−1.35)
Log (pop)	−0.068	0.076	0.026	−0.013	0.119
	(−0.41)	(0.43)	(0.19)	(−0.10)	(0.89)
Log (pop)^2	0.003	−0.014	−0.005	−0.013	−0.020
	(0.17)	(−0.65)	(−0.31)	(−0.82)	(−1.34)
Log (y)	0.132	0.114	0.199	−0.007	−0.001
	(1.90)	(1.25)	(3.20)	(−0.07)	(−0.01)
Log (y)^2	0.107	0.084	0.066	0.053	−0.020
	(2.38)	(1.84)	(1.64)	(1.44)	(−0.42)
Enrollment		0.003			
		(1.33)			
Fuel export		0.540			
		(0.66)			
Tariff		0.001			
		(0.35)			
NTB frequency		−0.002			
		(−0.94)			
FX premium		−0.002			
		(−0.94)			
Log (inflation)		−0.081	−0.096	0.010	0.020
		(−1.74)	(−3.14)	(0.20)	(0.41)
Credit rating				0.015	0.01
				(2.35)	(1.70)
Trade/GDP					0.370
					(2.14)
Adj. R2	0.52	0.62	0.66	0.72	0.66
F	7.96	5.20	10.90	11.95	9.28
SSE	1.59	0.92	1.09	0.85	1.03

Note: Values of *t*-statistics in parentheses; 5% significance level is 2.1, 10% level is 1.7.

dowments include enrollment in primary education as a proxy for human capital, and the ratio of fuel exports to GDP as a proxy for natural resources. No explicit physical capital index is included because the per capita income variable presumably captures much of this variation. The policy factors used include two measures of trade barriers (tariffs and the frequency of nontariff barriers), a measure of distortions in currency markets (the average black market premium for foreign exchange), and the average inflation rate as a proxy for macroeconomic stability.

The large number of possible explanatory variables included in this relationship introduces considerable noise, and so the results of model 2 are not very strong. Only the inflation rate is near statistical significance.

Model 3, therefore, simplifies the relationship by including only the four "Chenery factors" and the inflation rate.

The fourth model further expands this relationship by adding a survey-based index of perceived creditworthiness as published by *Institutional Investor* magazine. Higher values of this index (which ranges from 0 to 100) denote greater creditworthiness. The results show that the creditworthiness index has considerable explanatory power and, once introduced, renders even the inflation variable insignificant. In other words, creditworthiness captures whatever information is contained in the inflation rate, and more. A problem with this specification, however, is that respondents to the *Institutional Investor* survey used to produce the index may have taken the vibrancy of a country's stock market into account in judging creditworthiness. This would introduce simultaneity bias into the analysis.

Finally, the fifth model introduces trade linkages as a separate explanatory variable. The theoretical rationale for this variable lies in the "commitment" and "openness" hypotheses advanced above; an open economy is more likely to allow future repatriation of capital and to retain a favorable policy regime. The trade variable proves to be the strongest explanatory factor for stock market capitalization—stronger even than the creditworthiness variable. Moreover, it is difficult to imagine that simultanteity could significantly cloud this relationship.

Implications of the Empirical Analysis

A considerable portion of the international variance in stock market capitalization appears to be due to differences in per capita income and in various indicators of the policy environment. Comparisons of alternative models show that a survey measure of creditworthiness is a better predictor of stock market capitalization than inflation as an index of macroeconomic stability, and that trade exposure is an even stronger explanatory factor than creditworthiness.

These relationships are summarized usefully in table 6.8, which presents pairwise correlations for various measures of openness and policy. The table shows strong positive correlations among various aspects of an open economy: trade, foreign direct investment, and market capitalization. It also shows generally positive correlations among distortions: tariffs, frequency of nontariff barriers, black market premiums, and inflation. Finally, it shows negative relationships between openness and distortions. Economic growth is also correlated positively with openness and negatively with distortions.

East Asia's experience fits neatly within this explanatory framework. East Asian economies have consistently pursued less distorting economic policies than other low- and middle-income countries, and most have

Table 6.8 Correlation of external linkages and protection

	trade/GDP	FDI/GDP	Equity/GDP	Tariff	NTBs	Black market premium	Inflation
Trade/GDP	1	0.82	0.85	−0.52	−0.35	−0.27	−0.45
FDI/GDP		1	0.60	−0.39	−0.27	−0.18	−0.33
Equity/GDP			1	−0.51	−0.40	−0.36	−0.42
Tariffs/GDP				1	0.52	0.19	0.24
NTB Frequency					1	−0.11	0.17
Black market premium						1	0.32
Inflation							1
Growth	0.49	0.38	0.52	−0.20	−0.09	−0.48	−0.61

Note: 10% significance level is 0.26, 5% is 0.32, and 1% is 0.45. Sample was 27 developing market economies.

adopted export-oriented growth strategies. Some of the region's most open economies have also been the most successful in developing active equity markets and attracting foreign portfolio investment. The large stock-market capitalizations of Hong Kong, Singapore, and Malaysia exemplify these relationships; each economy is unusually open and has been unusually effective in attracting foreign portfolio equity.

Portfolio Inflows and Macroeconomic Management

Although many elements of the policy environment discussed above are desirable quite apart from their role in attracting and retaining foreign portfolio investment, a high degree of integration into international capital markets also places significant constraints on a country's options for domestic macroeconomic management while opening domestic markets to additional external shocks. For East Asia, the importance of this aspect of internationalization has been underscored by the events of 1997.

The goal of attracting and retaining internationally mobile funds may prevent a government from using policies that might otherwise be considered desirable.[13] For example, a monetary stimulus that reduces domestic interest rates is likely to cause a reduction or reversal of inflows, especially flows generated by those seeking high current yield. Likewise, a change in external market conditions may trigger outflows of highly mobile capital unless domestic monetary authorities are willing to raise domestic interest rates. In October 1997, as the turmoil in Southeast Asia spread to Hong

13. The basic mechanisms are highlighted in the classic Mundell-Fleming analysis of the relative effectiveness of alternative macroeconomic policies under fixed and flexible exchange rates. The analysis is particularly applicable to flows motivated by short-term yield rather than diversification concerns.

Kong's markets, officials raised interest rates in an effort to offset pressure on the exchange rate. Of course, similar policy constraints are implied by the possibility of domestic capital flight. Indeed, the case of Mexico illustrates the potential for shifts in domestic policy to trigger both domestic capital flight and repatriation of domestic savings from abroad.

As the events of 1994 and 1997 illustrate, the presence of highly mobile portfolio investment makes it harder for monetary authorities to defend a pegged exchange rate once investors begin to believe the rate is likely to change in the near future. For somewhat different reasons, Mexico in 1994 and a number of Asian and Latin American developing countries in 1997 had developed perceptibly overvalued exchange rates. In several of these countries, efforts to defend overvalued exchange rates with high short-term interest rates, combined with extensive foreign currency borrowing throughout the economy, led to banking-system crises. These examples are structurally similar to scenarios in countries otherwise as diverse as Israel, Norway, and Thailand (Kaminsky and Reinhart 1996).

In addition to problems that arise when portfolio flows are highly sensitive to short-run market conditions, net capital flows that are large relative to other balance-of-payments items put pressure on the exchange rate in a floating-rate regime and on the domestic monetary base in a fixed-rate regime. Large capital inflows, even when expected to persist over a long period, thus complicate the task of maintaining a macroeconomic environment and real exchange rate conducive to growth. Capital-importing countries must choose between allowing the nominal exchange rate to appreciate or engaging in foreign exchange intervention. In practice the issue is the extent to which nominal exchange rate adjustment is permitted; there are few if any instances in which accommodation has been made entirely through movements of a freely floating exchange rate. When intervention is used, a further choice is whether to sterilize the effects on the monetary base. A country's other circumstances determine the best choices, for example, whether the real exchange rate is initially undervalued or overvalued relative to purchasing power parity, whether economic growth and success in reducing domestic inflation has increased the demand for money, and whether increased spending brought about by the inflows is concentrated on investment or consumption.

Several developing countries that have attracted large portfolio capital inflows have experienced substantial exchange rate appreciations. Real appreciation of the exchange rate can sabotage fledgling industries by undermining their international competitiveness, as illustrated by the predevaluation problems of Mexico and Argentina. In both cases, the exchange rate was pegged as part of a "nominal anchor" stabilization strategy. The real appreciation reflected domestic inflation, which was fed by the increased demand from capital inflows. Typically such economies eventually face severe pressures to depreciate or contract, and most have experienced sharp reversals of capital inflows.

A number of other countries, including most Asian capital importers except for the Philippines, have avoided real appreciation via domestic inflation through a variety of means, including fiscal and monetary restraint, trade liberalization, and enhanced saving incentives. Interestingly, an IMF study showed no correlation between private capital inflows and real appreciation for a sample of sixteen major private capital recipients in Latin America, central Europe, and Asia (Dadush and Brahmbhatt 1995). The data are consistent with the hypothesis that real appreciation brought about by capital inflows is associated primarily with domestic inflation rather than nominal appreciation. In economies that have avoided real appreciation, new demand generated by the capital inflows has been offset through reductions in other domestic spending, thus helping to control inflationary pressures.

In addition to insulating the domestic economy from macroeconomic consequences of capital flows, capital-importing countries sometimes act directly to discourage inflows, especially inflows conducive to future volatility. To limit its reliance on highly mobile foreign funds, a country can reduce the potential for funds seeking high short-term yields by restricting some types of capital inflows directly, as have most Asian countries, or by taxing either investment flows or the investment income generated by them. A small tax on inflows (a Tobin tax) has little effect on long-term investments but makes a significant dent in the return available to funds with a very short time horizon. A different approach is to reduce risk-adjusted short-term yields through small but very frequent movements in the nominal exchange rate, as Chile has done. This approach is especially potent for currencies without well-developed facilities for hedging foreign exchange risk.

Looking to the Future

Investors in developed countries have become increasingly cognizant of the potential advantages as well as the risks of diversification into emerging market securities. At the same time that the policy environment for investment has been improving in a number of important emerging markets, policy makers have become painfully aware that private capital flows in both directions and that investors can react very quickly and sometimes even overreact to new information. Together, these trends suggest that growth of portfolio equity flows will continue, but the path is not likely to be smooth. Stock prices in emerging markets tend to be volatile, and they declined sharply in 1994 and again in 1997. New investors recently drawn to Asian markets by the promise of high returns are bound to have been disappointed; the pace of future flows may show a corresponding decline, at least for a while. However, the primary rationale for emerging market investment is not exceptional return, but diversification. Even so, when growth resumes, investors will surely be more alert to the large differences in the regulation of securities transactions in developed and developing countries, thus putting pressure on emerging stock markets to speed their implementation of institutional and legal reforms.

The Risk of Capital Flight

A key policy concern raised about the desirability of equity portfolio flows into developing countries is the fear that a sharp market decline will drive foreign investors away from a particular market—a fear that is well grounded in recent experience. Unlike bank loans or foreign direct investments, portfolio investment can be readily liquidated when expectations change.

The argument is valid, up to a point. Vigorous, open equity markets imply that assets will be competing against others throughout the world, and factors that make the assets of a particular country more or less attractive relative to others will be rapidly reflected in prices. The implications for volatility, however, are unclear. Although a market might be sheltered from international shocks if it is made inaccessible to foreign investors (and domestic investors are not allowed to invest abroad), it will be more exposed to fluctuations in domestic income or productivity. On the other hand, although the sharp reversals experienced by several emerging markets in the recent past appeared to reflect inappropriate policy approaches to handling international capital flows, reversals in other countries were due to abrupt changes in investor sentiment based on market developments elsewhere, in other words, contagion effects.

A central consideration in the case of portfolio equity investment is that even if large asset price changes occur, they do not affect the productivity of the physical capital created by the investment and may not even be accompanied by net outflows of portfolio capital. This is because price rather than quantity adjustments play the key role in restoring equilibrium in asset markets. As the value of foreign positions declines, foreigners investors will become more willing to hold their existing shares, in anticipation of future price increases. In the unlikely event that foreign investors do sell in panic, the result could be favorable to the domestic economy. Massive foreign sales would depress the value of shares and the country's currency and thus transfer ownership to domestic investors on attractive terms. But for the same reasons, an investor flight is bound to exacerbate the problems of maintaining a fixed exchange rate.

To be sure, a broad decline in the foreign currency value of a country's equity shares is likely to diminish the flow of additional portfolio investment, at least for a time. This is a consequence, however, not of capital flight itself, but of the decline in perceived investment prospects indicated by the fall in share prices. The same reduction in new flows would likely have occurred with any other channel of capital inflow.

A more subtle advantage to the host country of foreign equity investment is that under adverse conditions the foreigner investors will have a stake in reestablishing the productivity of the country and its enterprises, rather than simply ensuring that they receive all contractual payments. Thus, the interests of foreign investors, as expressed through influence in either the domestic or the international policy process, are more likely to coincide with the country's own general economic interests. Whatever the objective merits of the bailouts in 1994 and 1997, it is evident that private foreign investors pushed hard for measures that would maintain growth in the affected economies.

Incomplete Integration and Excess Returns

Although the consequences of a meltdown in equity prices can be contained, there is a strong theoretical rationale for expecting future average rates of return in emerging markets to diminish. If emerging markets were fully integrated with those of the advanced nations, prices of bonds and equities would simply reflect expected returns and their variance. But emerging markets are not fully integrated into world capital markets, and this helps to explain why their returns have appeared to be unexpectedly high in the past.

One reason why historical returns were high was the cost of market information. It is difficult and expensive to judge the prospects of new enterprises in new markets. Investors will therefore wish to add securities from the new markets to their portfolios only to the extent that anticipated returns exceed those available elsewhere by enough to offset the cost of information. This information premium may be substantial in economies where reporting requirements are minimal, and issuing firms are often newly privatized and operating within a newly established policy regime.

The information premium may be substantial even for securities that could be called the emerging blue chips: stocks and bonds issued by large, established companies with assured growth as per capita income rises, in sectors such as telephone, electric power, real estate, construction, and banking. Information premiums should fall as financial disclosure norms become similar to those of the advanced countries and as new firms and policy regimes establish longer track records. The profitability of monopolized blue chip sectors may also fall if new policy regimes are market oriented to the extent of encouraging entry by new competitors.

A second reason for high historical returns involves restrictions on market access. Whereas more and more emerging markets now encourage foreign investors, governments have typically restricted access in the past. Like other nontariff barriers, such limits create rents for those who are on the inside. If foreign portfolio purchases are limited to a single closed-end fund, as was the case in some Asian markets, the rents will show up as a premium on fund shares over the value of the assets it holds. This market-access premium may be captured by fund organizers or early purchasers of the fund's shares. As the market is liberalized, the premium will shrink, lowering the return to foreign investors, while domestic investors enjoy excess returns as domestic valuations of companies climb to achieve parity with international valuations.

A third reason for high historical returns is that the opportunities for investment in some attractive markets were small relative to investor interest. As table 6.5 shows, the ratio of market capitalization to GDP has varied markedly among the markets usually grouped together as emerging. Among the more advanced markets such as Korea, the recent increase in portfolio inflows reflects liberalization of access and/or improved policy environment. Among newly emerging markets such as China, the international demand for assets may well exceed the market's current capacity to issue shares; in this case a further availability premium is embedded in the prices of securities available to meet increasing demand.

These premiums, each reflecting a different type of barrier to global portfolio diversification, are either unavailable to foreign investors with no special access to local securities, or will diminish as global market integration proceeds. As a consequence, future (obtainable) risk-adjusted returns are not likely to exceed returns elsewhere. Putting this another way, the returns achieved by early entrants into a particular emerging market are likely to overstate what will be available to later investors in the same market. Market participants who invest in expectation of excess returns are likely to be disappointed and may therefore moderate their emerging market investments.

At the same time, progress toward global market integration is likely to raise the correlation between the U.S. market and emerging stock markets. However, because domestic conditions and exchange rate movements are important determinants of short-run fluctuations in the U.S. dollar yields of securities issued abroad, even a high degree of market integration will not eliminate the benefits of international diversification (table 6.4 shows a correlation of only .33 between total returns in the U.S. and other developed-country stock markets).

Implications for Future Flows

Even before the dust has settled from 1997's market turmoil, some conclusions may be drawn regarding private capital flows in general and portfolio equity in particular. The first is that, whereas a healthy banking and financial system is important to the growth of any developing country, the need is greatest for countries that wish to tap international capital markets. The second is that overall market conditions, not only domestic conditions, influence investor sentiment, with the impact of contagion between markets potentially greatest for countries relying heavily on mobile foreign portfolio capital. Finally, although the benefits and costs of fixed exchange rates have been debated for decades, the disruptive parity changes in 1997 add weight to the evidence favoring exchange rate arrangements with some degree of flexibility.[14]

The 1997 performance of emerging equity markets notwithstanding, the long-term outlook for the growth of emerging-market equity investments remains favorable. These flows represent both an attractive instrument of diversification for developed-country investors and a desirable source of capital for developing-country enterprises. From the viewpoint of capital-importing firms and countries, portfolio equity flows have attractive risk characteristics relative to other types of external finance. Moreover, many countries have adopted precisely the policies that stimulate the development of equity markets—macroeconomic stability and openness—because these are now widely recognized as essential for economic growth. That these policies were already prominent in East Asia is one reason why the region led in attracting portfolio equity capital.

Whether the events of 1997 lead to a sustained slowdown in East Asian development remains to be seen, and the region's future growth rates will surely affect the valuations that private investors place on East Asian equities. The lessons of 1994 and 1997 may also lead to more widespread use of policy measures to dampen the volatility of international capital movements. But the global equity market is here to stay.

References

Chenery, Hollis, and Moises Syrquin. 1975. *Patterns of Development, 1950–70*. London: Oxford University Press.

Chuhan, Punam, Stijn Claessens, and Nlandu Mamingi. 1993. "Equity and Bond Flows to Latin America and Asia: The Role of External and Inter-

14. The alternative is an arrangement like the planned European Monetary Union, where the use of a single money precludes any possibility of a parity change, and thus speculation on the imminent occurrence of such a change.

nal Factors." Policy Research Working Paper No. 1160, World Bank, Washington, D.C.

Cline, William R. 1995. *International Debt Reexamined*. Washington, D.C.: Institute for International Economics.

Dadush, Uri, and Milan Brahmbhatt. 1995. "Anticipating Capital Flows Reversals." *Finance and Development* 32(4):3–5December.

Eichengreen, Barry, and Albert Fishlow. 1996. "Contending with Capital Flows: What is Different about the 1990s?" New York: Council on Foreign Relations.

IFC (International Finance Corporation). 1993. *Emerging Stock Markets Factbook 1993*. Washington, D.C.: International Finance Corporation.

———. 1997. *Emerging Stock Markets Factbook 1997*. Washington, D.C.: International Finance Corporation.

IMF (International Monetary Fund). 1995a. *Balance of Payment Yearbook 1995*. Washington, D.C.: International Monetary Fund.

———. 1995b. *Private Market Financing for Developing Countries*. Revised. Washington, D.C.: International Monetary Fund.

Kaminsky, Graciela L., and Carmen M. Reinhart. 1996. "The Twin Crises: The Courses of Banking and Balance-of-Payments Problems." International Finance Discussion Paper No. 544, Board of Governors of the Federal Reserve System, Washington, D.C.

"Resilence of Developing Country Markets Masks Changes in Capital Flows." 1996. *IMF Survey*, February 19, p. 57.

World Bank. 1995. *World Development Report, 1995*. Washington, D.C.: World Bank.

———. 1996a. *Financial Flows and the Developing Countries*. New York: Oxford University Press.

———. 1996b. *World Debt Tables 1996*. Washington, D.C.: World Bank.

———. 1997a. *Global Development Finance 1997*. Washington, D.C.: World Bank.

———. 1997b. *World Development Report, 1997*. New York: Oxford University Press.

7

Central and Eastern Europe: Financial Markets and Private Capital Flows

Dorothy Meadow Sobol

The resurgence of private capital flows to developing countries beginning in the late 1980s did not initially benefit the countries of central and eastern Europe. With the collapse of communist governments throughout the region beginning in 1989, most countries in the region were absorbed in a political and economic upheaval unimaginable only years earlier, as they sought to undo decades of central planning and transform their economies into ones based more on market principles. In this environment, it is understandable that private foreign capital was slow to enter any of these countries. Not until the efforts of these countries to free up their economies and introduce macroeconomic and structural reforms began to bear fruit did private foreign investors begin to take significant note of this region in their investment decisions.

Today, although the amount of private capital entering central and eastern Europe is still a very small fraction of that provided to all developing countries, it has nonetheless begun to flow (figure 7.1, table 7.1). Whereas the countries in central and eastern Europe as a group were running capital account deficits in the early 1990s, this situation turned around beginning in 1992, as reform programs in a number of countries started to take hold (figure 7.2).[1]

There are a few caveats, however. For one, the bulk of the private capital flowing into central and eastern Europe in recent years has been concen-

The author thanks Kate Kisselev for superb research assistance, and Warren Moskowitz and Adam Posen for helpful comments. The views expressed are the author's and do not necessarily reflect those of the Federal Reserve Bank of New York or the Federal Reserve System.

1. For the three countries in this study—Hungary, Poland, and the Czech Republic—the combined capital account swung from near balance in 1992 to surpluses of $10.9 billion in 1993, $10.4 billion in 1994, and $17.6 billion in 1995, before falling off to $7.5 billion in 1996. Poland's surplus beginning in 1992 stemmed from the exceptional financing it received from its official creditors in the Paris Club.

Figure 7.1 Direction and composition of private capital inflows. See table 7.1 for the data on the Czech Republic, Hungary, and Poland.

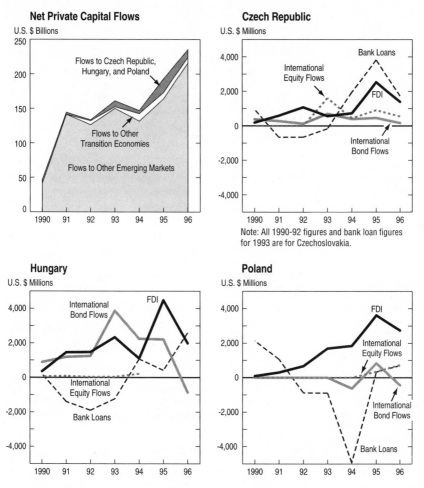

Sources: IMF *Balance of Payments Statistics Yearbook;* IMF *International Financial Statistics;* IMF *International Capital Markets;* IMF *Private Market Financing for Develping Countries;* BIS *The Maturity, Sectoral, and Nationality Distribution of International Bank Lending;* National Bank of Hungary *Monthly Report;* National Bank of Poland *Information Bulletin.*

trated in relatively few countries. Of these, the most important are Hungary, Poland, and the Czech Republic.[2] These countries therefore form the focus of this chapter.

2. By some accounts, these three countries accounted for 90 percent of net capital inflows into eastern Europe in 1995 (UNECE 1995).

Table 7.1 Composition of private capital inflows (millions of US$)

	1990	1991	1992	1993	1994	1995	1996
Bank loans							
Czech Republic[a]	955	−656	−652	−163	1953	3832	1727
Hungary	200	−1395	−1899	−1234	1068	411	2597
Poland	2138	1061	−882	−891	−4929	324	698
Total	3293	−990	−3433	−2288	−1908	4567	5022
Net foreign direct investment							
Czech Republic[a]	187	586	1073	564	732	2531	1394
Hungary	354	1462	1479	2339	1095	4476	1986
Poland	89	298	665	1697	1846	3617	2741
Total	630	2346	3217	4600	3673	10624	6121
International portfolio investment							
Czech Republic[a]	375	277	129	3205	846	137˙	721
Hungary	956	1277	1275	3919	2464	2212	−869
Poland	0	0	0	1	−624	1177	301
Total	1331	1554	1404	6225	2686	4760	153
of which, International equity investment							
Czech Republic[a]	0	0	0	1608	450	911	551
Hungary[b]	68	91	33	46	214		
Poland	0	0	0	1	0	346	732
Total	68	91	33	1655	664	1257	1283
of which, International bond investment							
Czech Republic[a]	375	277	129	697	396	460	170
Hungary	888	1186	1242	3873	2250	2212	−869
Poland	0	0	0	0	−624	831	−431
Total	1263	1463	1371	4570	2022	3503	−1130
Grand total	5254	2910	1188	8537	4451	19951	11296

Sources: IMF, *Balance of Payments Statistics Yearbook,* IMF, *International Financial Statistics* (*IFS*), IMF, *International Capital Markets,* IMF, *Private Market Financing for Developing Countries;* BIS, *The Maturity, Sectoral and Nationality Distribution of International Bank Lending;* National Bank of Hungary, *Monthly Report;* National Bank of Poland, *Information Bulletin.*
[a] Data are for Czechoslovakia from 1990–1992. Bank loans in 1993 are also for Czechoslovakia.
[b] Comparable data for 1995 and 1996 are unavailable because the National Bank of Hungary has revised its balance of payments methodology.

Second, the evidence is as yet only preliminary and the data far from comprehensive. Nonetheless, the findings to date suggest that these three countries, as well as many others in the region, should benefit from private capital inflows for many years. Whether they will be able to do so, however, will be a function of both their ability and their willingness to adhere to market-oriented reforms and carry out often politically difficult restructuring measures. For those able to hold to such a course—and lucky enough to avoid or overcome the political backlashes likely to accompany the im-

Figure 7.2 Capital account reversal in the 1990s.

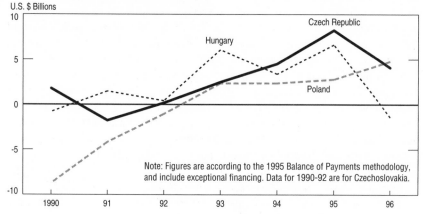

Capital and Financial Account Balances

Note: Figures are according to the 1995 Balance of Payments methodology, and include exceptional financing. Data for 1990-92 are for Czechoslovakia.

Sources: IMF *Balance of Payments Statistics Yearbook;* IMF *International Financial Statistics.*

plementation of their policies—foreign private capital should be forthcoming. Nevertheless, the competition for capital is fierce. And, in this era of globalized markets, when investment decisions are often made within minutes, markets will not be slow to respond to those who are perceived to lag, falter, or fail in their reform and restructuring efforts.

By focusing on the three major recipients of private capital flows to central and eastern Europe thus far, I seek to identify the nature and composition of private capital flowing into the region in recent years, and some of the factors driving these flows. In addition, I explore some of the problems these inflows have raised, how policy makers are responding, and what the prospects are for continuing inflows over the coming years. One conclusion seems clear. Although some market participants may continue to view the region as a single entity, many increasingly appear to be distinguishing among the countries when making their investment decisions.

Composition of Private Capital Flows

In broad terms, private capital flows consist of three basic elements: lending by commercial banks, foreign direct investment (typically defined as an equity investment of 10 percent or more in a foreign firm), and portfolio investment through bonds and equities. Portfolio investment through bonds takes place when foreigners invest in the money and capital markets of another country and when public or private entities, including governments, raise funds in a foreign market or the international markets. Equity flows are generated when foreigners buy shares in firms that are listed on another country's stock exchange and when private or publicly owned firms in one country issue shares in the markets of another country or in the international markets through the use of depositary receipts.

On a net basis, the flow of private capital from these three sources to Hungary, Poland, and the Czech Republic rose from an estimated $5.3 billion in 1990 to over $8 billion in 1993 before dropping off to about $4 billion in 1994 with the collapse in international bond markets and Poland's agreement with its commercial bank creditors that entailed write-offs of a portion of its bank debt.[3] Inflows in 1995 surged to almost $20 billion before falling back to an estimated $11 billion in 1996. As elsewhere in the developing world, bank flows ceased to dominate private sector financing to the countries of central and eastern Europe in the 1990s. Between 1990 and 1994, Hungary and the Czech Republic, combined, amortized more bank debt than they took on. In Poland's case, debt was forgiven. Offsetting the declines in bank lending have been notable increases for all three countries in foreign direct investment and, for Hungary in particular, portfolio inflows.

Also noteworthy is the extent to which the changes taking place in the composition of private capital flows to these three countries during the 1990s shifted from those considered to be debt-creating (such as bank lending and portfolio investment through bonds requiring repayment) to those considered to be of longer duration and to entail no direct repayment obligation (such as foreign direct investment and portfolio investment through equities). Between 1990 and 1996 the share of bank and bond finance provided to the three countries as a share of their total private sector inflows fell from 87 percent to 34 percent. No country was more affected by these shifts than Poland, which on a net basis saw its debt-creating flows as a share of total private inflows fall from 96 percent in 1990 to about 23 percent in 1995, and 7 percent in 1996, following its 1994 commercial bank debt-reduction agreement and marked increases in foreign direct investment.

These broad patterns, of course, mask important differences among the three countries. The following sections cover some of these similarities and differences.

---

3. As part of its agreement with its commercial bank creditors, Poland was granted a 50 percent reduction in the net present value of its bank debt. Although not counted here as such, the debt forgiveness this agreement entailed ought properly to be thought of as a capital inflow.

Figure 7.3 Bank lending in the 1980s and 1990s.

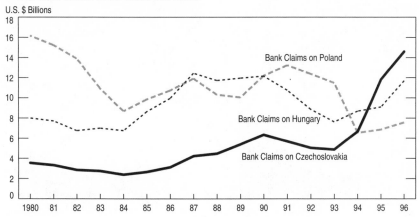

BIS Bank Claims in the 1980s and 1990s

Source: BIS *The Maturity, Sectoral, and National Distribution of International Bank Lending.*

Commercial Bank Lending

Throughout the 1980s and into 1990, commercial banks continued to lend to many countries in central and eastern Europe, including Poland, Hungary, and the Czech Republic (figure 7.3). Beginning in the early 1990s, however, bank lending to these countries began to slow markedly as economic and financial conditions deteriorated following the collapse of communist regimes in 1989 and 1990, and amortizations in both Hungary and the Czech Republic began to offset new inflows on a net basis. The falloff in bank lending was, to be sure, most notable in the case of Poland, where new lending net of amortizations fell from an inflow of $2.1 billion in 1990 to an outflow of $900 million in 1993, prior to the country's implementation of its commercial bank or so-called Brady agreement in October 1994.

Beginning in 1994, however, bank lending to both Hungary and the Czech Republic began to revive, and these inflows continued in 1995 and 1996, as did flows to Poland. In the Czech Republic, net increases in bank flows that started in 1994 have been very pronounced. During 1995 and 1996, net claims by BIS-reporting banks on Czech borrowers rose by $5.6 billion. The bulk of these credits have been short term in nature (figure 7.4). The attraction of these credits to Czech borrowers has been their lower interest rates and longer maturities than those available from domestic banks.

Figure 7.4 Maturity of BIS bank claims.

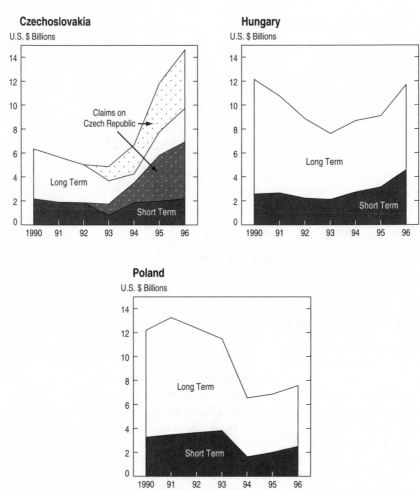

Source: BIS *The Maturity, Sectoral, and National Distribution of International Bank Lending.*

Among economists, there is some disagreement about the nature of this increased foreign borrowing by Czech institutions. On the one hand, the increased borrowing may reflect a substitution of foreign for domestic credit, motivated by inefficiencies in the domestic financial system—in particular, wide margins between domestic deposit and lending rates. On the other hand, the increased borrowing may simply reflect a genuine shortage of credit in the economy, despite the fact that interest rate spreads, particularly with respect to the deutsche mark, though still wide,

Figure 7.5 Dollar and deutsche mark returns on local investments.

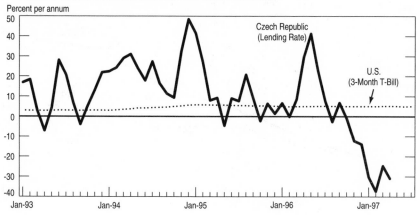

Annualized Ex Post Dollar Returns on Local Investments

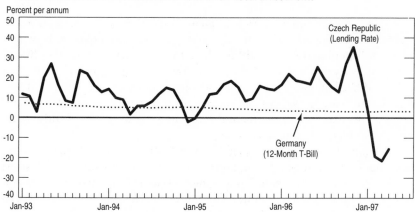

Annualized Ex Post Deutsche Mark Returns on Local Investments

Sources: IMF *International Financial Statistics;* Bloomberg L. P..

have generally been declining (figure 7.5). To one group of International Monetary Fund (IMF) economists, the credit shortage hypothesis is more consistent with the evidence: economic activity has strengthened over the past several years, increasing the real demand for money (Calvo, Sahay, and Vegh 1995, 19–20).

To counter some of the effects of these bank inflows, including the upward pressure they put on the real exchange rate (figure 7.6), as well as to deter those inflows that were more speculative in nature, the Czech mone-

Figure 7.6 Real effective exchange rates.

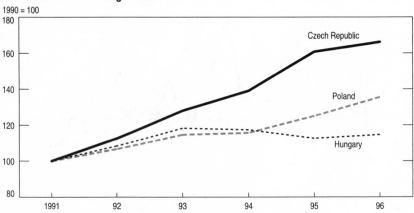

Real Effective Exchange Rates

Sources: IMF *International Financial Statistics;* PlanEcon.

tary authorities adopted a variety of measures. Chief among these, the central bank introduced a more flexible foreign exchange policy in February 1996, by widening the band within which the koruna was allowed to fluctuate from +0.5 percent to +7.5 percent. By bringing a greater measure of risk to the exchange rate, the authorities sought to reduce speculative inflows and ease growth of the money supply ("Prague Eases Exchange" 1996). This decision followed a series of earlier measures the central bank had put in place for similar reasons.

For example, in April 1995 the central bank announced that it would no longer buy and sell foreign exchange at uniform rates but instead would charge a fee based on a percentage of the intermediaries' exchange rate. Further, in August it limited commercial banks' borrowing abroad to no more than 30 percent of their short-term assets, or Kc 500 million ($19 million). At the same time, it unified reserve requirements for sight and time deposits at 8.5 percent (from 12 percent and 3 percent, respectively), raised the discount and Lombard rates, and announced that short-term borrowing by commercial banks would be slowed through administrative procedures (Girocredit 1995, 41). In October 1995, the government made the koruna fully convertible for current account transactions and partially liberalized capital account transactions by allowing Czech residents for the first time to purchase real estate and make direct investments abroad.

Ultimately, however, none of these measures proved sufficient. Faced with a mounting trade deficit, which rose to a record 7 percent of gross domestic product (GDP) in 1996, and a speculative attack on the koruna, the Czech monetary authorities were obliged to allow their currency to float in late May 1997. To dampen the inflationary effects of the devaluation, the authorities raised the discount rate to 13 percent from 10.5 percent and announced cabinet changes to shore up confidence in the koruna and the government. At the same time, the authorities cut the koruna's link to the dollar and deutsche mark, opting to peg their currency to the deutsche mark alone, but they would not disclose how widely they planned to allow the koruna to fluctuate ("Czechs Abandon Currency Link" 1997).

A welcome development for Poland in 1994 was to regain access to the syndicated lending market after years of protracted arrears and debt-servicing difficulties. Following the country's Brady-type debt reduction agreement with banks in October 1994, which among other things, reduced the net present value of its bank debt by 50 percent, a state utility company received five-year term financing of $113 million from a syndicate of European banks (IBRD 1994–1995, 11–12).

Like the Czech Republic, Poland also faced mounting inflows of foreign exchange over the past several years. Market participants believe that the bulk of these foreign exchange inflows, which reached an estimated $5 billion to $6 billion in 1994, represent revenues from domestic sales of goods and services to foreigners, primarily Russians, Ukrainians, and Germans, who come to Poland to shop and benefit from comparatively more attractive prices. Because of Polish balance-of-payments accounting procedures, however, data on these inflows were not well captured until January 1996.[4] Although the inflows from this border trade have led to dramatic increases in Poland's reserves and contributed to strong output growth, they have also put upward pressure on the real exchange rate.

In response to these inflows, the Polish authorities opted in mid-May 1995 to float the zloty by widening the band within which the currency is allowed to fluctuate to 14 percent. The authorities also chose to continue the monthly devaluation rate of 1.2 percent. In the four weeks before the central bank's decision, an estimated $1.5 billion flowed into the country in anticipation of a currency revaluation (Podkaminer 1995, 32–33). To discourage further inflows of speculative funds, the authorities lowered interest rates substantially. In addition, on June 1, 1995, the zloty was made fully convertible for current transactions in line with the IMF's Article VIII guidelines. Nevertheless, in December 1995, the authorities revalued the zloty by 6 percent and in January 1996 they lowered the monthly devaluation rate to 1 percent (Creditanstalt 1996a, 37).

---

4. Beginning in January 1996, these previously unclassified transactions, notably stemming from cross-border trade, are no longer counted as short-term capital transactions but instead are shown on the current account (Creditanstalt 1996b, 33).

One feature of bank lending that applies particularly in the case of Hungary has been the increasing use banks have made of various risk-reducing techniques in their lending decisions, including the cofinancing of loans with some of the major international financial institutions. In February 1993, for example, Hungary arranged a $375 million loan facility, with the participation of the European Bank for Reconstruction and Development (EBRD), in connection with a road transport project that was secured by toll revenues (CEC 1994, 3). In June 1995 MATAV, the Hungarian telephone company, entered negotiations to syndicate a $300 million loan that was being arranged by the EBRD, the International Finance Coporation (IFC), and the Deutsche Bank of Germany ("MATAV to Syndicate" 1995).

Finally, it is interesting to note that the Czech Republic has been offered some of the best borrowing terms among developing-country borrowers. For example, whereas weighted average spreads for developing-country borrowers tended to rise between 1990 and 1994—from an average of 64 basis points over Libor to 100 basis points over Libor (IMF 1995a, 41)— the Czech Republic saw its spreads narrow dramatically over this period. In 1994, two of the country's major banks, Obchodni and Komercni, were able to raise funds at 65 to 70 basis points over Libor, well below the average for developing-country borrowers. In May 1995 CEZ, the state-owned power utility, broke new ground by arranging a $100 million, three-year syndicated credit from Sumitomo Bank at just 25 basis points over Libor, when average spreads to developing countries had risen to about 107 basis points (IMF 1995c, 26). Obchodni Bank achieved comparable spreads in a $75 million three-year credit it arranged with Societé Generale (Economist Intelligence Unit 1995, 5). By 1996 most borrowers in the region were witnessing a downward trend in margins as well as a lengthening of maturities. The National Bank of Hungary, for example, saw its spread on a $350 million five-year credit fall to 20 basis points over Libor in November 1996, the lowest ever for a Hungarian borrower, whereas the previous year it had to pay 50 basis points over Libor for a similar credit ("Cost of Borrowing" 1996).

Foreign Direct Investment

One of the main factors assisting the transformation of the central and eastern European countries has been foreign direct investment. Because it is generally longer term in nature, this form of investment can help to encourage structural change and modernize obsolete production facilities while bringing with it such indirect benefits as the transfer of technology, management, and marketing skills. Practically nil in 1989, foreign direct investment has grown markedly throughout central and eastern Europe, almost doubling between 1994 and 1995 to about $14 billion for the region as a whole ("Foreign Investment in Eastern" 1996), of which two-thirds went to Poland, Hungary, and the Czech Republic. Its rapid rise is not surprising given the sudden opening of the economies in the region and the massive privatization programs initiated by some. A substantial portion of these investment flows, however, has to date been concentrated in one country—Hungary, which accounted for about 42 percent of the total net flows to the three countries between 1990 and 1996.

Generally, direct investment inflows to central and eastern Europe have not taken place through "green field" operations in which new facilities are created from scratch. In fact, the OECD estimates that investment in this form has accounted for only 20 percent of all such flows to the region. Instead, most direct investment inflows have entailed either taking over existing companies or taking holdings in existing companies. Surveys have shown that investment in the region thus far has been motivated primarily by the desire for access to the domestic markets. Low wages have also been cited as an attractive feature, as have such factors as comparative political stability and a skilled labor force ("Piling into Central Europe" 1996).

The sectors that have interested foreign investors have varied across countries (figure 7.7). In Hungary, manufacturing has played a major role. In the Czech Republic, investments in transport and telecommunications have been particularly significant. In Poland, foreign direct investment has flowed largely to the electrical engineering sector, the food industry, and the financial sector.

By virtually all measures, Hungary has surpassed all other countries in the region in attracting foreign direct investment since 1990 (figure 7.8). Market-based reforms progressively implemented since 1968 together with its close proximity to Austria have given Hungary an edge and made it a low-cost production site for exports to western Europe (All Busy on the Western 1995). Between 1990 and 1996 the country accumulated $13.2 billion in foreign direct investment, almost double the $7.1 billion for the Czech Republic and well over the $11.0 billion for Poland. As a share of GDP, these inflows between 1990 and 1996 reached 4.8 percent in Hungary, compared with 2.7 percent in the Czech Republic and 1.5 percent in Poland. In terms of annual flows on a per capita basis, Hungary again outdistanced its neighbors, with inflows averaging $160 per year over the 1992–1994 period, compared with $77 for the Czech Republic and $36 for Poland. Both Poland and the Czech Republic, however, made considerable strides in attracting new direct investment inflows in 1995, and these continued in 1996, although at a somewhat reduced pace. Interestingly, the Czech Republic offers no tax concessions to attract foreign direct investment, whereas Poland and Hungary do.

Figure 7.7 Foreign direct investment by sector.

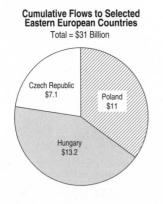

Cumulative Flows to Selected Eastern European Countries
Total = $31 Billion

Czech Republic $7.1

Poland $11

Hungary $13.2

Cumulative flows in U.S. $ billions from 1990 to 1996.

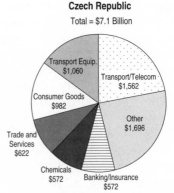

Czech Republic
Total = $7.1 Billion

Transport Equip. $1,060

Transport/Telecom $1,562

Consumer Goods $982

Other $1,696

Trade and Services $622

Chemicals $572

Banking/Insurance $572

Cumulative FDI in U.S. $ millions from 1990 to 1996.

Hungary
Total = $13.2 Billion

Telecom $1,847

Energy $1,583

Industry $6,398

Commerce $1,319

Other $1,187

Financial Sector $857

Cumulative FDI in U.S. $ millions from 1990 to 1996.

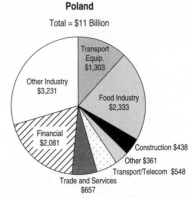

Poland
Total = $11 Billion

Transport Equip. $1,303

Other Industry $3,231

Food Industry $2,333

Financial $2,081

Construction $438

Other $361

Transport/Telecom $548

Trade and Services $657

Cumulative FDI in U.S. $ millions from 1990 to 1996.

Sources: IMF *International Financial Statistics;* Economist Intelligence Unit *Country Reports;* Reuters.

Also influencing the levels of direct investment inflows to Hungary, Poland, and the Czech Republic have been macroeconomic developments in each country over the past several years (figure 7.9). Hungary, whose reform efforts started as early as 1968, has recorded steady, if sometimes slow, progress in developing a market economy. Despite large fiscal and current account deficits, which the government began to address through the introduction of an austerity program in March 1995 coupled with a devaluation and an import tax surcharge, the country has never failed to service all of its external debt (figure 7.10). Tight monetary and fiscal

Figure 7.8 Foreign direct investment by country.

Cumulative Flows from Major Investors

Total = $31 Billion

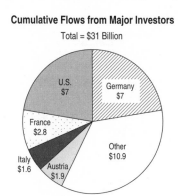

Cumulative FDI from 1990 to 1996 in U.S. $ billions.

Czech Republic

Total = $7.1 Billion

Cumulative investment in U.S. $ millions from 1990 to 1996.

Hungary

Total = $13.2 Billion

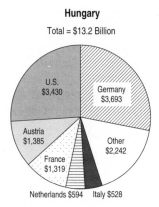

Cumulative investment in U.S. $ millions from 1990 to 1996.

Poland

Total = $11 Billion

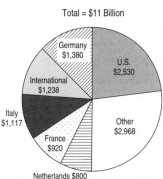

Cumulative foreign direct investment in U.S. $ millions from 1990 to 1996. "International" includes the EBRD as well as multinational corporations.

Sources: IMF *International Financial Statistics;* Economist Intelligence Unit *Country Reports;* Reuters.

policies pursued by the Czech Republic since reform began in 1989, and low levels of external debt contributed to a domestic environment conducive to long-term economic growth, although significant structural problems remain, for example, in the corporate and financial sectors, and a mounting trade deficit has been worrisome. After difficulties in some key areas of its economy in the early 1990s, including a sharp run-up in inflation following price liberalization, Poland has seen its economy re-

Figure 7.9 Indicators of macroeconomic performance.

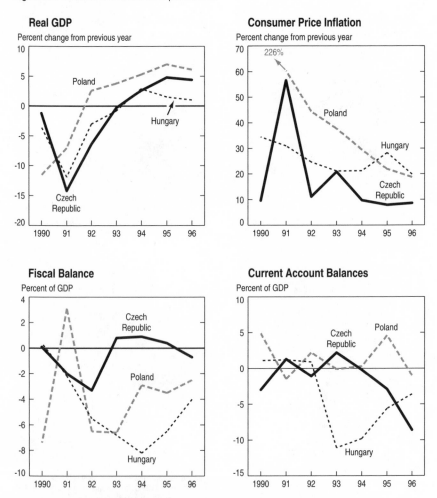

Sources: IMF *International Financial Statistics;* Economist Intelligence Unit *Country Reports;* National Bank of Poland *Information Bulletin;* Czech National Bank; *CNB Monthly Bulletin;* EBRD 1997.

cover strongly over the past four years, fueled by strong export growth and private sector activity as well as the normalization of relations with its external creditors.

Integral to these broad macroeconomic and structural reforms have been efforts since 1990 on the part of all three countries to reduce the share of state holdings in the economy. The magnitude of the privatization efforts undertaken by each country may be seen by the fact that, as of

Figure 7.10 External debt.

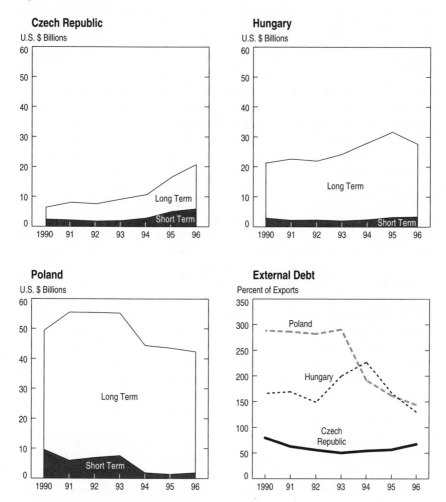

Sources: IBRD *World Debt Tables;* IMF *International Financial Statistics;* PlanEcon; National Bank of Hungary *Monthly Report;* National Bank of Poland *Information Bulletin;* BIS.

1996, the private sector contributed 75 percent to the GDP of the Czech Republic, 73 percent to that of Hungary, and 60 percent to that of Poland.

There are clear differences among the countries, however, in the privatization course each has chosen and its implications for the participation of foreign finance. Although the World Bank calculates that foreign participation was most marked in the privatization efforts of countries in Europe and central Asia, with an estimated 57 percent of sales revenues stemming from foreign sources between 1988 and 1993 (IBRD 1994–1995, 125), this finding appears most applicable to Hungary, but considerably less so to the Czech Republic and Poland.

Hungary

Unlike the programs in Poland and the Czech Republic, the privatization program in Hungary has been dominated by sales for cash. When communism collapsed in 1989, the Hungarian government, which had been introducing many market elements to its economy since 1968, opted for a market privatization program combined with generous tax incentives to attract foreign investors. It opened up large sectors of the economy and sold them primarily to Western firms. General Electric, Unilever, and Electrolux all bought out existing companies. Ford and General Motors built new ones. The drive to sell state assets culminated in late 1993 with the sale of a 30 percent stake in MATAV, the state telephone company, to a German-American consortium for $875 million, one of the region's largest privatizations to date.

After having spent most of the 1990s aggressively pursuing privatization and attracting considerable foreign investment inflows in the process, the country began to falter in 1994 when it saw its revenue from foreign direct investment fall by more than $1.2 billion from its 1993 level. In part this decline is misleading in that almost one-third of the 1993 inflows stemmed from the MATAV sale. Nonetheless, a change in government in March 1994 and a lack of political consensus on the desirability of foreign participation in the disposition of the government's remaining holdings (valued at roughly $14 billion) stalled the privatization program considerably in 1994 and much of 1995.

A new privatization law passed in May 1995, helped revive activity. The law merged the two existing privatization agencies into the State Privatization and Holding Company (APV Rt) and charged the agency with selling most of the remaining state companies by 1997. Under the new law, the finance minister was no longer in control of privatization, and parliament was given final say in privatization decisions considered to be "vital to the nation." At the same time, despite considerable opposition, the government committed itself to bringing several medium-sized companies to market over the remainder of 1995, including the oil and gas utility (MOL), five regional gas suppliers, and a major broadcasting company. The government's success in meeting its goals far exceeded expectations. Initially, the government had hoped for privatization revenues on the order of $1.5 billion for 1995. Instead, by year end, the government was able to realize a record $3.5 billion in privatization revenues and a total of $4.5 billion in foreign direct investment (Creditanstalt 1996b, 26). The government's successful privatization efforts continued in 1996. By 1997, the privatization process was nearly complete, with major industries having been restructured by new Western owners, providing Hungary with some of the best-run companies in the region ("Hungary's Sacrifices" 1997).

The Czech Republic

As in Hungary, foreign direct investment flows to the Czech Republic have also been related to the country's privatization program, although in the Czech Republic the relationship has been somewhat less direct. The Czech privatization program consisted of two waves. In the first wave, which began in 1991, a direct auction method was used for small privatizations. Foreigners were not allowed to bid at the initial auction but could do so— and did—if no domestic buyers offered bids. In the second wave of privatization, which was completed in early 1995, the country handed out vouchers to all Czech residents, who could use them to purchase shares either directly on the stock exchange or in newly formed investment funds. Again, no foreign participation was involved in the initial distribution, but foreigners could subsequently purchase shares from Czech residents.

As a result, the Czech Republic has been extremely successful in attracting foreign direct investment inflows even though it offers no specific tax concessions. Although revenues from foreign direct investment fell rather sharply in 1993, the drop was associated primarily with uncertainties surrounding the country's split with the Slovak Republic on January 1. By 1994, the flows returned such that, by the end of 1996, the country had attracted a total of over $7 billion in foreign direct investment since 1990, over 40 percent of this in 1995 alone.

As elsewhere in the region, however, the government continues to retain major stakes in some key sectors of the economy, including the banks, utilities, and oil refineries, but like Hungary, it too has demonstrated over the course of 1995 and 1996 its commitment to gradually reducing its role in many of these sectors. For example, in late June 1995, it sold a 27 percent stake in SPT Telecom, the telephone company, for which it received $1.45 billion from a consortium led by a Dutch firm, making this sale the largest privatization in the region since the $875 million share offering in Hungary's MATAV in 1993 ("Czech Telecom Stake" 1995). In addition, the government has begun to privatize its oil refineries. Three Western oil companies—Royal Dutch Shell, Conoco, and Agip of Italy—agreed in September 1995 to buy 49 percent of the two main refineries for $173 million and to invest an additional $480 million over the next five years. A new state holding company, Unipetrol, retains a 51 percent stake in the refineries ("Czech Oil Refinery" 1995).

One long-term issue that may discourage foreign investment relates to the ownership structure of Czech enterprises. Although much of the economy is in private hands, a major portion of ownership rights is concentrated in a comparatively small number of private investment funds created as part of the voucher privatization program. Most of these investment funds, in turn, are owned by the major banks. As a result, ownership of Czech enterprises is not as widespread as had been envisaged. Moreover, this ownership structure raises the potential for conflicts of interest on the part of fund managers who, when faced with market pressures, may be tempted to maximize earnings at the expense of the long-term development interests of their funds' portfolios. The comparatively low unemployment rate in the Czech Republic—3.5 percent in 1996, compared with 10.5 percent in Hungary and 13.6 percent in Poland—suggests that the necessary restructuring of Czech enterprises has not yet been undertaken in part because of these ownership arrangements (Creditanstalt 1995b, 8).

Poland

In contrast to developments in both Hungary and the Czech Republic, foreign direct investment was slow to get under way in Poland following the introduction of the country's shock therapy program in 1990. With the fixing of the exchange rate in early 1991, the economy began to stabilize, and foreign investment did flow into Poland. Nevertheless, the amount was relatively modest given the size of the country's economy, by far the largest of the three countries. Although foreign investment has grown steadily over the 1990s, the bureaucratic hassles stemming from the fact that a number of enterprises may report to more than one ministry tended to discourage investors and precluded more substantial inflows.

In addition, the country's privatization program did little until 1995 to promote the inflow of foreign direct investment. Prior to 1995, the Polish privatization program was largely voluntary, relatively slow to be implemented, mostly confined to small- and medium-sized businesses, and considerably delayed by a lack of a political consensus on its aims and methods. Of the 8,400 state firms registered in August 1990, only 2,290 small- and medium-sized firms and 135 large firms were privatized by the end of 1994. Of this total, 961 were sold in 1991, compared with only 294 in 1994 ("Poland: Set Loose" 1995).

This situation began to change in the middle of 1995. After a three-year delay, the government agreed in July to launch its long-planned mass privatization program, signing management contracts with fund management companies to manage fifteen national investment funds (NIFs). The NIFs, which are partly managed by foreign fund managers and 85 percent owned by the adult population, received 60 percent of the shares of over 500 privatized companies. The government reserved 15 percent of the remaining shares for the employees of the companies; it planned either to hold the balance of the shares or distribute them to local authorities and suppliers.

Under the terms of the privatization plan, one fund served as lead manager for each enterprise privatized, receiving one-third of the shares offered in that company. The remaining shares were then distributed equally among the other funds. Using a lottery system, each fund was allowed to bid on those companies it wished to lead-manage. The lottery took place in early 1996. To encourage the investment funds to take a longer-term interest in the enterprises whose shares they hold, the government allowed them, for a specified time period, to reconfigure their portfolios if they wished (Girocredit 1995, 9). In addition, beginning in late 1995, the government allowed all adult Poles (29 million people) to purchase at a nominal price of 20 zloty each ($8) participation certificates that could be converted into shares in each of the fifteen funds. These shares became tradable on an over-the-counter market in early 1996 and were listed on a special market of the Warsaw Stock Exchange in July 1996. This was preliminary to the listing of the individual funds on the Warsaw Stock Exchange in 1997 ("Fibremaker Gives Dress" 1996). By mid-1997 almost 26 million adult Poles had purchased vouchers, which were declared valid until 1998. Once the vouchers were registered with stockbrokers, they could be exchanged for shares in each of the fifteen funds ("Poles Leaping toward Privatization" 1997).

Although the mass privatization program may bring little immediate revenue to the country, it holds the promise of attracting foreign investment in the coming years. At the same time, it also permits a rapid sell-off of state assets in the face of a shortage of capital among the population. Nonetheless, aspects of the new program continue to be mired in political controversy. For example, parliament and not the privatization minister has the right to veto all privatization decisions involving key sectors of the economy, such as banks, oil and gas, and insurance. The legislation that created the program barely survived the president's veto, which parliament voted to override in October 1995. Poland's privatization program is likely to remain highly politicized, but it does open the way to advance the restructuring process of Polish enterprises.

Under new government leadership, the privatization program for 1996 was on track, with the government moving forward in its plans to sell a minority stake in Polska Miedz, a copper producer expected to be valued at $2 billion, which would make this transaction the largest privatization in the region to date ("Polish Privatization Plan" 1996). In addition, in early 1996, the government announced plans to privatize over seven years most of the country's electrical generating and distribution sector ("Poland Plans Power" 1996). In midyear it allowed two foreign banks to take majority control of their respective Polish partners ("Poland Allows Foreign" 1996). At the same time, the government faced some potential conflicts with foreign investors, stemming from the dismissal in May 1996 of two U.S. managers of one of the funds ("U.S. Fund Managers" 1996).

Portfolio Investment

Portfolio investment is undeniably the most significant new development in the provision of private capital to developing countries in the 1990s. Launched by the efforts of pension funds, insurance companies, mutual funds, and other institutional investors located primarily in the United States and the United Kingdom, to diversify their portfolios in the late 1980s, portfolio investment has probably grown at a faster rate than any other source of private capital flows to developing countries. The countries of central and eastern Europe, however, have only just begun to benefit from inflows from this source. Moreover, the activity that has been reported to date vis-à-vis the region has almost always assumed the form of bond flows and not equity flows, despite the fact that the bulk of emerging market mutual funds' global portfolio investment takes place through equity and not bond investment (IMF 1995a, 39). Of the central and eastern European countries, Hungary continues to dominate activity in these markets.

One caveat to note in considering portfolio investment to the region is the relative paucity of data and the uncertain reliability of the information that is available. To date, there has been no systematic compilation of statistics on portfolio flows by an international organization. Much of the data that do exist have been obtained from diverse and often inconsistent sources (CEC 1994, 6). In addition, balance-of-payments statistics in individual countries often do not distinguish portfolio flows from other capital flows. Moreover, most countries lack systematic methods for recording secondary market transactions in domestic market bonds and equity. Therefore, recorded foreign activity in these markets may be significantly understated.

Bonds

Since 1990, an estimated 72 percent of all private capital flowing into central and eastern European in the form of portfolio investment has taken place through bonds. As noted earlier, portfolio investment through bonds occurs in two ways, and both merit discussion. First, public or private entities can issue securities in the domestic market of a foreign country or in the international markets. Thus far, most of the activity concerning the countries of central and eastern Europe has taken this form. Second, nonresidents can invest in the money or capital markets of another country. This form of bond investment is only just beginning in central and eastern Europe. Some data are available for international purchases by these countries in foreign markets, but only anecdotal evidence is possible in the case of foreign purchases in these countries' domestic markets.

Hungarian, Czech, and Polish Bonds Issued in Foreign Markets

Of all the central and eastern European countries, Hungary has been the most active participant in the international capital markets during the first half of the 1990s. On average, it raised more than $1 billion a year in the Eurobond market until 1993 when, taking advantage of favorable market conditions, it raised a spectacular $3.9 billion. Mounting fiscal and current account deficits prompted its need for finance. According to some estimates, Hungary alone accounted for as much as 83 percent of all international bonds issued by all countries in the region between 1989 and 1994 (CEC 1994, 5).

In addition, Hungary has also been able to access the Euroyen and Samurai market and, in 1993, for the first time, the U.S. dollar or Yankee bond market. Although until late 1996 Hungary lacked the investment grade ratings from some of the international credit rating agencies that both Poland and the Czech Republic enjoyed,[5] the fact that the country has long been committed to market-based reform and serviced its external debt strictly according to schedule despite some unfavorable conditions has been important to its generally positive reception in the international markets (Creditanstalt 1995c, 17).

Like Hungary, the Czech Republic began to access the international capital markets before the fall of its communist government. The amounts the country has raised, however, have been far more modest than those raised by Hungary, averaging about $350 million per year between 1990 and 1996. Following the dissolution of Czechoslovakia on January 1, 1993, the Czech National Bank tapped the Eurobond market for the first time in April 1993, issuing a three-year $375 million Eurobond to help rebuild the reserves depleted by speculation against the koruna in connection with the breakup of the country (CEC 1994, 5–6). Notwithstanding the Czech Republic's investment grade ratings, which it received in March 1993, spreads for dollar-denominated issues for both the Czech Republic and Hungary were comparable at about 275 basis points over U.S. Treasuries in 1993, although spreads for the Czech Republic fell sharply the following year (figure 7.11).

Poland, by contrast, was able to access the international capital markets only after it had normalized relations with its commercial bank creditors in

---

5. The Czech Republic saw its investment grade ratings upgraded in the fall of 1995, to Baa1 in September by Moody's and to A in November by Standard and Poor's. Whereas Poland has had an investment grade from Moody's since June 1995 (Baa3), it was rated below investment grade by Standard and Poor's (BB) until April 1996 when it was upgraded by two notches to investment grade BBB–. Hungary is rated investment grade by both these rating agencies: Baa3 by Moody's in December 1996 and BBB– by Standard and Poor's in October 1996. It was given investment grade status by two other rating agencies earlier in 1996: IBCA in April and by Duff and Phelps in June (Credit Rating Boost 1996).

Figure 7.11 Yield spreads on sovereign borrowing.

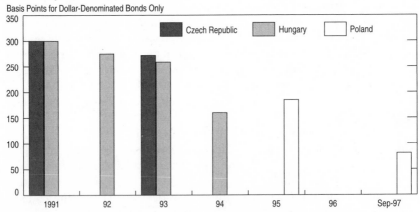

Sources: IMF *Private Market Financing for Developing Countries;* Bloomberg L. P.

1994. It made its debut offering in the Eurobond market in June 1995, raising $250 million for five years at a spread of 185 basis points over comparable U.S. Treasuries—a lower spread than that achieved by other comparably rated borrowers (Greece and South Africa) ("Poland's Debut Meets" 1995). The offering followed close on the heels of the country's having been awarded an investment grade rating by Moody's. With some $15 billion in reserves, Poland sought mainly to test its standing in the international debt markets. In July 1996, following its upgrade to investment grade by Standard and Poor's, the country further tested the markets by issuing its first deutsche mark–denominated Eurobond, a five-year DM 250 million ($165 million) offer at a spread of 65 basis points over comparable German government bonds. This spread was roughly in line with secondary market spreads on its dollar-denominated Eurobond, whose price had risen sharply over the year with the yield spread over U.S. Treasuries falling from 185 basis points to about 70 basis points ("Investors Snap Up" 1996).

Although the vast majority of developing-country borrowers in the international capital markets during the 1990s were nonsovereigns, all of the borrowing by Hungary and most of that by the Czech Republic between 1990 and 1994 was undertaken by sovereigns.[6] As privatized companies are restructured, however, and the corporate sector strengthened, some of

6. In November 1994 CEZ, the state-owned power company, became the first corporation in the region to enter the Eurobond market with a $150 million issue at a spread of 110 basis points (IMF 1995c, 21).

the major firms in these countries have begun to access the international capital markets. In March 1996, for example, Poland's export development bank (Bank Rozwoju Eksportu) issued a $50 million three-year floating-rate note with a spread of about 150 basis points ("Polish Bank Plans" 1996). In April, the Czech Republic's Komercni Banka raised $250 million with a spread of 78 basis points over U.S. Treasuries ("Komercni Banka Eurobond" 1996). And in May, Poland's Bank Handlowy issued $100 million three-year bonds at 88 basis points over comparable U.S. Treasuries ("Bank Handlowy Three-Year" 1996). One year later, in only the fourth Eurobond by a Polish borrower, Bank Handlowy was able to issue $150 million three-year bonds at 60 basis points over comparable U.S. Treasuries ("Bank Handlowy Taps" 1997).

One development of note was that in October 1995 the Czech koruna became the first postcommunist currency in which borrowers can tap the Eurobond market. General Electric Credit Corporation was the first borrower to raise funds denominated in koruna, with a Kc 2 billion ($76 million) issue of three-year bonds. A second issuer, the Nordic Investment Bank, raised Kc 1.5 billion ($58 million) later in the month. Both these issues followed the decision by the Czech parliament in September to approve the full convertibility of the koruna for current account transactions, and a significant liberalization of the currency for capital account transactions. Interest rate differentials enabled these borrowers to fund their operations in the Czech Republic more cost-effectively in the international markets than they could have in Czech local markets ("Czech Koruna Broadens" 1995). In December 1995, the World Bank became the largest issuer of koruna-denominated bonds, issuing Kc 2.5 billion ($96 million) two-year bonds at a spread of 600 basis points over domestic German paper ("World Bank Launches" 1995). The Bank placed a second issue in May 1996 for Kc 1.5 billion ($54 million) (Czech National Bank 1996). As of February 1996, borrowers can also tap the Eurobond market in Polish zloty ("First Zloty Eurobond" 1996). The IFC, the EBRD, ING Barings, and British Midland have all issued zloty-linked bonds in anticipation of the full convertibility of the zloty.[7]

Foreign Access to Hungarian, Czech, and Polish Money
and Capital Markets.

Evidence of private capital inflows to the domestic markets of countries in central and eastern Europe is by necessity anecdotal. Comprehensive data do not exist. Nonetheless, there are indications that foreign investors have

---

7. The Polish authorities eased constraints on direct investment flows in April 1996. They planned a further dismantling of controls beginning in January 1997 to allow Polish citizens to buy stocks on the international markets (Poland to Ease 1996).

begun to take note of both the government securities markets and corporate bond markets in some of these countries, especially those where regulations affecting foreign access to these markets and the ability to repatriate investment income have been liberalized (table 7.2) (CEC 1994, 7).

Since 1993, Hungary in particular has been easing restrictions on the ability of foreigners to participate in its treasury markets. In view of its substantial fiscal and current account deficits, it has sought to attract additional funds to help finance these deficits. Foreign participation to date, however, has been modest. For example, in the first Hungarian treasury issue made available to them in May 1994, foreigners took only HUF 104 million ($1.02 million) of the HUF 8.8 billion ($86 million) offered (Girocredit 1995, 18–19).

Corporate bond markets in Hungary and the Czech Republic have also begun to attract the interest of foreign investors. The bulk of these investments, however, has been arranged through private placements with the issuers—either local subsidiaries of multinational companies or state-owned firms and banks. As a result, there is virtually no secondary market trading in these bonds. Some market participants estimate that total portfolio investment in koruna-denominated securities amounted to Kc 28 billion ($10.8 million) at the end of 1994 (Creditanstalt 1996, 9). Were the Czech government to lift its prohibitions against allowing domestic borrowers to issue short-term debt denominated in hard currency, a greater pool of foreign investors might be attracted to the local market, prompting the development of a secondary market (*Business Eastern Europe* 1995b, 7). Finally, new investment funds geared to attracting foreign investment have been formed in recent years. One such fund in Hungary, capitalized at HUF 330 million ($2.6 million), was launched by the Austrian bank Creditanstalt Bankverein. In addition, two local Czech brokers have also launched similar funds geared to attracting foreign participation ("Central European Economic" 1995). By early 1996, plans were in place by the Templeton Fund to raise $300 million to invest in central and eastern European government debt instruments ("Debt Fund Planned" 1996).

Equities

Portfolio investment through equities takes place when nonresidents purchase shares on the stock exchange of a foreign country or when private or publicly owned firms issue shares in the international markets or the domestic market of a single country through the use of global or American depositary receipts. To date, the bulk of activity in portfolio investment through equities for the central and eastern European countries has taken place through nonresident direct purchases on the stock exchanges of these countries rather than through the issuance of shares in the inter-

Table 7.2 Exchange rate regime and capital account restrictions

	Exchange rate regime	Capital account restrictions
Czech Republic	The koruna has fluctuated under a managed floating exchange rate regime since May 1997. Previously, the koruna had been pegged to a basket consisting of the deutsche mark (65%) and the dollar (35%) and allowed to fluctuate by plus/minus 7.5% around central parity. The koruna has been fully convertible for current account transactions under the IMF's Article VIII guidelines since October 1995. The currency is also convertible for many capital and financial account transactions, and the authorities are working toward full convertibility.	*Inflow:* There are no restrictions on foreign direct investment or equity purchases in the Czech Republic by nonresidents, except that licenses may be required and some restrictions apply to purchases of various financial institutions. Purchases of real estate by noncitizens are restricted. Czech companies may accept credits from nonresident banks. *Outflow:* Czechs are allowed to purchase real estate abroad and make direct investments abroad. Restrictions apply to purchases by Czechs of foreign securities, the issue of foreign securities on the Czech market, and the provision of credit to nonresidents (outside of credits from the state, those with a term of over five years, for the purpose of direct investment, or between persons).
Hungary	The forint is pegged to the deutsche mark (70%) and the dollar (30%). As part of an austerity package introduced in March 1995, the forint was devalued by 9% and a crawling peg system of devaluation in line with inflation was introduced. The forint is allowed to fluctuate by plus/minus 2.25% around the central rate. The forint has been convertible for current account transactions in line with IMF Article VIII guidelines since January 1996.	*Inflow:* Foreign direct investment in the form of joint ventures is mostly unrestricted, but purchases of more than 10% of a bank's equity require licenses. Restrictions apply to nonresidents' purchases of Hungarian real estate. Foreigners may purchase Hungarian bonds, but licenses are required for original maturities under one year. Licenses are required for most lending to Hungary. *Outflow:* Licenses are required for some direct investments abroad. The sale of investment-grade OECD-country securities in Hungary is unrestricted, but restrictions apply to other countries' securities. Licenses are required for most lending to nonresidents.
Poland	The zloty is pegged to the dollar (45%), the deutsche mark (35%), the pound sterling (10%), the French franc (5%), and the Swiss franc (5%). The central exchange rate is devalued in line with inflation under a crawling peg system. Since May 1995, the zloty has been allowed to fluctuate by plus/minus 7% around the central rate. The zloty has been convertible for current account transactions under the IMF's Article VIII guidelines since June 1995.	*Inflow:* Foreign direct investment in Poland is mostly unrestricted. Foreign investment in Polish securities is mostly unrestricted. Restrictions apply to residents' issue of short-term securities abroad. Restrictions apply to nonresidents' purchases of real estate in Poland. *Outflow:* Poles may make foreign direct investments in OECD countries and certain other countries freely. Restrictions apply to nonresidents' issue of short-term securities in Poland. Licenses are required for lending to nonresidents when maturities are shorter than one year. Restrictions apply to purchases of real estate abroad.

Source: International Monetary Fund, *1997 Annual Report on Exchange Arrangements and Exchange Restrictions.*

national markets by firms in these countries (CEC 1994, 5). As privatization efforts proceed, however, and firms continue their necessary restructuring, equity investment is likely to grow markedly. A stronger corporate profile will not only enhance the attractiveness of these countries' stock markets to foreign investors but also make firms seeking to issue shares abroad more appealing. Foreign interest in these equity markets has been facilitated by the inclusion of these countries in emerging-market indexes over 1995 and 1996 ("Emerging-Nation Markets" 1996; "Elusive Benchmark of Emerging" 1996).

Foreign Purchases of Shares in Czech, Polish, and Hungarian Markets

The striking growth in emerging-market mutual funds, which numbered some 900 by the end of 1994, has made direct purchases of shares in developing-country stock markets an increasingly important source of portfolio investment in the 1990s. Mutual fund purchases of developing-country equities are estimated to have grown from almost $6.5 billion in 1990 to more than $58 billion in 1994 when, despite turbulent market conditions in many developing countries, these funds continued to grow rapidly (IMF 1995c, 26). According to market participants, virtually all mutual funds today hold investments in central and eastern Europe, compared with only 68 percent in 1991 (Chang 1995, 6).

The IMF lists Hungary as the only country to which equity funds are specifically directed. By the end of 1994, it reports, there were three closed-end equity funds for Hungary, with a combined net asset value of $200 million (IMF 1995a, 48–51). Because many mutual funds combine both equity and bond holdings and are global or regional in focus, it is impossible to reach a comprehensive estimate of the amount of equity they hold in any given country.

Nonetheless, the booms in the Czech, Polish, and Hungarian equity markets, particularly from the second half of 1993 until early 1994, again in 1996, and especially for Hungary for most of 1997, clearly suggest a significant presence of foreign investors (figure 7.12). The Budapest Stock Exchange, for example, estimates that foreigners, mainly institutional investors, account for between 50 percent and 70 percent of the exchange's turnover and investments (Budapest Stock Exchange 1995, 6). In the Polish market, foreigners are estimated to account for about 25 percent of turnover and 20 percent of market capitalization (CEC 1994, 6–7).

Some have argued that increased equity investment in the region largely reflects the resale to foreigners of stocks received by domestic residents during the mass privatization of state enterprises in 1991 and 1992 (Calvo, Sahay, and Vegh 1995, 17). This observation appears to be particularly rel-

Figure 7.12 Indicators of stock market performance.

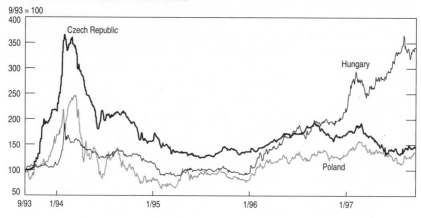

Stock Market Indices in Dollar Terms

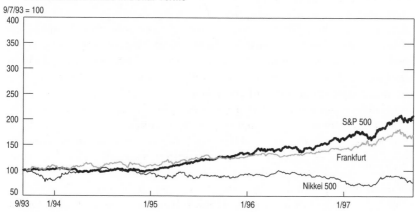

Stock Market Indices in Dollar Terms

Sources: Datastream; Bloomberg L. P.

evant to the Czech Republic, whose stock exchange opened in April 1993 just prior to the completion of the first wave of privatization in May 1993. By the fall, local mutual fund managers reportedly began to offer blocks of shares to international fund managers once it became apparent that the holdings were relatively inexpensive, especially when compared with Polish shares, at a time when prospects for the Czech economy looked relatively favorable (CS First Boston 1994, 5).

The performance of stock markets in these countries to date has been anything but predictable. After registering huge run-ups in 1993, stock markets in Hungary, the Czech Republic, and Poland pulled back, often unevenly, over the course of 1994 as increases in U.S. interest rates beginning in February made returns on these investments relatively less attractive and domestic demand slackened. From where it stood in February 1994, the Prague stock market had lost two-thirds of its market value by the fall of 1995, while the Warsaw market also suffered a major decline ("Eastern European Stock" 1995). In Budapest, the stock exchange fell to a fifty-two-week low in January 1995 and gradually moved up over the year, but at a considerably reduced level. By early 1996, however, after two years of strong export-led growth and privatization programs actively under way in both Hungary and Poland, most of these markets had begun to turn around, with markets in Poland, Hungary, and the Czech Republic all registering gains ranging from 41 percent to 49 percent in the first quarter of 1996 ("Market Place" 1996).

These gains were broadly maintained through much of 1996 in all three countries, although share prices fell sharply in the Czech Republic after September as a result of a worsening in the macroeconomic outlook and a banking crisis that stemmed from a series of failures of small banks in late summer ("Banking Crisis Besets Prague" 1996). By contrast, in Hungary, marked improvement in macroeconomic performance over 1996 and into 1997 led to a surge in share prices, with the Budapest index rising over 130 percent in dollar terms in 1996. Gains continued in 1997 after a moderate correction early in the year ("Bull-Run Continues" 1997).

The resurgence in equity markets in the region led Europe's largest independent fund manager, Mercury Asset Management, to launch the first equity fund for central and eastern Europe in January 1996. The open-end fund, based in Luxembourg, planned an initial capitalization of DM 30 million to 40 million ($20 million to $30 million) and to allocate roughly 70 percent of its funds to Poland, Hungary, and the Czech Republic ("Eastern Europe Fund" 1996). In addition, in mid-1996, an affiliate of Deutsche Bank, DBG Eastern Europe, launched a private equity fund capitalized at Kc 900 million ($32.7 million) to provide development capital to companies in the region. The aim of this fund was to provide finance for management buyouts and buyins, acquisitions and joint ventures, and improvements in the quality of earnings and management ("Fund Set Up" 1996).

When looking at the performance of the equity markets in these countries, it is useful to bear in mind how very recently they have come into operation and how very much still needs to be done to strengthen not only the markets themselves but also the banking and financial systems of which they are integral parts.[8] The Prague market opened in April 1993, the Warsaw market in mid-1992, and the Budapest market in June 1990. There is little dispute that these markets lack breadth and liquidity, making any large-scale trade impossible to execute without significantly moving the price of the stock. Problems and glitches abound.

Hungary

The Hungarian market listed only forty-four stocks at the end of 1996 and, although in operation longer than either the Czech or Polish exchange, continues to have a smaller market capitalization than either of these countries (figure 7.13). Because of political differences surrounding the country's privatization process, only a handful of major privatizations were effected for a good part of 1995, the first major one being the successful offering of shares in July 1995 in OTP Bank, the national savings and commercial bank. However, the government's renewed commitment to an active privatization program in the fall of 1995 and its unexpected success in exceeding its goals led to a sharp increase in the market capitalization of its stock exchange. This rose from less than $2.6 billion in October 1995 to $3.8 billion by May 1996 and $5.3 billion by the end of 1996. Daily turnover also increased dramatically, averaging about $5 million in May 1996, which is over four times the average daily figure for 1995 (Creditanstalt 1996b, 30), and rose to $9 million by the end of 1996.

Over the past several years, the Hungarian government has undertaken some specific steps to help strengthen the country's stock market. In 1994, it established a fully operational clearinghouse and share depository that has reduced settlement time on trades. An efficient settlement system can help to improve surveillance and regulatory control, thereby contributing to investor confidence and increased volume of cross-border transactions (IMF 1995b, 32).

During March 1995, the government took two additional steps to improve the breadth and transparency of the Budapest Stock Exchange. First, it opened an unregulated market (UM) that is able to use the regular stock exchange facilities after official trading hours. The UM market, which was formed by the agreement of thirty-three stock exchange members, is not official; listing, disclosure, and trading requirements do not apply to the stocks traded there. Since opening, eleven stocks have been admitted and trading has been sporadic. Second, the government allowed trading in cer-

---

8. More formal statistical analysis is required to assess the performance of these markets fully. In broad terms, the IMF has found evidence of volatility spillovers from U.S. markets to emerging-country stock markets and has determined that these spillovers are strongest when portfolio flows have been most volatile (IMF 1995a, 119).

Figure 7.13 Indicators of stock market performance.

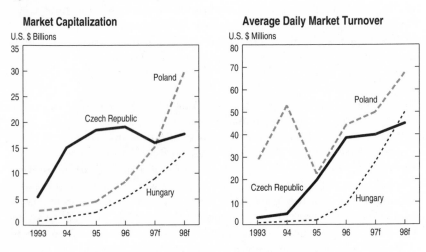

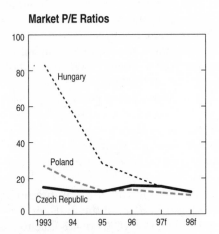

Source: ING Barings *Emerging Markets Weekly Report.*

tain derivative products to take place on the Budapest exchange, with a total of five contracts made available (Creditanstalt 1995b, 19).

Investor confidence in Hungary has been boosted in 1996 and 1997 not
only by the measures the government has taken to improve the country's
stock exchange but also by the improved performance of the economy, including renewed growth and declining inflation, the introduction of currency convertibility in January 1996, the approval of an IMF $387 million
standby program in March 1996, and acceptance as an OECD member at

the end of March 1996, the second ex-Soviet bloc country to be admitted. The market continued to strengthen in 1996 and into 1997 with the privatization of TVK, a chemical producer, and the further privatization of MOL, the oil producer, and MATAV, the state telephone company. In June 1996, Cofinec, a central European packaging company, became the first non-Hungarian firm to be listed on the Budapest Stock Exchange ("Hungarian Share Issue" 1996).

Poland

Like its Hungarian counterpart, the Polish stock exchange has also suffered from comparative thinness. As in Hungary, this situation began to change in 1996, driven by strong economic growth, the persistent influx of foreign capital, and the implementation of the mass privatization program in mid-1995. With only forty stocks listed in October 1995 and a market capitalization of roughly $4.3 billion, the Polish stock exchange had fifty-eight companies listed by August 1996 and a market capitalization of over $7.0 billion, which rose to $8.4 billion by the end of 1996. Still, Poland's stock exchange was more than twice as small as the Czech exchange even though its economy was almost four times larger. After more than four years of trading, there are few open-end mutual funds, the main one being the Boston-based Pioneer Group's Pioneer First Polish Trust Fund, which began operations in July 1992.

Domestic restrictions on fund activities—rather than market concerns—have tended to hold back the development of funds. Until 1996, Polish residents were prohibited from holding any investments abroad. This meant that mutual funds could invest only in domestic securities, which until the end of 1995 comprised fewer than fifty stocks and a small array of government debt issues. Moreover, a regulation requiring trust funds to employ at least two licensed investment advisers in a country where only twenty-two had been licensed as of early 1995 made new applications for setting up funds scarce ("Central European Economic" 1995, 32).

Further, until the middle of 1995, the Warsaw Stock Exchange tended to be dominated by retail investors, who began to leave the market after heavy losses in 1994. Domestic institutional investors such as banks and insurance companies were mostly absent, as were foreign investors, who were largely deterred from entering the market between 1994 and mid-1995, owing in part to uncertainties stemming from political tensions between the president and the parliament.

With the government's decision to implement its mass privatization program in May 1995, these factors began to change. By year-end, shares in over 400 companies were added to the Warsaw Stock Exchange, a development that clearly contributed to improving the market's liquidity. Driven by strong foreign interest, in part resulting from 7 percent real growth in

1995 as well as sharply declining inflation, the Warsaw exchange saw its average daily turnover catapult from as low as $21 million in late October 1995 to over $44 million by the end of 1996. Moreover, the National Investment Funds are expected to help stimulate corporate restructuring by deepening the stake each fund has in the success of the companies in its portfolio. This too should add to foreign interest in Polish equities. In addition, Poland has the most stringent disclosure requirements of all countries in the region, obliging companies listed on the exchange to report not quarterly, as is typical elsewhere, but monthly. A new securities law in 1995 that established strong penalties for securities offenses such as the falsifying of information in prospectuses has also helped improve investor protection rights (IMF 1995b, 32).

Foreign involvement in the Warsaw Stock Exchange should deepen further as a consequence of the decision by the government in early 1996 to allow foreigners to sell investment fund units, stocks, and securities with a maturity of more than one year up to an overall total of ECU 200 million ($250 million) after obtaining permission from the Polish Securities Commission ("Poland to Ease" 1996). In addition, domestic residents are expected to be able to widen their portfolios, particularly toward the manufacturing sector, as soon as their certificates have been exchanged for shares in the fifteen National Investment Funds in 1997 and the shares are traded in an organized market (Creditanstalt 1996b, 37).

The Czech Republic
The Czech stock market, by contrast, faces a rather different set of problems as it struggles to cope with over 1,700 listed stocks as of March 1, 1995, following the completion of the second wave of voucher privatization in February. With a market capitalization of over $19 billion by the end of 1996—the region's largest—and an economy whose performance would suggest that the stock market should be strong, the Prague Stock Exchange faced notably slack demand for most of 1995. This was true as well for the market created at the same time for small investors, called the RM system. In large part, the sluggishness of these markets stemmed from the absence of a significant foreign presence in an environment characterized by inefficiency, fragmentation, and a lack of transparency. This situation began to change in 1996 as foreign investors returned to the stock exchange and were mainly responsible for the market's upward surge in the first half of 1996 (Creditanstalt 1996b, 25).

Nonetheless, market activity continues to be dominated by a handful of regularly traded companies—CEZ, SPT Telecom, and Komercni Banka—that account for more than 55 percent of the market's turnover (bonds account for 25 percent) and 57 percent of its capitalization. On average, only 677 issues trade daily, which is no more than 40 percent of the total

1,700 companies listed (Creditanstalt 1996c, 11). Added to these difficulties is the fact that voucher privatization basically created a large and fragmented body of shareholders but no active investors. The fifteen largest investment funds manage an estimated 40 percent of the assets distributed; many of these funds are owned by the country's major banks, which remain largely state owned (Gilibert and Steinherr 1995, 7).

In addition, the bulk of share trading, 80 percent by some estimates, takes place outside the organized exchanges in over-the-counter markets, in part because settlement time is faster and in part because prices on the official exchanges are not allowed to fluctuate by more than a specified amount on any trading day (Czech National Bank 1995, 4). Thus, public prices bear little relation to over-the-counter trades, leading to a serious lack of transparency that keeps away many domestic and foreign investors.

These weaknesses have convinced market participants and the authorities of the need for changes. In a fall 1995 initiative intended to encourage market transparency a group of brokerage firms agreed on a voluntary code committing them to report over-the-counter trades on a daily basis. In addition, in September 1995, the authorities introduced new measures to limit the number of stocks that can be listed on the main exchange and to improve disclosure requirements for all traded stocks. The plans call for a primary and a secondary exchange for listed stocks, plus a third exchange to function as a free market. Whether a company is listed on one of the main exchanges depends on its trading volume and the amount of its publicly traded shares. Investment funds, too, are subject to similar requirements. Reporting requirements are far stricter for companies and funds that trade on the primary exchange, although disclosure requirements are imposed on all. Any company that fails to fulfill these conditions may be transferred to the free market (Creditanstalt 1995a, 2–3).

The authorities put in place two additional initiatives in early 1996. The first was the introduction of continuous trading on the Prague Stock Exchange of the exchange's five most liquid stocks (SPT Telecom, Komercni Banka, CEZ, Ceska Sporitelna, and Komercni Banka Investincni Fund). This measure, which had been planned for over a year, was intended to facilitate market liquidity and may be followed by continuous trading in other issues before year-end (Creditanstalt 1996b, 25).

Second, planned improvements in investor protection laws, which, among other things, require disclosure of those holding more than 10 percent in any company, were also put in place in April 1996 when parliament approved an amendment to the country's securities act. Among its other provisions, the new legislation required companies listed on the Prague exchange to publicize their annual results within three months after the end of their fiscal year and to provide semiannual reports. Broadly, the legislation was intended to strengthen foreign confidence in the Czech markets and boost their transparency, which has lagged that of both the Polish and Hungarian markets (Creditanstalt 1996b, 25).

In addition to its disclosure and investor protection requirements, new securities legislation that took effect in July 1996 also provided for the possibility of transforming investment funds into different types of companies. Investment funds may not hold more than 20 percent of their assets in any one company. But if these funds elect to become managerial companies, which they may now do with the consent of three-quarters of their shareholders, they may be permitted to acquire majority stakes in Czech companies and, for the first time, manage the assets of pension funds. This means as well that they are no longer subject to investment fund regulations and oversight by the ministry of finance ("The Czech Republic" 1996, 43; "Czechs Plan Tighter" 1996).

Not addressed until early 1997, however, was the fact that most trades on the Prague Stock Exchange continued to take place outside the official markets, so that prices on the exchange often varied widely from those the investors were paying ("Czech Capital Markets" 1996). This issue was addressed in February 1997 when the authorities began to require daily instead of weekly reports on trades and prices in the over-the-counter markets. At the same time, the authorities created a new securities office that is expected to become independent within a year ("Czechs Act to Beef" 1997).

As early as the fall of 1995, it was clear that foreign investors had begun to take note of some of these prospective stock market changes. In October, a U.S. investor opted to invest $140 million through a newly created investment fund, the Stratton Fund, which contributed importantly to the market's liquidity and was intended to give fresh impetus to corporate restructuring ("U.S. Investor Revives" 1995). Moreover, in December, Bankers Trust, in an arrangement with Ceska Sporitelna, bought a forty percent stake in two Czech voucher funds, paying Kc 6.7 billion ($252 million) in notes due in 2000, making this investment the largest single investment in the region's equity markets ("Bankers Trust to Sell" 1995). Finally, two principal U.S. investors in the Czech market agreed in July 1996 to create a joint investment vehicle targeted not just at Czech companies, but also at others in the region. With a net worth of roughly $1.4 billion, the new company, Daventree, planned to seek stakes of more than fifty percent in companies in the region, before restructuring and selling them ("Bermuda Businessmen" 1996; "Investment Marriage" 1996).

Issues of Czech, Polish, and Hungarian Shares in Foreign Markets

Another source of equity flows, although far more modest than direct purchases by foreigners, has been the issuance of shares in foreign markets by Hungarian, Polish, and Czech firms between 1990 and 1994. Available

IMF data show that Polish firms raised $1 million in 1993 and Czech firms $10 million in 1994 (IMF 1995c, 25).

Hungarian firms have been far more active. They issued shares abroad totaling over $400 million between 1990 and 1994, roughly half of which were placed in 1994 (IMF 1995c, 25). The greater amount of share issuance abroad by Hungarian firms is explained in large part by the fact that most securities listed on the Budapest exchange also trade in markets outside Hungary, primarily in Austria, Germany, and the United Kingdom. Of the forty companies listed on the Budapest Stock Exchange in March 1995, twenty-eight were also listed on foreign exchanges, accounting for 91 percent of the Budapest exchange's total capitalization at the time. In addition, foreign ownership accounted for 57 percent of the capital held by these twenty-eight companies, and in some of these companies it exceeded 90 percent. A few Hungarian shares also trade in the United States (Budapest Stock Exchange 1995, 6).

As for recent activity, the Czech Republic's Komercni Banka offered $32 million in nonvoting depositary receipts to international investors in May 1995 (Czech National Bank 1995, 4) and made available a second tranche a year later, bringing to $140 million the total of the bank's shares held in global depositary receipts ("Komercni Banka in Further" 1996). Another Czech bank, Ceska Sporitelna, raised $48.5 million in early June 1996 ("Ceska Sporitelna Raises" 1996). Two large Polish companies, Optimus and Mostostal Export, raised $14 million in the first half of 1995 by these means, and Bank Gdanski, as part of its privatization, became Poland's first financial institution to offer shares to foreign investors through global depositary receipts ("Polish Bank Makes" 1995). In July 1995, Hungary's OTP Bank completed an international private placement for 20 percent of its shares ("Stake Placed" 1995, 16).

It is not surprising that private capital has only recently begun to flow into the countries of central and eastern Europe. After all, 1994 was the first year since 1989 that all three of the countries examined here—Hungary, the Czech Republic, and Poland—began to see some of their liberalization and restructuring efforts bear fruit as each registered significant gains in real growth. Private inflows allowed the three countries to incur a combined current account deficit of $9.5 billion over the 1990–1996 period and to accumulate almost $34 billion in reserves (figure 7.14). By enabling these countries to run larger current account deficits than would otherwise have been possible, the capital inflows contributed to an improvement in the countries' living standards, "directly through a greater variety (and higher quality) of imports of final goods and indirectly through imports of high quality capital and intermediate goods" (Calvo, Sahay, and Vegh 1995, 23).

Figure 7.14 External position of central European countries.

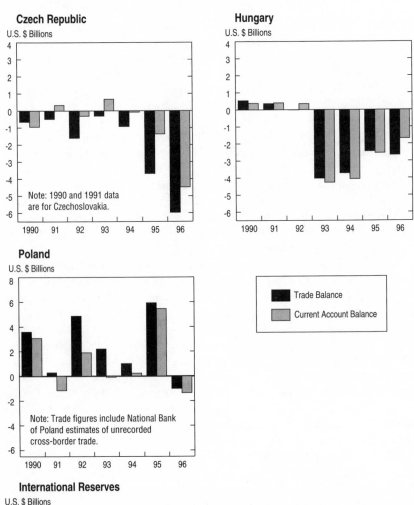

Czech Republic

U.S. $ Billions

Note: 1990 and 1991 data are for Czechoslovakia.

Hungary

U.S. $ Billions

Poland

U.S. $ Billions

Note: Trade figures include National Bank of Poland estimates of unrecorded cross-border trade.

■ Trade Balance

▨ Current Account Balance

International Reserves

U.S. $ Billions

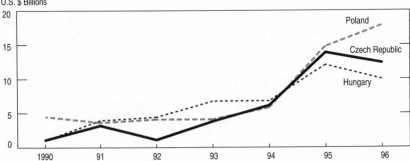

Poland

Czech Republic

Hungary

Sources: IMF *International Finacial Statistics;* IMF *Balance of Payment Statistics Yearbook;* National Bank of Poland *Information Bulletin.*

Nevertheless, as has been widely noted in the literature, capital inflows also bring concerns, one of the most important of which is a potential loss in competitiveness in global markets owing to real exchange rate appreciation. Of course, countries have a variety of policy options to mitigate the effects of capital inflows on their domestic economies, but none is without drawbacks, whether sterilizing inflows, reducing fiscal deficits, or imposing temporary capital controls.

What is of fundamental concern is how the imported capital is ultimately being used. If the capital goes to finance current consumption, it fails to contribute to the productive capacity of the economy and therefore cannot promote growth in the long run. But if the capital goes primarily to finance investment, there are few reasons for concern, assuming the investment is productively used and improves export-earning capacity. By this means, countries are able to earn the necessary foreign exchange to service their ongoing borrowing.

To date, the evidence on the uses of imported capital by the central and eastern European countries is mixed. Saving and investment rates clearly fell in all three countries in the early years of the postcommunist economic transformation (figure 7.15). This was to be expected, as households were obliged to draw on savings to maintain consumption levels or avoid seeing too sharp a falloff in consumption in the face of widespread cutbacks in state subsidies.

There are indications that investment levels are beginning to increase, although they are still far below those that prevailed before the transformation process got under way, particularly in the Czech Republic and Poland. Although Poland and the Czech Republic currently face gaps between saving and investment levels—the current account deficit that must be financed with foreign funds—the gap for Hungary, which had been the most pronounced, has recently been reversed.

What then should countries do if they wish to preserve the benefits of continued private capital inflows at the same time as they minimize the costs? The basic policy prescriptions are no less relevant for the countries of central and eastern Europe than they are for other developing countries. Avoidance of large external debt positions and attention to other aspects of macroeconomic stability reduce the risks of investing in these countries. To the extent that these reduced risks result in favorable credit ratings, countries may find their access to private capital eased and the price they must pay for it lower.

Structural reform remains crucial as well. Only with an infrastructure provided by a well-functioning banking and financial system will capital be allocated efficiently and money flow to its most productive uses. The amount of work that lies ahead for all countries in central and eastern Europe in these respects will be a challenge for many years. Progress will re-

Figure 7.15 Saving and investment ratios.

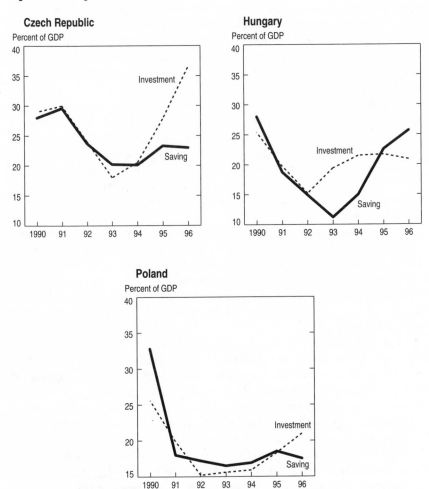

Sources: IMF *International Financial Statistics;* Reuters.

quire, among other things, modernization of telecommunications facilities, more efficient payment and settlement systems, recapitalization and privatization of the banking system, clarification of property rights, improvements in accounting and disclosure standards and investor protection laws, and development of sound supervisory and oversight institutions. Measures to boost labor mobility and improve pension systems are also needed (IBRD 1996). All of these reforms require time. What is most significant is that for Hungary, Poland, and the Czech Republic, the initial steps seem to be well under way.

The fact that private capital has begun to flow into these countries, despite the many challenges that they still confront, is a market vote of confidence in the potential these countries offer. If the countries, in turn, are able to hold firm to their course and not be swayed or felled by political backlashes, they stand to be the beneficiaries of potentially substantial inflows of private capital from abroad for many years to come.

References

"All Busy on the Western Front." 1995. *Business Eastern Europe,* October 30, p. 5.

"Bankers Trust to Sell Czech Shares to Western Funds." 1995. *Financial Times,* December 18.

BIS (Bank for International Settlements). *The Maturity, Sectoral and National Distribution of International Bank Lending.* Various issues.

"Bank Handlowy Taps Short-Dated Sector." 1997. *Financial Times,* May 1.

"Bank Handlowy Three-Year Offer Heavily Oversubscribed." 1996. *Financial Times,* May 1.

"Banking Crisis Besets Prague." 1996. *Financial Times,* November 11.

"Bermuda Businessmen Link to Fund Eastern European Groups." 1996. *Financial Times,* July 9.

Budapest Stock Exchange. 1995. "Five Years of the Budapest Stock Exchange," June. Budapest: Budapest Stock Exchange.

"Bull-Run Continues in Budapest." 1997. *Financial Times,* June 2.

Business Eastern Europe. 1995. September 4.

Calvo, Guillermo A., Ratna Sahay, and Carlos A. Vegh. 1995. "Capital Flows in Central and Eastern Europe: Evidence and Policy Options." Working Paper WP/95/57, International Monetary Fund, Washington, D.C.

CEC (Commission of the European Communities). 1994. "Private Capital Flows to CEECs and NIS." *European Economy* 3 (Supplement A, March): 1–9.

———. 1995. "Saving and Investment in Transition Countries." *European Economy* 7 (Supplement A, July): 1–15.

"Central European Economic Review." 1995. *Wall Street Journal Europe,* February, p. 32.

"Ceska Sporitelna Raises $48.5 Million with GDR Issue." 1996. *Financial Times,* June 3.

Chang, Joyce. 1995. "Looking for Value Outside of Latin America." Paper presented at Salomon Brothers Emerging Markets Seminar, August 15, New York.

"Cost of Borrowing in Hungary at New Low," 1996. *Financial Times,* November 29.

Creditanstalt. 1995a. *Central and Eastern Europe. Monthly Market Review* (July). Vienna: Creditanstalt.

——. 1995b. *Central European Quarterly.* Vol. 2. Vienna: Creditanstalt.

——. 1995c. *Central European Quarterly.* Vol. 3. Vienna: Creditanstalt.

——. 1996a. *Central European Quarterly.* Vol. 1. Vienna: Creditanstalt.

——. 1996b. *Central European Quarterly.* Vol. 2. Vienna: Creditanstalt.

——. 1996c. *Central European Quarterly.* Vol. 3. Vienna: Creditanstalt.

"Credit Rating Boost for Hungary." 1996. *Financial Times,* June 11.

CS First Boston. 1994. *Czech Stock Guide 1994* (January). Prague: CS First Boston.

"Czech Capital Markets Reformed." 1996. *Financial Times,* April 26.

"Czech Koruna Broadens Eurobond Currency Base." 1995. *Financial Times,* October 10.

Czech National Bank. 1995. *CNB Monthly Bulletin* (August). Prague: Czech National Bank.

——. 1996. *CNB Monthly Bulletin* (June). Prague: Czech National Bank.

"Czech Oil Refinery Deal Signed." 1995. *Financial Times,* June 19.

"The Czech Republic, the Second Time Around." 1996. *The Banker,* February.

"Czechs Abandon Currency Link with U.S. Dollar." 1997. *Financial Times,* May 27.

"Czechs Act to Beef Up Securities Laws, But Some Worry Changes Are Cosmetic." 1997. *Wall Street Journal,* February 7.

"Czechs Plan Tighter Bourse Rules." 1996. *Financial Times,* April 9.

"Czech Telecom Stake Sold for Record $1.5 Billion." 1995. *Financial Times,* June 29.

"Debt Fund Planned for Central and Eastern Europe." 1996. *Financial Times,* January 12.

"Eastern European Stock Markets Start to Attract Notice." 1995. *New York Times,* October 6.

"Eastern Europe Fund from Mercury." 1996. *Financial Times,* January 18.

EBRD (European Bank for Reconstruction and Development). 1997. *Transition Report 1996.* London: European Bank for Reconstruction and Development.

Economist Intelligence Unit. 1995. *Country Report on the Czech Republic and Slovakia, Third Quarter.* London: Economist Intelligence Unit.

——. *Country Reports.* London: Economist Intelligence Unit. Various issues.

"Elusive Benchmark of Emerging Markets." 1996. *Financial Times,* July 15.

"Emerging-Nation Markets to Receive Big Lift from New Indexes Created by World Bank Unit." 1996. *Wall Street Journal,* June 20.

"Fibremaker Gives Dress Rehearsal for Privatised Poland." 1996. *Financial Times,* July 18.

"First Zloty Eurobond." 1996. *Financial Times,* February 7.

"Foreign Investment in Eastern Europe Doubles." 1996. *Financial Times,* March 25.

"Fund Set Up for Central Europe." 1996. *Financial Times,* May 17.

Gilibert, Pier Luigi, and Alfred Steinherr. 1995. "Changing Investor Base, New Instrument and the Adjustment Process in the Emerging Markets Crisis of 1994–95." Paper presented at the conference on Private Capital Flows to Emerging Markets after Mexico, Institute of International Education and the Oesterreich National Bank, September 7–9, Vienna.

Girocredit. 1995. *Eastern European Chronicle* (January–February). Vienna: Girocredit.

"Hungarian Share Issue Well Received." 1996. *Financial Times,* July 9.

"Hungary's Sacrifices Begin to Pay Off." 1997. *Wall Street Journal,* July 16.

IBRD (International Bank for Reconstruction and Development). 1994–1995. *World Debt Tables 1994–95. External Finance through Privatization.* Vol. 1. Washington, D.C.: International Bank for Reconstruction and Development.

———. 1996. "From Plan to Market." *World Bank Development Report,* June.

IMF (International Monetary Fund), *Balance of Payments Statistics Yearbook.* Various issues. Washington, D.C.: International Monetary Fund.

———, *International Financial Statistics.* Various issues. Washington, D.C.: International Monetary Fund.

———. 1995a. *International Capital Markets,* August.

———. 1995b. *Private Market Financing for Developing Countries,* March.

———. 1995c. *Private Market Financing for Developing Countries,* November.

———. 1997. *Annual Report on Exchange Arrangements and Exchange Restrictions.* Washington, D.C.: International Monetary Fund.

ING Barings. *Emerging Markets Weekly Report.* New York and London: ING Barings. Various issues.

"Investment Marriage Made in the Bahamas." 1996. *Financial Times,* July 10.

"Investors Snap Up DM 250 Million Polish Eurobonds." 1996. *Financial Times,* July 10.

"Komercni Banka Eurobond." 1996. *Financial Times,* April 29.

"Komercni Banka in Further GDR Issue." 1996. *Financial Times,* May 13.

"Market Place." 1996. *New York Times,* April 5.

"MATAV to Syndicate $300 Million Loan." 1995. *Financial Times,* June 21.

National Bank of Hungary, *Monthly Report.* Budapest: National Bank of Hungary. Various issues.

National Bank of Poland, *Information Bulletin.* Warsaw: National Bank of Poland. Various issues.

"Piling into Central Europe." 1996. *Business Week,* July 1, p. 42.

PlanEcon. *PlanEcon Report.* Washington, D.C.: PlanEcon. Various issues.

Podkaminer, Leon. 1995. *Transition Countries: Economic Developments in Early 1995 and Outlook for 1995 and 1996.* Vienna Institute for Comparative Economic Studies, pt. 1, no. 219. Vienna.

"Poland Allows Foreign Buyers for Some Banks." 1996. *Financial Times*, July 1.

"Poland Plans Power Sell-off over Seven Years." 1996. *Financial Times*, March 13.

"Poland's Debut Meets Strong Demand." 1995. *Financial Times*, June 28.

"Poland: Set Loose the Dogs." 1995. *The Banker*, May, p. 25.

"Poland to Ease Capital Flows." 1996. *Financial Times*, March 28.

"Poles Leaping toward Privatization." 1997. *Financial Times*, May 13.

"Polish Bank Makes Its Debut in London." 1995. *Financial Times*, December 20.

"Polish Bank Plans $50 Million International Bond Issue." 1996. *Financial Times*, March 28.

"Polish Privatization Plan Survives Cabinet Changes." 1996. *Financial Times*, February 8.

"Prague Eases Exchange Controls." 1996. *Financial Times*, February 29.

"Stake Placed in Biggest Hungarian Bank." 1995. *American Banker*, July 10.

UNECE (United Nations Economic Commission for Europe). 1995. *Economic Survey of Europe*. New York: United Nations.

"U.S. Fund Managers Furious at Polish Sacking." 1996. *Financial Times*, May 3.

"U.S. Investor Revives Czech Stocks," 1995. *Financial Times*, October 23.

"World Bank Launches Record Czech Koruna Issue." 1995. *Financial Times*, December 21.

8

Foreign Investment and Political Economy in Russia

By Gail Buyske

Russia's inability to attract foreign investment has been a long tale of woe, replete with investors being erased from shareholder registries, companies such as IBM withdrawing due to insurmountable tax problems, and joint venture investors being manipulated out of their investments by their Russian partners. Yet, in 1996 and the first ten months of 1997, foreign investors contributed significantly to record-setting stock market growth of approximately 175 percent and 135 percent, respectively; as of mid-1997 fourteen Russian companies had issued American Depository Receipts (ADRs), and Prime Minister Chernomyrdin announced to the world's top financiers that Russia aimed to achieve 20 billion dollars in annual foreign investment by the end of this century.[1]

Do these positive developments indicate that the Russian foreign investment picture has changed significantly, and if so, how? I argue that an understanding of the foreign investment environment in Russia requires looking within the state and society to study the players that create and influence foreign investment policy. It also requires analyzing the institutional structure of the economy in which the foreign investment is made. This chapter unavoidably refers to events current in the fall of 1997, in an effort to illustrate the broader and more lasting themes concerning foreign investment in Russia.

In applying this analytical framework to Russia, it becomes clear that the most significant change in the 1996–1997 period was the ascendance of a reform team, headed by deputy prime minister Anatoliy Chubais, that saw foreign investment as a key to introducing greater competitiveness into the

---

1. The dollar-adjusted stock market figures are in Brown 1997; Chernomyrdin's speech, presented in Davos, Switzerland, is translated by David Crouch and reprinted in *Russia Review* (Chernomyrdin 1997).

Russian economy. Despite the team's impressive accomplishments, however, the most significant challenge has yet to be achieved: reversing the historic lack of a domestic constituency for foreign investment, particularly within the private sector. Without the development of such a constituency, the efforts of the reform team will last only as long as their tenure in office, and the environment for foreign investment in Russia will remain as unpredictable as it has been historically. Therefore I explore the political and institutional aspects of the foreign investment environment in Russia and the challenges entailed in creating an effective "pull" policy for potential foreign investors.[2]

The Current Status of Foreign Investment in Russia

The single most noteworthy characteristic of foreign investment in Russia is that it has been very low. Estimated foreign direct investment (FDI) for 1996 was $1.6 billion, with cumulative inflows over the previous five-year period of $5.1 billion, or a mere $34.00 per capita. These five-year per capita figures are lower than those of thirteen countries in eastern Europe, with the exception of only Macedonia. Russia's figures are particularly bleak by comparison with Hungary, the star regional performer, which boasts a five-year cumulative FDI per capita of $1,288.00 (European Bank for Research and Development 1997, 12, table 4). It is still too early to determine whether estimated FDI of $2 billion in the first half of 1997 reflects the beginning of a positive trend for Russia (Interfax 1997).

Portfolio investment in Russia, by contrast, leaped from under $1 billion in 1995 (Mileusnic 1996) to a reported $7.5 billion in 1996 (Bush 1997, 14), and approximately $4.5 billion in the first half of 1997 (Interfax 1997). Major contributing factors have been Russia's booming stock market, the partial opening of the profitable Russian treasury bill market to foreign investors, and Yeltsin's victory in the presidential elections of June 1996.

Even these strengthening figures, however, pale when compared with those of China, which is arguably the most relevant comparison for Russia because of China's large size, central planning legacy, extensive resources, and still-to-be-realized potential. In 1995, FDI in China of $35.8 billion and portfolio investment of $2.8 billion accounted for 5.5 percent of Chi-

---

2. "Pull" factors are related to the inherent attractiveness of the emerging market economy receiving foreign investment, in particular its foreign investment policies and the characteristics of its economy. "Push" factors refer to the economic and regulatory conditions within the developed market economies from which the foreign investment is made, in other words, if the conditions in the developed markets are not favorable for investment, funds are pushed out of those markets into emerging markets.

nese gross domestic product (GDP).[3] Comparable total investment figures for Russia were under 1 percent of GDP in 1995 and 2.7 percent in 1996 (or approximately 2.2 percent when Russia's shadow economy is taken into account) (World Bank 1997, 102, table 10). The enormous difference in FDI figures is particularly relevant because of the more permanent nature of FDI compared to portfolio investment, and its longer-term impact on a country's economy. Russia clearly has a long way to go to achieve Chernomyrdin's expectations and to pose significant competition to other emerging economies as a foreign investment location.

Why has Russia's share of foreign investment historically been low relative to that of other countries undergoing economic transitions? A study undertaken in 1995 at the request of the Analytical Center of the President of the Russian Federation concluded that the major obstacle to foreign investment in Russia was the shortcomings in its legal system, and in particular, concern over weak contract law and the enforceability of shareholder rights. The second and third largest disincentives, respectively, were economic risk and political risk (Halligan and Telplukhin 1995). Economic risks are defined in the study as high inflation, tax issues, currency risk, lack of business education by Russian counterparts, and low consumer demand.

A more recent 1997 survey of forty global market specialists showed little progress. Over 70 percent of the respondents rated the Russian government's efforts to develop and enforce "shareholder-friendly" legislation as only fair or poor, and 63 percent cited political instability as the primary investment risk. Fifty-nine percent of the respondents claimed a low degree of confidence in Russian accounting standards, which is a reflection of economic risk (Broadgate Consultants 1997). I believe that future survey results will not be markedly different unless a domestic constituency for foreign investment is created in Russia.

The Legal and Regulatory Environment for Foreign Investment

In this section I outline very briefly some of the key aspects of the legal and regulatory environment for foreign investment in Russia. This discussion is not intended to be a comprehensive treatment of this highly complex topic; its purpose is to provide a general framework for the arguments presented later in this chapter. I discuss recent positive trends, significant pending legislation, and specific restrictions on foreign investment in Russia.

3. The 1996 Chinese FDI figure was an even higher $42 billion. The 1996 figure is cited in Williams 1997.

There have been two recent positive developments for foreign investors in Russia. One has been the gradual removal of quantitative restrictions on foreign investment in Russia's lucrative government securities (GKO) market. Although the yield for foreign investors is still capped below that available to domestic investors, it is nevertheless attractive. Furthermore, effective as of 1998, all current restrictions on repatriating GKO profits will be removed.

Signs of a potentially emerging positive trend are also visible in Russia's privatization program, which earned a notorious reputation worldwide for the insider dominated "loans-for-shares" program that began in 1995 and appears to have ended in 1997. The Chubais team has committed to conducting the remaining privatizations on a fair and transparent basis. The assets still available, which include significant stakes in several oil companies, are of interest to many foreign investors. Also with regard to privatization, it should be noted that there were no restrictions on foreign participation in Russia's voucher privatization program, which was completed in mid-1994. However, there were logistical complications that made foreign participation a major challenge.

Whether this positive trend will continue depends on the fate of three pieces of legislation under consideration by the Duma. The first of these is the attempt by the Yeltsin administration to revise Russia's infamous tax regime. Russia has an overwhelming array of more than 200 types of taxes, which, if they were all paid, would easily put most companies out of business. According to the *Wall Street Journal,* for example, taxation was the primary reason why IBM Corporation closed its Russian computer production facility after two years of production (Banerjee 1996). The streamlined tax code under consideration in the Duma reduces the number of taxes to below thirty and eliminates all tax privileges, among other changes. The debate over this new tax code has already been protracted, however, and shows every sign of continuing in this vein.

Second is yet another draft investment law, which is intended to replace the outdated law of 1991. While a 1996 draft appeared to be moderately favorable to foreign investors, provisions in the draft that received its first Duma hearing in May 1997 caused an experienced American lawyer to call the draft "significantly flawed." Its shortcomings include weak grandfathering protection, the prohibition of international arbitration, and the lack of any significant inducements for foreign investors (Pettibone 1997).

Another long-lived and controversial piece of legislation was the originally much heralded production-sharing agreement (PSA) for foreign investment in the oil and gas industry. This law was adopted at the end of 1995 and was expected to facilitate foreign investment of over $60 billion in Russia's oil and gas industries. Two of several shortcomings in the final version of the law, however, were that all production sharing in "strategic" zones (which were not defined) must be approved by parliament, and that any production-sharing agreement can be amended if "circumstances change" (Lukyanov and Comerford 1996). As a result, PSAs for only 9 out of 250 identified locations have been approved since the adoption of this law. Efforts to amend the law and adopt the related framework legislation have been underway since this the law's passage.

Regarding explicit restrictions on foreign investment, there are three noteworthy limitations. With the exception of the long list of restricted and banned activities in the draft foreign investment law, the following restrictions are comparable to those established in other emerging markets:

1. As already noted, there are currently restrictions on foreign purchases of Russian government securities (GKOs).
2. The level of foreign participation in the banking sector, both in the form of foreign banks having a physical presence in Russia and in the form of purchases of Russian bank shares, is limited in the banking law by a ceiling that is controlled by the Duma (Article 12; "On Banks and Banking" 1995). The current ceiling is 12 percent of total Russian bank capital. It is important to note that there are no other explicit restrictions on foreign participation in Russia's equities market, although the related regulations, particularly those concerning the related foreign currency transactions, have historically been extremely burdensome. Considerable progress has been made to simplify these procedures.
3. The draft law on foreign investment enumerates the sectors of the economy in which foreign investment is either banned or restricted. Whereas some of these sectors, such as those related to defense or the environment, are reasonably included, the total of more than 100 restricted or banned activities is unusually—and prohibitively—high.

As this overview illustrates, the legal and regulatory environment for foreign investment in Russia is at a potential turning point. In a best-case scenario, the reform team would be able to push through a new tax code, a hospitable new foreign investment law, and an improved production-sharing law. However, although a congenial body of laws is a prerequisite to foreign investment, the political environment in which those laws are implemented is critical as well.

The Political Environment for Foreign Investment

To convey an understanding of the challenges in creating an effective pull policy for foreign investment in Russia, it is necessary to outline the positions of the major players in the foreign investment policy-making process in Russia.

As a result of the ascendance of the Chubais reform team, the executive branch is currently the major proponent of foreign investment in Russia. As I stress, however, this attitude reflects the reform agenda of a single individual, First Deputy Prime Minister Chubais, with the support of President Yeltsin. Should Chubais fall from grace, as he has in the past, the complexion of the executive branch's position on foreign investment is vulnerable to change as well.

Ministries that are clear supporters of foreign investment include the Ministry of Finance, headed by Chubais himself; the Ministry of Energy, headed by Deputy Prime Minister Nemtsov, a reformer equally as dedicated as Chubais; the GKI (privatization ministry); the Federal Securities Commission (which has ministerial status); and the Ministry of Economy. All of these organizations were headed by current or former Chubais protégés as of the fall of 1997.[4]

Not only are the heads of these organizations committed to the same reform principles as Chubais, but foreign investment assists the agenda of each of them to breathe greater competitiveness into their respective economic spheres. Russia's Federal Securities Commission, for example, has always viewed foreign investors as an important ally in building a level playing field for capital market participants, and in particular as a counterweight to Russia's powerful banks. Foreign investment assists the GKI as well in its efforts to create a transparent privatization process and maximize privatization revenue. The Ministry of Economy has also benefited from the current reform mode; although it has explicit responsibility for facilitating foreign investment and coordinating the government's foreign investment–related activities, it has historically not played a significant policy-setting role. More recently, however, with the focus on market-oriented reforms, this ministry has been carving out a more prominent position.

In contrast to the above, there are several entities within the executive branch that represent economic sectors that are highly vulnerable to the increased competition that foreign investment would entail. Although these organizations are not actively involved in creating framework foreign investment policies, they have an influential voice within the state apparatus. These entities include the ministries and other state entities related to the military-industrial complex and to heavy industry, as well as the Ministry of Agriculture.

---

4. Relations between Chubais and Dimitriy Vasiliev, director of the Federal Securities Commission, have cooled as a result of the struggle between the commission and the Russian central bank over the issue of bank participation in Russia's capital markets.

Russia's central bank is an important entity whose position on foreign investment is less readily identified. Under the leadership of Sergei Dubinin, the most professional of Russia's central bank governors to date, the central bank appears to be focusing on its monetary management responsibilities, with its position on foreign investment deriving from that primary responsibility. Periodically, however, the central bank makes an inexplicably hostile gesture toward foreign investors, leaving observers wondering about its underlying motivation.

In the fall of 1997, for example, when foreign investors in Russia were already anxious about the Asian emerging market contagion effect on Russia, the central bank announced unexpectedly that it would cease doing business with eleven major foreign financial institutions because of their failure to honor their securities transactions obligations. Russian banks were advised to follow the central bank's example. Not only did the so-called failures turn out to be standard market practice, but central bank department head, Irina Yasina, told *Kommersant Daily* that "we didn't give much thought to [the effect of our announcement on] the securities market" (Rushaylo 1997).

This inexplicable behavior recalled a similar event in 1995, when a xenophobic internal central bank memo found its way to the press. The memo, written by Andrei Kozlov, at that time a department head and now one of the bank's vice chairmen, argued that a proposal to restrict the activities of Russian banks on the capital markets was advocated by supporters of American financial institutions. According to excerpts in the *Financial Times*, these supporters were said to have a "thought-out strategy" to "seize strategic control in the division of property and the process of foreign investment in Russia" (Freeland 1995). Although this memo may have been the by-product of the central bank's long-standing and acerbic dispute with the securities commission over the role of Russian banks in Russia's securities markets, its release, like the more recent central bank announcement, reflects a remarkable lack of concern for foreign investor sentiment.

A final important player in the executive branch is Prime Minister Chernomyrdin, whose responsibilities extend to the legislative branch as well. As prime minister, Chernomyrdin officially supports foreign investment; he created some fanfare in the fall of 1994 with the formation of Russia's Foreign Investment Council, a high-level consultative body of senior Russian policy makers and seventeen major foreign investors.

However, as a politician and head of the right-of-center political party, Our Home is Russia, Chernomyrdin must be sensitive to nationalist and protectionist sentiments. Reflecting these pressures during the 1996 presidential campaign, Chernomyrdin was quoted by the *Wall Street Journal* as saying that "foreign states and transnational oil companies are trying to subordinate the [former Soviet states] to their rules of the game, to their economic interests" (World Wire 1996).

The ephemeral nature of executive branch policy making is reflected in the fact that Russia's prime minister could make such a public statement less than a year before the ascendance of the Chubais reform team. It is also worth noting, moreover, that Chernomyrdin was previously the chief executive of Gazprom, Russia's gas monopoly behemoth. As I discuss later, Russia's oil and gas sector has historically not welcomed foreign investment.

With regard to the Duma, the strongest and most readily identifiable lobby is in clear opposition to foreign investment. The members of this group include the Communist Party (35 percent of seats), the ultranationalist Zhirinovsky and his Liberal Democratic Party (11 percent), and the protectionist Agrarian Party (4 percent of seats). An illustrative *Moscow Times* op-ed piece by Communist Party Deputy Viktor Ilyukhin stated that "specialists warn that . . . foreign companies and banks will . . . buy up between 70 and 80 percent of the shares in Russian enterprises during the second stage of privatization. . . . If these tendencies continue . . . Russia's economy, natural resources and industrial potential may end up under the control of foreign firms and foreign governments" (Ilyukhin 1995).

As for other groups in the legislative branch, Yavlinsky's Yabloko Party and Gaidar's Russia's Choice Party could reasonably be expected to support foreign investment, because they are both headed by individuals who have a strong intellectual commitment to the development of a market economy. Neither, however, is impervious to lobbying. Even Gaidar, for example, was convinced to support the controversial limits on foreign bank activities that were established in 1993 when he was still prime minister. As of the fall of 1997 these two promarket groups accounted for approximately 12 percent of the Duma's members. Even in combination with Chernomyrdin's Our Home is Russia Party (12 percent of seats), it would be quite a battle for these promarket groups to force through any foreign investment legislation. Given the lack of a domestic private sector constituency for foreign investment, which is discussed later, an astute politician could reasonably wonder whether it is really worth it.

The Private Sector

The lack of a domestic constituency for foreign investment is the pivotal characteristic of the foreign investment environment in Russia. Such a constituency, if it existed, would have two key characteristics: (1) the potential to benefit substantially from foreign investment, and (2) sufficient political and financial clout to influence the policy-making process. Although there are two groups that meet these requirements, both of them have historically resisted foreign investment.

Russia's oil and gas sector is one of two groups whose position on foreign investment is critical. As the source of almost 50 percent of Russia's exports, the sector's financial weight is unmatched. The sector also has strong political connections: for example, Prime Minister Chernomyrdin was formerly the head of Gazprom; central bank chairman Dubinin was previously a director of Imperial Bank, Russia's seventeenth largest bank, in which Gazprom is a significant shareholder; and Deputy Director of the National Security Council Berezovsky owns a significant share of Sibneft, Russia's seventh largest oil company.

Furthermore, it is well documented that Russia's oil and gas sector would benefit substantially from increased foreign investment. A 1996 study undertaken by the Russian Academy of Sciences together with the Petroleum Advisory Forum (a trade group for foreign oil companies) concluded that the implementation of six large PSAs would expand Russian GDP by $450 billion (the 1996 GDP was approximately $360 billion) and create an average of 400,000 new jobs a year (Gordon 1997a). Furthermore, in the absence of foreign investment, Russian oil production is projected to fall to 3.6 million barrels a day within the next five years, down from 6 million barrels a day in 1997 and 12 million barrels a day in 1987 (Gordon 1997a).

Rather than seeking such investment, however, the industry on the whole avoids it. Recent examples include the suspicious breakdown of negotiations concerning a $28 billion Amoco project in which Amoco had already invested $100 million, and the annulment, due to unspecified "legal irregularities," of a multi-billion-dollar project awarded to Exxon in competitive bidding (Gordon 1997a).

The second relevant group is Russia's banking sector. The political weight of Russia's top bankers has been extensively documented. They are widely acknowledged, for example, to have played the key role in financing Yeltsin's 1996 presidential campaign, as well as in bringing Chubais back from political exile to run that campaign. In a much-referenced interview, Boris Berezovsky, one of Russia's wealthiest entrepreneurs, told the *Financial Times* in the fall of 1996 that acknowledgment of the bankers' support was evidenced by his own appointment as deputy director of Russia's National Security Council, and the appointment of Vladimir Potanin, chairman of Oneximbank, Russia's fourth largest bank, to a deputy prime minister position (Freeland, Thornhill, and Gowers 1996). The influence of these financiers has become so widely acknowledged that Russians commonly refer to the *semibankirshchina,* or the "era of the seven bankers."[5]

For Russia's banks, The principal advantage of increased foreign investment is the opportunity to intermediate those funds, which have the po-

5. These seven bankers are Berezovsky. Potanin, Khodorkovsky of Bank Menatep, Gussinsky of Most-Media (which includes Most-bank). Smolensky of Stolichny Bank, and Aven and

tential to be in the tens of billions of dollars. In addition, Russian banks are positioned to benefit from the associated economic growth of foreign investment; one study estimates that each dollar of FDI in an emerging economy is associated with $0.50 to $1.30 in additional domestic investment (Chuhan, Perez-Quinos, and Popper 1996). Russian banks could intermediate this "multiplier effect" investment as well.

Given the identifiable advantages of foreign investment, why would these two powerful groups not support it? In the case of the oil and gas sector, the answer is fear of losing control. For the senior management of these organizations, this fear extends beyond the prosaic concern over job loss to the fear of losing myriad other benefits that senior managers can reap in Russia's still vacuum ridden corporate governance environment. The classic example is provided by Rem Vyakhirev, current chairman of Gazprom, who signed a secret trust deed with the government in 1994 that, among other benefits, enabled Gazprom's management to vote a 35 percent block of shares according to the management's wishes. ("How Now, Cash Cow," 1997) The actual agreement could not even be located until Deputy Prime Minister Nemtsov raised it as a public issue in a television interview (Thornhill 1997b). (The agreement has since been amended.)

Russia's bankers have potentially even more to lose. First, they are tantalizingly close to the seat of power. Second, Russia's banks have been able to take advantage of their close state ties, together with a relatively closed domestic economy, to amass extensive holdings in Russia's corporate sector. These holdings take the form of financial industrial groups (FIGs) or other conglomerate arrangements that link banks and enterprises.[6]

Many of these conglomerates have been spearheaded by banks, with oil and gas investments as part of their portfolio. Examples include Oneximbank's majority holding in Sidanco, Russia's fourth largest oil company, and the majority holding of Bank Menatep, Russia's ninth largest bank, in Yukos, Russia's second largest oil company. In addition, however, the oil and gas companies have also created their own "industrial financial groups." Examples are provided by Gazprom, with investments in Bank Imperial and National Reserve Bank (Russia's tenth largest bank), and by Lukoil, with an investment in Bank Imperial.

Friedman of the Alfa Group (which includes Alfa Bank). It should be noted that Berezovsky's original financial base was the national car dealership Logovaz, which he founded. Berezovsky's banking interest, Obedinnennyi Bank, is considerably smaller than the other six banks.

6. FIGs are formed on the basis of Russia's 1995 Law on Financial-Industrial Groups to "realize investment or other projects and programs aimed at increasing competitiveness, broadening the market of goods and services, improving efficiency of production, and creating new jobs" (Article 2). The law allows FIGs to apply for preferential treatment in such areas as taxation, financing, and depreciation. At least half of Russia's twenty largest banks are involved in formal FIGs or FIG-like arrangements.

These holdings were acquired by a variety of methods, including through Russia's voucher privatizations. Russia's banks have also successfully fought their way into Russia's capital markets, backed by the central bank in its ongoing battle with the securities commission over control of those markets. As a result of the banks' efforts, there are no significant restrictions on the banks' ability to trade and invest in corporate securities, particularly by means of subsidiaries or holding company structures.[7]

But the most significant investment boon for the banks, as well as the most egregious example of the payoff for the banks' support of the Yeltsin administration, was the much-publicized loans-for-shares program. In this series of transactions, which began in 1995, major banks acquired significant holdings in major industrial assets at below-market prices in overtly insider transactions. One of the many examples is Bank Menatep's $309 million acquisition of 78 percent of Yukos, Russia's second largest oil company, in an auction managed by Bank Menatep itself. (As of mid-1997 Yukos' market capitalization was over $4.5 billion.) Bank Menatep went so far as to predict in advance of the auction that it would be the winner (Gulyayev 1995).

Finally, it should be noted that the banks have not limited themselves to investments in industry and natural resources; they have also expanded quite deeply into the newspaper and television industry. A partial list of examples includes the Most-Media Group's (whose Most-bank is Russia's eleventh largest bank) controlling ownership in the television station NTV (also 30 percent owned by Gazprom), and its investments in the daily newspaper *Sevodnya* and weekly magazine *Itogy;* Oneximbank's investments in the daily newspapers *Izvestiya* and *Komsomolskaya Pravda* (Gazprom also owns 20 percent), and its founding of the weekly magazine *Russkiy Telegraf;* and Berezovsky's 20 percent holding in TV6 and 8 percent holding in ORT, the majority state-owned television station.

Under the current scenario, therefore, increased foreign investment poses the risk to Russian bankers that this comfortable, profitable, and protected environment will be destroyed. Foreign banks in particular pose a significant threat; whereas Russia's banks are major players in their home territory, they are surprisingly small by international standards. For example, the *combined* total assets of Russia's ten largest banks as of the end of 1996 were the equivalent of approximately 22 percent of the total assets of the Chase Manhattan Bank on the same date.[8] It is not surprising that Russia's banks were adamant about limiting the presence of foreign banks in

---

7. Russian banks are prohibited by central bank regulations from making equity investments that, in total, exceed 25 percent of bank capital. The creation of other corporate structures, together with the lack of a requirement for the banks to consolidate subsidiaries for accounting purposes, has easily allowed the banks to sidestep this requirement.

8. As was noted, Russian banks are not required to consolidate their subsidiaries.

Russia; in 1993, for example, pressure from the banks forced Yeltsin to retroactively reduce the scope of eight foreign bank licenses that had already been issued.[9]

In the context of resistance to foreign investment, it is also important to note the attitude of a third group, the Russian population at large, including that of the managers of medium and small enterprises in less influential sectors of the economy. The first factor to stress is that the Russian corporate sector continues to be largely hostile to any outside shareholders, whether domestic or foreign. As of 1996, outsiders were the majority owners of only 19.8 percent of Russian companies, compared to majority employee ownership of 64.7 percent. This majority employee ownership figure actually represents an increase from 59.0 percent in 1995 (Blasi, Kroumova, and Kruse 1997, 193, table 5). It would appear that the results of a 1995 study of managers of privatized companies conducted by Andrei Volgin, chairman of the Moscow Shareholders' Rights Committee, remain relevant. According to the *Financial Times,* this study revealed that 90 percent of the managers did not want to raise additional capital because they placed a higher priority on retaining control of their companies (Thornhill 1995).

The second factor to consider is that historic Russian nationalism, combined with disappointment—and even resentment—with the failure of the mature market economies to make the expected contribution to the Russian economic transition, makes foreign investors particularly suspect. As one former senior minister acknowledged off the record, no matter how much the government stresses the advantages of foreign investment, such as increased employment and the fact that foreign investors are putting their own money at risk, the Russian population remains intuitively suspicious. While this third category does not constitute an identifiable interest group, as do the oil and gas sector and the banking sector, its attitude also does not facilitate the foreign investment environment.

The Outlook

In view of this bleak scenario, how can the recent upward trend in foreign investment figures be explained? From the investor side, the main incentives have been the perceived decline in political risk following Yeltsin's reelection, combined with a belief that Russia represents one of the world's last undervalued markets. However, it takes two to tango; the most noteworthy change on the Russian side is that Russian entities themselves have begun to seek foreign investors more actively. The issuance of ADRs by

9. Pressure from the European Union ultimately resulted in Yeltsin's lifting of the retroactive limitations on foreign banks from countries that had investment protection treaties with Russia.

fourteen Russian companies as of mid-year 1997 is a particularly striking illustration of this trend, because these instruments are aimed specifically at foreign investors.

The key question that all foreign investors and the Chubais team, or any subsequent reform team, should ask is: why are Russians turning to foreign investors? The deceptively simple answer, for now, is that they need the money. As a result of the successful deficit-reducing budgets of 1996 and 1997, there is less money in the Russian economy to fund projects. Governments at all levels must now scrutinize their expenditures more carefully. Russian banks, which were never a significant source of funding in any case, must now cope with the declining treasury bill yields caused by lower inflation. As a result of this tighter financial environment, barter transactions are estimated to account for up to 50 percent of all commercial transactions in Russia, and according to Russian newspaper *Rossiyskaya Gazeta,* investment in fixed capital is under 20 percent of the 1990 level ("Financier's Column" 1997).

The simple fact that Russian companies (as well as all levels of government) need more money, however, is insufficient to develop the necessary constituency for foreign investment. The benefits of foreign investment are maximized when the foreign investor contributes more than just money. Foreign investment can also result in technology transfers and, perhaps even more important but less quantifiable, the transfer of "knowledge capital."

The World Bank describes knowledge capital as "the possession of highly specialized, intangible assets, such as knowledge about how to produce cheaper or better-quality products at given input prices, ability to innovate, special skills in design, styling, promotion, marketing, or sales, or possession of a trademark or brand with a strong customer following" (World Bank 1997, 38). Knowledge capital is intrinsic to a company and therefore cannot be effectively transferred by sale, leasing, or imitation. Yet knowledge capital is considered to be a growing factor in a company's success. In the United States, for example, measured intangible capital (training, research and development, etc.) was the approximate equivalent of physical stock in the mid-1970s, but by 1990, it exceeded physical stock by 15 percent (World Bank 1997; Abramovitz and David 1996).

A simple example of the impact of knowledge capital can be provided by comparing two cases. In one case McDonald's invests $1 million in a chain of Russian restaurants. The owner of the restaurant has made it clear to McDonald's that he knows his business and simply needs a source of equity capital that is currently unavailable from Russian sources. In the second case, McDonald's invests only $500,000 and spends the other $500,000 to send its staff and senior management to the restaurants in the chain to work with the Russians on a daily basis.

It is not difficult to predict that, even without a specific technology transfer, the investment in the second case will have a more profound impact on the Russian economy, as the accumulated expertise of the McDonald's staff is conveyed to the Russian employees in myriad, often imperceptible, ways. It should be stressed that this expertise concerns not just the restaurant business, but is specific to how McDonald's manages the restaurant business. It is knowledge that is unique to McDonald's employees. No amount of classroom training, translation of manuals, or hiring of consultants can transfer this knowledge capital as effectively as the investor itself.

Until the difference between these two investment effects is fully appreciated by the Russian corporate sector, there will be no constituency for foreign investment in Russia. Until then, Russian companies will seek foreign money only when there is a shortage of domestic money. Furthermore, because of the control concerns already outlined, these companies will deliberately seek to structure their foreign funding in a way that minimizes the potential nonfinancial impact of the funding. As a result, not only will the Russian economy not experience the full benefit of this funding, but the more extensive advantages of foreign investment will not be demonstrated.

A brief review of the foreign investment figures cited earlier illustrates this phenomenon. Russian FDI has shown little growth between 1991 and 1996. The 1996 FDI figure was $1.6 billion, compared with $42 billion in China. The real growth has been in portfolio investment, which increased from under $1 billion in 1995 to a reported $7.5 billion in 1996. Although these figures should be treated as approximations, both because of data accuracy problems and because an investment that is recorded as a portfolio investment might have FDI intentions or characteristics, the relevant point is that the growth has been in investments that are typically characterized by ease of exit.

What might cause this scenario to change in favor of the foreign investor? Should estimated FDI of $2 billion in the first half of 1997 be considered the beginning of a positive trend? Ironically, the answer lies in the Russian banking sector, which has lobbied successfully in the past to limit foreign competition within its own industry. The Russian banking sector is currently as a crossroads. The top Russian banks have amassed enormous financial resources, including extensive industrial holdings, and they are at the pinnacle of political power. Where will they go next?

One scenario calls for more of the same. The names of the players will inevitably change, but the rules of the game will be the same: the banks will have a close—and closed—partnership with the state, characterized by bank support for specific political figures and projects, in return for preferential treatment by the state.

The second scenario is that the banks themselves will destroy this cozy relationship as a result of the inevitable competition between them. Rather than limiting themselves to competing for state spoils, one or more banks may deliberately turn to other arenas of competition. Foreign investment is one such arena.

A harbinger of this development could be the highly controversial purchase of 25 percent of the shares of Svyazinvest, Russia's telecommunications monopoly, in the summer of 1997 by a consortium headed by Oneximbank. The consortium included several foreign investors, most notably among them George Soros, who contributed close to $1 billion to the $1.9 billion deal (Banerjee 1997). The controversy was multifaceted, but the relevant issue for this discussion is Oneximbank's claim that the losers were bitter because the sale had been awarded to the highest bidder, rather than through the usual backroom deal. Another significant aspect of this purchase is that Oneximbank could not have financed the purchase on its own. Not only were Oneximbank's total assets at the beginning of 1997 under $4 billion, but Oneximbank also had to finance its loans-for-shares-related purchase of 38 percent of Norilsk Nickel, the world's largest nickel producer, one month later. Oneximbank was forced to turn to foreign sources of funds to afford its Svyazinvest purchase.[10]

A pivotal question is whether Soros and the other investors will play an active or passive role in managing the Svyazinvest investment and therefore whether Svyazinvest—and even Oneximbank—is able to benefit from the broader and less tangible features of foreign investment. As of the fall of 1997, the outlook was moderately positive, particularly because Oneximbank was in the process of merging its investment banking arm with Renaissance Capital, a maverick investment banking firm founded by aggressive former staff of Credit Suisse First Boston. More than any of the other large Russian banks, Oneximbank has positioned itself to play two games: the internal Russian political game and the competitive foreign investment game.

Still, the fate of foreign investment in Russia, and the possible development of a constituency for this investment are likely to remain a sideshow to the other major issues that are currently playing out. Most notably, the relationship among Russia's top banks, and their relationship with the state, turns primarily on the presidential elections scheduled for the year 2000. If the banks cannot agree on a single promarket candidate for this

---

10. The bank also issued a $200 million Eurobond in July. Note also that the Norilsk Nickel acquisition, at a cost of approximately $620 million, including related buyer obligations, was arguably a return to the backroom deals; Oneximbank paid an estimated effective price of $8.85 per share, compared with the market price of $15.00 (Thornhill 1997a).

election, there is a serious risk that a conservative (antimarket) candidate could win the presidency. While the banks are continuing to compete with each other for a variety of spoils, this much more fundamental issue looms.

One must remember that the bank-state relationship is a two-way street; should one or more banks decide to break away and seek their fortune by spearheading genuine competition in the Russian economy, a prerequisite for success is that the state allow this to happen. The downside for the state is that such a development would reduce its current ability to influence the banks' activities.

As of the fall of 1997, the messages on this topic were mixed. President Yeltsin made a much publicized speech in which he stressed that "the state [will not] tolerate any attempts to bring pressure on it on the part of the business community and the banks" (Gordon 1997b). This pronouncement was accompanied by a number of related statements by Chubais and Nemtsov. Chubais, in a representative statement, was quoted in *Nezavisimaya Gazeta* as asking rhetorically, "What kind of capitalism are we building? Do we want two, three, five or ten giant financial structures to chart Russia's development and make political decisions to be advised to the authorities later on?" (1997). Nevertheless, at the associated meeting with six of Russia's top bankers, Yeltsin also raised the possibility of meeting more frequently with the banks in the future. As some observers noted, this could be the precursor to the development of an industrial policy in Russia characterized by continued close cooperation and the fostering of mutual interests between the banks and the state. In other words, both options remain open.

In summary, the environment for foreign investment in Russia has always been characterized by considerable—and conflicting—noise. One major Russian company is on an investor road show while another is erasing shareholders from its registry; a powerful administration figure proclaims Russia's sincere intent to facilitate foreign investment while the Duma drafts inhospitable legislation. Beyond this noise and beyond even the activities and pronouncements of any specific administration, the question to ask is: where is the domestic constituency for foreign investment? The players to follow in answering this question are in Russia's banking sector. The players may change in the future, but the key question remains the same.

References

Abramovitz, M., and P. A. David. 1996. "Technological Change and the Rise of Intangible Investments: The U.S. Economy's Growth Path in the Twentieth Century." In *Employment and Growth in the Knowledge-Based*

Economy. Paris: Organization for Economic Cooperation and Development.

Banerjee, Neela. 1996. "IBM's Plan to Close Venture in Russia is New Black Mark for Investment There." *Wall Street Journal,* February 29, p. A14.

———. 1997. "Svaz: Fair or Fixed?" *Russia Review,* August 25, p. 18f.

Blasi, Joseph R., Maya Kroumova, and Douglas Kruse. 1997. *Kremlin Capitalism: The Privatization of the Russian Economy.* Ithaca, N.Y.: Cornell University Press.

Broadgate Consultants, Inc. 1997. *International Investment Trends: Russia.* Broadgate Consultants, Inc., New York. Duplicated.

Brown, Jeffrey. 1997. "Russia Keeps Up Momentum." *Financial Times,* October 20, p. 26.

Bush, Keith. 1997. "The Russian Economy in June 1997." Center for Strategic and International Studies, Washington, D.C. Duplicated.

Chernomyrdin, Viktor. 1997. Translated by David Crouch. *Russia Review,* February 24, 1997, pp. 20–22.

Chuhan, P., G. Perez-Quiros, and H. Popper. 1996. *International Capital Flows: Do Short-Term Investment and Direct Investment Differ?* Washington, D.C.: World Bank and International Finance Corporation.

European Bank for Research and Development. 1997. *Transition Report Update 1997.* London: European Bank for Research and Development.

"Financier's Column." 1997. *Rossiyskaya Gazeta,* September 25.

Freeland, Chrystia. 1995. "Moscow Suspicion Grows." *Financial Times,* January 19, p. 3.

Freeland, Chrystia, John Thornhill, and Andrew Gowers, 1996. "Wealthy Clique Emerges from Kremlin Gloom." *Financial Times,* October 31, p. 2.

Gordon, Michael R. 1997a. "The Gusher That Wasn't in Russia." *New York Times,* September 5, p. D1f.

———. 1997b. "Yeltsin Moves to Insure Greater Free-Market Competition." *New York Times,* September 25, p. A3.

Gulyayev, Michael. 1995 "Menatep Sets Sights on Yukos Takeover." *Moscow Times,* November 10, p. 1f.

Halligan, L., and P. Teplukhin. 1995. "Investment Disincentives in Russia." Analytical Center of the President of the Russian Federation, Moscow. Duplicated.

"How Now, Cash Cow." 1997. *Economist,* November 29, p. 65.

Interfax, September 25, 1997.

Ilyukhin, Viktor. 1995. "Russia's Security Crisis. *Moscow Times,* weekly edition, June 18, p. 22.

Lukyanov, Sergey, and Mike Comerford. 1996. "Oil Law Still a Mess." *Russia Review,* January 15, p. 21.

Mileusnic, Natasha. 1996. "Bust Looms for Brokers as Market Slows." *Moscow Times,* February 20, p. 10.

Nezavisimaya Gazeta. 1997. "Yeltsin Goes to Oryol to Claim Global Power Role for Russia." September 18. Reprinted in *Johnson's Russia List,* September 18, 1997.

"On Banks and Making Activities in the Russian Federation." 1995.

Pettibone, Peter J. 1997. "Draft Russian Law on Foreign Investment May Restrict Investors." *Eastern European Newsletter* 7 (July):122–124.

Rushaylo, Pyotr. 1997. "Bank Rossii Svoikh." *Kommersant Daily,* November 18, p. 1.

Thornhill, John. 1995. "Cash Stays under the Bed." *Financial Times,* April 10, Russia supplement, p. 4.

——. 1997a. "Banking Chief Plays by New Rules of Russian Finance." *Financial Times,* August 7, p. 2.

——. 1997b. "No Standing on Ceremony as Yeltsin Seizes the Moment." *Financial Times,* December 3, p. 2.

Williams, Frances. 1997. "Foreign Investment Builds Up." *Financial Times,* September 23, p. 4.

World Bank. 1997. *Global Economic Prospects and the Developing Countries.* Washington, D.C.: World Bank.

World Wire. 1996 "Russia Sees Energy Threat." *Wall Street Journal,* May 14, p. A17.

9

Alternative Approaches to Financial Crises in Emerging Markets

Jeffrey D. Sachs

Developing countries fall into international financial crises for a variety of reasons, including fiscal profligacy, exchange rate mismanagement, international financial shocks, financial liberalization, and weaknesses in the domestic banking sector. Market expectations may play an independent role in a financial crisis by triggering a self-fulfilling financial panic. International public policy should be aimed first and foremost at avoiding financial crises but must also be prepared to ameliorate financial crises after they begin.

Despite ample experience with financial crises in the past decade, there are still serious differences of opinion with regard to how best to avoid them and properly manage them whenthey occur. These differences relate to the appropriate roles of exchange rate policy, banking policy, fiscal policy, and the international institutions. Here I review the lessons of the past decadeto draw some policy conclusions for developing-country governments and international institutions such as the International Monetary Fund (IMF), World Bank, and Bank for International Settlements (BIS).

Avoiding International Financial Crises

At the risk of gross analytical oversimplification (and in lieu of formal models), I focus on three main types of international financial crises that plague emerging market economies:

The information in this chapter was prepared as background for discussion during meetings at the Bank for International Settlements in Switzerland, December 1995. The paper was not updated to include the East Asian crisis of 1997–1998. For details on the most recent crisis, see Radelet and Sachs 1998.

1. *Fiscal crises.* The government abruptly loses the ability to roll over foreign debts and attract new foreign loans, possibly forcing the government into rescheduling or default of its obligations.
2. *Exchange crises.* Market participants abruptly shift their demands from domestic-currency assets to foreign-currency assets, depleting the foreign exchange reserves of the central bank in the context of a pegged exchange rate system.
3. *Banking crises.* Commercial banks abruptly lose the ability to roll over market instruments (i.e., certificates of deposit [CDs]) or meet a sudden withdrawal of funds from sight deposits, thereby throwing the banks into illiquidity and possibly insolvency.

Although these three types of crises are logically distinct and in some cases come in a pure form, they often arrive in combination because common underlying shocks or market expectations are likely to operate simultaneously in the market for government bonds, the foreign exchange market, and the market for bank assets.

Regardless of the type of financial crisis, we find four distinct triggering mechanisms. The first is an *exogenous shock* to markets, causing market agents to reassess the ability of the government, the central bank, or the commercial banks, to meet various intertemporal commitments. For example, the collapse of the terms of trade of an oil-rich country may call into question the debt-servicing capacity of the government, thereby reducing its creditworthiness. Or a terms-of-trade collapse might lower domestic prices, in turn undermining the solvency of the banking system and thereby provoking a banking crisis. Frequently, a rise in world interest rates undermines the ability of the government or the banks to obtain further loans.

The second possible cause of financial crisis is an inadvertent *policy shock*, in which a policy reform in one market triggers an adverse market reaction in another part of the economy. For example, money market liberalization might cause a rise of money market interest rates, which in turn leads to disintermediation of the commercial banks, and then to a banking crisis. Alternatively, if the government was borrowing at low domestic interest rates, internationalization of financial markets might cause a hardening of terms for government borrowing, leading to a fiscal crisis.

The third possible cause of crisis is the *exhaustion of borrowing limits*, whether by the government, the central bank, or the commercial banks. All market borrowers have borrowing limits determined by their intertemporal solvency and institutional constraints (e.g., prudential limits on borrowing that govern the borrowers and the creditors). In some cases, these limits produce boom-bust cycles in which the borrower incurs debts very quickly up to the borrowing limit and then suddenly is unable to borrow further beyond that point. This may lead to a crisis of the borrower itself (if the arrival at the borrowing limit is not properly anticipated) or to a crisis among other borrowers in the economy, if the sudden cutoff of funding leads to a sharp shift in market conditions.

Suppose, for example, that after the end of capital controls, a country's commercial banks borrow very heavily in international capital markets, until their borrowing limit is reached. Initially the borrowing will lead to a boom in domestic spending, as the banks intermediate a large flow of foreign loans. This initial boom will also tend to produce a real exchange rate appreciation. Once the banks are fully borrowed, the inflows stop, the domestic credit markets tighten, domestic demand declines. and there is almost surely the need for an exchange rate depreciation to reverse the preceding appreciation. This kind of boom-bust cycle in bank borrowing abroad contributed to the onset of the 1994–1995 financial crises in Argentina and Mexico.

The fourth possible cause of crisis is a *self-fulfilling panic.* In almost all financial markets, asset prices may be subject to multiple "rational" equilibriums, including highly adverse equilibriums such as government bond crises, foreign exchange crises, or banking crises. Self-fulfilling panics are well known and have been discussed and debated for nearly two centuries, even if there remain important differences of opinion about their likelihood and frequency. Consider three cases of panic, one for each of our paradigmatic financial crises.

A self-fulfilling fiscal crisis emerges when the markets "rationally" expect the default of an illiquid but solvent government borrower (Sachs 1995b; and Sachs, Tornell, and Velasco 1996a). Suppose that the government has a solvency limit of $100 billion (equal to the discounted value of future taxation that can be devoted to debt servicing) and a current debt of $50 billion in short-term liabilities. Suppose also that the maximum debt-servicing capacity in any one year is far below $50 billion. Individual creditors will be happy to roll over their claims on the government and even increase their exposure if they are confident that other creditors will continue to lend. But if a panic begins, and each creditor believes that the other creditors will withdraw their short-term claims, then the individual creditors will also call in their claims. The government will find itself unable to borrow and may be pushed into default because it is unable to come up with $50 billion in short-term revenues.

A self-fulfilling foreign exchange crisis can similarly arise (Obstfeld 1996). Suppose that the government is defending a mildly overvalued exchange rate, trading off higher unemployment for lower inflation in the short term. An exchange rate attack begins in which market participants believe that the central bank will choose to devalue to reduce short-term unemployment. To defend the exchange rate, the central bank would have to raise interest rates sharply, which would do grave damage to the banking system and the real economy. Therefore, the central bank decides to forego a defense of the currency and resets the rate at a more competitive level in line with the sudden shift in market expectations. In this way, there may be two rational market expectations: no devaluation (and no panic), or panic followed by devaluation.

A self-fulfilling banking panic is the most familiar (Diamond and Dybvig 1983). A bank's business is to engage in maturity transformation, taking on short-term liabilities and long-term assets. This maturity transformation exposes banks to the possibility of a bank run. Individual depositors begin a panicked withdrawal of funds, based on the belief that other depositors are also withdrawing their funds. Each depositor knows that the bank lacks the funds in the short-run to meet all demands for withdrawals. In this way, an otherwise solvent bank can be pushed into insolvency.

Based on theory and recent experience, can we draw certain policy prescriptions about how to avoid financial crises, other than the obvious ones of fiscal discipline, realistic exchange rate policy, banking supervision, and the like? I think the answer is yes, with the proviso that a full treatment of the issues here requires a vastly more detailed analysis and argumentation. There are, nonetheless, several general lessons that can be gleaned from recent cases.

Exchange Rates

Strictly pegged exchange rates raise the risks of financial crises, and therefore should be used only in very specific circumstances.

Consider the various sources of financial crises. Adverse external shocks (e.g., a fall in the terms of trade), a rise in world interest rates, or a shift in world demand against a country's exports, tend to require a real depreciation that is extremely difficult to achieve through internal deflation (as opposed to currency depreciation). Similarly, the exhaustion of external borrowing limits (as when a government has accumulated a heavy load of foreign debt) typically requires the shift from current account deficit to current account surplus, which in turn requires a real exchange rate appreciation.

Market participants know that pegged exchange regimes are fragile in the face of adverse external shocks, therefore, they are likely to speculate against pegged rates in the face of such shocks. Either the defense of the pegged rate will prove very costly as a result of such speculation (as in Argentina in 1995), or more likely, the market pressures will lead to the abandonment of the pegged rate (as in several European countries in the exchange rate mechanism [ERM] in 1992, or Mexico in 1994). Obstfeld and Rogoff (1995) offer similar conclusions.

Perhaps less obviously, self-fulfilling panics are much easier to handle or can be obviated entirely by implementing floating exchange rate regimes instead of pegged rate regimes. Consider the case in which the government owes debts of 50 billion in local currency such as pesos, with a solvency limit of 100 billion pesos. As noted earlier, a self-fulfilling panic can ensue, even though the government is not at its solvency limit, if each creditor believes that other creditors will stop lending. The government is pushed into default. In a floating exchange rate regime, the central bank can stop the panic by standing behind the government, promising to offer credits to the government so that the government can avoid default on its market debts. The knowledge that the central bank stands ready to provide credit to the government to prevent a default is enough to rule out a default as a rational equilibrium. Under fixed rates, by contrast, the central bank would be less able or willing to act as a lender of last resort, unless of course, the central bank has 50 billion pesos worth of foreign exchange or an international line of credit in that amount.

For the same reason, a bank panic is much more likely in a fixed exchange rate regime. In the event of a banking panic, the central bank can act as a lender of last resort in a floating regime, but not under a pegged rate regime without jeopardizing the exchange rate peg itself. Wigmore (1987) has argued that the failure of the Federal Reserve to protect the U.S. banking system in the winter of 1932–1933 was the result of the Federal Reserve's fears that lender-of-last-resort credits to the banks would undermine the link of the U.S. dollar to gold. In this way, the commitment to the gold standard opened the U.S. to a self-fulfilling banking panic. Similarly in 1995 Argentina's strict currency board arrangements opened it to the threat of a banking crisis because the Argentine central bank was unable to act as a lender of last resort.

What, then, are the appropriate circumstances for a pegged exchange rate regime for an emerging market? The first and very rare case is a true optimal currency union with one or more countries. In this case, a common central bank can act as lender of last resort for the whole union. Note that many cases of "permanent" exchange rate pegs, such as the CFA Franc peg in West Africa, or the dollar peg in Liberia, were not even remotely appropriate as optimal currency areas, and therefore produced situations of prolonged currency overvaluation.

A second exceptional case for pegging may be an extremely open and diversified economy with an extremely flexible labor market. Such an economy can adjust to external shocks through internal deflation if necessary, rather than depreciation. Also, by virtue of diversification, such an economy may be less likely to be hit by serious external shocks than an economy highly specialized with respect to a few export goods, particularly natural resources. Hong Kong and Estonia, both of which use currency boards, are possible examples. Even in these cases, however, there is still the need to maintain a lender-of-last-resort mechanism. It is rarely recognized but extremely pertinent that Hong Kong has relied on the Bank of China to serve as a lender of last resort in the event of banking crises.

A third exceptional case for pegging, at least in a temporary manner, arises in the wake of hyperinflation or in the case of the introduction of a new national currency, as in the successor states of the Soviet Union and Yugoslavia. In both cases, the economy tends to be undermonetized, with extremely low ratios of money supply (M) to gross domestic product (GDP). A temporary peg of the exchange rate serves several purposes: it increases confidence in a fragile currency; it stops a self-fulfilling flight from the new (or newly stabilized) currency; and most importantly, it provides an automatic mechanism for remonetization of the economy— through the balance of payments. Thus, after Estonia pegged the Kroon to the deutsche mark, Estonia ran a significant balance of payments surplus as Estonian households and firms repatriated foreign exchange to build up money balances in the new currency. Foreign reserves and the money supply rose by more than 10 percent of GDP in the first two years.

History has shown that the stabilization of a hyperinflation and the introduction of a new currency tend to be less costly in terms of lost output when a pegged rate is used rather than a floating rate (see Sachs 1995a for further discussion of this point). The floating rate deprives the economy of the mechanism for automatic remonetization, and the currency also seems to suffer from a lack of confidence relative to a pegged rate. At the same time, however, it is very important to switch from the pegged rate to a more flexible exchange rate arrangement (a float, crawling band, or some other flexible arrangement) as soon as the remonetization is substantially accomplished. If the pegged rate is maintained too long, then the economy is subjected to the problems noted earlier: inflexibility in the face of shocks (as in Mexico in 1994) and vulnerability to panics (as in Argentina in 1995 after the the Mexican crisis).[1]

---

1. It is at least arguable that Argentina presents a unique case. After forty years of chronic high inflation punctuated by episodes of hyperinflation the economic team in 1991 judged that only the straightjacket of a currency board could break the historical cycle of monetary disarray and the virtual complete absence of credibility of stabilization policies. The currency board arrangements have succeeded remarkably in reducing Argentina's inflation to low, single-digit rates, indeed Argentina has one of the lowest inflation rates in the world. Moreover, economically policy has become directed to vitally needed reforms of labor markets, public administration, social security, tax policy, public ownership, and other areas.

Thus, the undoubted costs of Argentina's monetary straightjacket, including the banking panic of 1995 and Argentina's high labor costs in international terms, must be balanced against the historic break in its deeply dysfunctional monetary policies over four decades. No other country failed for so long to find other institutional bases (central bank independence, pegged but adjustable exchange rates, etc.) to limit inflationary pressures. For that reason, few if any other countries should take Argentina's gamble on a strict currency

Dollarization

The central bank should discourage the dollarization of accounts in the domestic banking system. Similarly, the government should avoid the dollarization of its own short-term debts.

In many developing countries, particularly those recovering from high inflation, central banks often encourage reintermediation of the banking system by allowing dollar-indexed assets and liabilities. Even when these assets and liabilities are roughly balanced in overall totals (as is often required), there is usually maturity transformation, so the dollar liabilities are short term while the assets are longer term. The main problem is that the central bank is less able to act as a lender of last resort, even under floating exchange rates, because it must provide foreign exchange (dollars) in the event of a precipitous withdrawal of dollar balances. In many cases of dollar balances, therefore, dollar withdrawals are frozen when a bank run ensues; eventually, the dollar-denominated balances are converted into domestic currency with some degree of confiscation.

Similar logic militates against the reliance of governments on short-term dollar denominated debts such as the Mexican government's issuance of *tesobonos*, which played such havoc with Mexico in late 1994. Mexican government indebtedness was not extraordinarily high in late 1994 (perhaps 35 percent of GDP), but it was dollar denominated and very short term. Since dollar debts were much higher than dollar foreign exchange reserves at the end of 1994, a market panic could and did develop. Investors in Mexican government debts refused to roll over the outstanding *tesobonos*, and Mexico was pushed to the brink of default. Because the liabilities were dollar denominated, the Banco de México was unable to stand behind the government's obligations via a line of domestic credit to the government. There was, contrarily, much less, if any, risk of default on the government's peso-denominated liabilities. (See Sachs, Tornell, and Velasco 1996b for further details concerning the Mexican case.)

Currency Board Arrangements

As a corollary to avoiding pegged exchange rates and dollarization, currency board arrangements should also be avoided except in the case of very small, very open economies. Even then, the central bank should maintain some scope for lender-of-last-resort actions and arrange international lines of credit in advance to be able to respond to a future banking crisis.

---

board arrangement. The long-term consequences of Argentina's own bet on the currency board system are still to be seen.

"Permanently" fixed exchange rates have almost always provoked a serious crisis, whether in West Africa, Liberia, Panama, or more recently in Argentina (where the economy left a 20 percent unemployment rate in the 1995 crisis). They are an invitation to chronic overvaluation, banking crises, and often both together. Moreover, despite the claims made by Hanke and Schuler (1994) that currency board arrangements run smoothly despite the lack of a lender-of-last-resort facility, even Hong Kong had to rely on the Bank of China, in conjunction with the Hong Kong and Shanghai Banking Corporation, to act as a lender of last resort in the event of the failure of Ka Wah Bank in 1995 (see Jao 1992, p. 58 for details). And, of course, in 1995 Argentina required an emergency international loan package to help stave off an intense banking crisis (although see note 1).

Controls on Capital Inflows

The liberalization of controls on capital inflows should be managed gradually, to avoid a boom-bust cycle.

Many financial crises in the past ten years have been directly related to financial market liberalization, especially the elimination of controls on international financial movements. Crises linked to financial market liberalization include those in Argentina, Mexico, Venezuela, Israel, Sweden, and Norway. Each case has important distinctive features, but all exhibit a boom-bust cycle in which a sharp but temporary wave of capital inflow accompanied a pegged exchange rate. When the inflow subsided, the exchange rate needed to be devalued. The subsequent devaluation was often delayed until after a serious macroeconomic crisis had transpired.

The exact nature of the boom-bust cycle in capital inflows is hard to characterize precisely: Are these cycles rational? Are they based on myopic euphoria, which then bursts? In any case, the basic contours of the cycle are clear. Once capital controls are lifted, domestic banks and other financial intermediaries are able to tap the international capital markets. A sizable stock of foreign debt is rapidly accumulated until the banks and other intermediaries hit a borrowing limit, determined by their capital base and institutional rules. When the limit is hit, the borrowing slows dramatically.

This repeated experience probably justifies the decisions of countries such as Chile to liberalize gradually, so that domestic financial institutions cannot suddenly take on foreign debt. The borrowing limit is reached more gradually, and the boom-bust cycle is greatly damped if not eliminated. The real exchange rate does not appreciate as much as in the case of rapid liberalization, and the subsequent devaluation needed after the slowdown in capital inflows is much less dramatic. A reasonable pattern for the liberalization of capital inflows would probably allow immediate free movements of foreign direct investment (including repatriation of capital and profits), followed in sequence by liberalization of portfolio equity investment, long-term borrowing by nonfinancial enterprises, short-term borrowing by nonfinancial enterprises, and then finally, short-term commercial bank borrowing.

Prudential Standards

The BIS prudential standards for commercial banks are usually not sufficient for developing countries. More stringent capital:asset ratios should be encouraged, as well as rigorous minimum capital levels for banks.

Financial crises are stoked by undercapitalized banks, which are more vulnerable to self-fulfilling panics and more prone to excessively risky borrowing. (Raising the risk of the bank's portfolio effectively transfers wealth from the deposit insurance fund, usually provided by the government, to the bank's shareholders). Most emerging markets lack effective institutions for bank supervision, so the book value of bank capital often greatly overstates the amount of shareholder equity (e.g., bad loans may not be recorded expeditiously). Moreover, the ownership structure of banks in emerging markets typically adds to their riskiness. Nonfinancial companies own the banks, which in turn lend to the companies that own them. Moreover, bank licenses are frequently issued on the basis of party politics, nepotism, or corruption. For all these reasons, standard prescriptions for developed economies, such as a minimum capital:assets ratio of 8 percent, are likely to be grossly inadequate in the emerging markets context.[1]

Responding to International Financial Crises

Crisis prevention, alas, is only part of the story. Approximately 60 developing countries have experienced extreme financial crises in the past decade, in the form of debt defaults, debt reschedulings, or acute inflationary episodes. In the past two years, serious financial crises have hit Argentina, Latvia, Mexico, Turkey, and Venezuela, and lesser financial crises have hit many of the economies in transition. Dozens of developing-country governments are still grappling with heavy burdens of foreign indebtedness, and new proposals are in the works for easing the burdens of multilateral debts on the world's poorest countries.

The IMF was set up in 1944 in part to serve as a kind of international lender of last resort (ILLR), especially to provide temporary financing to help member governments maintain pegged exchange rates during a period of internal adjustment. With the collapse of the pegged exchange rate regime in 1971, that specific function has diminished (if not quite disappeared), but the IMF still plays the role of central arbiter of developing-country financial crises by providing advice, balance-of-payments lending, and coordination of debt-reduction operations.

Many financial crises in the past have been dependent on the IMF's procedures, which lack an adequate conceptual and institutional basis (Sachs 1994, 1995a), resulting in undue and costly inefficiency in the IMF's handling of international financial crises and its role as the ILLR. These arguments have been echoed by Eichengreen and Portes (1995), who concur with the need for revising the IMF's ILLR functions. It is analytically useful at this stage to examine the IMF's functions with respect to the three types of financial crises described in the previous section: fiscal crises, foreign exchange crises, and banking crises.

Fiscal Crises

In the past twenty years, dozens of developing country governments have experienced extreme financial embarrassment ranging from acute illiquidity leading to a temporary default on international obligations, to insolvency requiring a permanent cancellation of some portion of the government's foreign debt obligations. (Notice that domestic obligations are rarely defaulted because domestic-currency debts can be met through credits provided by the central bank at the cost of *indirect* partial repudiation via inflation). An elaborate, if not wholly successful, institutional pattern has emerged to handle sovereign financial distress, including IMF loans, Paris Club relief on bilateral credits, and London Club relief on bank credits.

An efficient system for financial workouts would offer the following features. First, it would reduce moral hazards, by rewarding countries for maintaining their debt servicing and punishing countries adequately for managing their affairs in a manner that leads to default on debt obligations. Second, it would ensure the effective functioning of the debtor government at all stages of the financial workout, from the onset of the crisis to its final resolution. Third, it would create mechanisms for coordinating the actions of creditors, to achieve an efficient arrangement for renegotiating the financial terms on the problem debts.

Twenty years of experience with the international debt crisis has demonstrated that current institutional arrangements do not meet these needs, although the international system has become more efficient over time. A 1995 IMF report (1995, p. 11) states, "Because there exists no well-defined and accepted legal process that is applicable in such cases, the process of debt resolution by involuntary restructuring is necessarily ad hoc with an uncertain outcome." The implications of the lack of a legal framework can be appreciated by comparing the ad hoc international arrangements with the legal structure that governs financial workouts under the bankruptcy laws of countries with advanced economies. The U.S. Bankruptcy Code's Chapter 9 (for municipalities) and Chapter 11 (for corporations) provide a particularly relevant contrast to the international arrangements because these chapters are explicitly designed to handle cases of financial restructuring rather than liquidation.

The U.S. Bankruptcy Code recognizes that efficient workouts require a regulatory environment for three stages of the workout. At the outset of insolvency (or at least the outset of creditor recognition of insolvency), the code provides for an automatic standstill on debt servicing. Creditors are not allowed to pursue legal remedies to seize assets or to force the payment of debts. The law recognizes that each creditor, acting individually, has the incentive to enter a "grab race" for assets, to their mutual detriment. The automatic standstill prevents the premature liquidation or impairment of the insolvent entity, thereby preserving the overall value of the entity, which benefits all the creditors.

The second stage is the time between the onset of the stay and the exit from bankruptcy through reorganization. During this interim period, the insolvent entity (whether a municipality or a corporation) will generally need access to new working capital. The prebankruptcy debt precludes a routine return to the capital markets, and high transaction costs among the current creditors normally precludes new lending from the existing creditors (because each creditor would like the *others* to make the emergency loans). The solution is debtor-in-possession (DIP) financing through the assignment of priority to the repayment of the new, emergency loans ahead of the prebankruptcy claims. The bankruptcy court must approve the DIP financing, to ensure that the new loans actually enhance the value of the entity, and thereby increase the value of the prebankruptcy debts. It is important to note that, unlike the IMF, the bankruptcy court does not dispose of any money itself; the court's ability to deliver working capital lies in its power to assign priority to new market borrowing by the insolvent entity.

The third stage of the workout is the final balance sheet reorganization (debt reduction, debt-service reduction, new loans, debt-to-equity swaps, etc.), which is usually combined with an operational reorganization (closure of loss-making units, divestiture, change in management, etc.). The key role of the bankruptcy law is to provide a negotiating framework that (1) brings all the parties together; (2) establishes mechanisms for across-the-board settlements involving all classes of creditors; and (3) discourages free-riding or holdouts by individual creditors, thereby pushing the process toward an expeditious resolution. The court has the power to accept nonunanimity among creditors during the confirmation of the reorganization plan, and to force the acceptance of a plan that is resisted by a particular group of creditors (a so-called cramdown). A plan is confirmed if it is accepted by two-thirds or more of each creditor class based on amount of claims, and by more than one-half of each creditor class based on the number of claimants.

By these standards, the shortcomings in the international system are clear. There is no automatic standstill. An insolvent government typically faces threatened or actual legal harassment by individual creditors for months or years after the onset of the crisis. The threats (for example, to seize airplanes, ships, and bank accounts, and to otherwise disrupt trade credit lines) usually do not subside until the final confirmation of a Paris Club and London Club deal, and by that time, individual creditors may have done great damage to the debtor government's effectiveness.

There is essentially no DIP financing other than the IMF lending (and perhaps other official lending) itself. Typically, only funds in the form of internationally mobilized taxpayer dollars under IMF supervision are available for short-term working capital. (Early on, the IMF orchestrated a few "involuntary lending" programs with the existing creditors, but these loans were very hard to arrange, and the IMF gave up by the mid-1980s. In the case of Mexico in 1995, for example, there was no active attempt to round up involuntary or voluntary private financing.) The fact that working capital depends on taxpayer dollars has important political economy ramifications. The IMF is naturally extremely hesitant to lend "other people's money" into a highly visible crisis. Therefore, there are typically very long delays between the onset of insolvency and the start of IMF lending. During this period, the debtor government is starved for working capital and often loses much of its capacity to govern. Russia during 1992 and 1993 is a vivid case of a government starved for working capital; the lack of capital undermined the economic reform program (see Sachs 1995a for details).

Finally, there are no effective rules to overcome free-riding and holdouts and ensure an expeditious overall settlement. The Paris Club and London Club have evolved norms of behavior to keep the major creditors fairly united. Nonetheless, there are still sharp divisions among various creditor classes (bilaterals versus multilaterals versus commercial banks versus suppliers; large banks versus small banks) that incite strategic moves among the creditors and in extreme cases lead to individual holdouts that significantly delay a debt-rescheduling or debt-reduction operation. The entire process requires a large input of time and energy from the U.S. Treasury and other leading finance ministries. Large, high-profile countries (e.g., Poland, Mexico, and Argentina) get more attention and more adequate remedies than smaller, less noticed countries.

On the basis of my earlier writings (Sachs 1994, 1995a) I have been interpreted by others as recommending an "international chapter 11, that is, an international bankruptcy court. This is too literal an interpretation of my critique of current arrangements. I am recommending that we recognize and attempt to establish the functional equivalents of the key bankruptcy code mechanisms: automatic standstills, priority lending, and comprehensive reorganization plans supported by nonunanimity rules. We do not need a literal bankruptcy court to move in the direction of implementing such mechanisms. We could begin with a clear statement of IMF operating principles regarding each stage of the workout. We could search for ways to establish emergency priority lending from private capital markets, under IMF supervision. The IMF and governments could recommend model covenants for inclusion in future sovereign lending instruments that would allow for emergency priority lending and efficient renegotiations of debt claims, should the future circumstances require them.

Foreign Exchange Crises

There is rarely a role for IMF lending in support of a particular nominal exchange rate of a member country. As the preceding analysis has stressed, pegged exchange rates are probably ineffective and unsupportable in most circumstances, especially in light of the high capital mobility now prevailing in the international economy. Of course, individual central banks may well have cause to intervene from time to time in their own currencies, but there is much less case for internationally coordinated interventions on behalf of a particular developing country.

There are, however, exceptions to this rule. International lending on behalf of a nominal exchange rate target makes sense when a government is attempting to establish confidence in a new national currency, or reestablish confidence in an existing currency that has suffered a bout of extreme inflation. In both cases, money:GDP ratios tend to be very low, and there is the risk of a self-sustaining collapse of the currency: market panic induces a flight from the currency, which in turn incites inflation and further currency flight. A descent into hyperinflation is at least a theoretical possibility and becomes more likely as the use of the national currency in the domestic economy (as evidenced by extremely low money:income ratios) becomes more tenuous. Note that before the Plan Real, Brazil exhibited a ratio of high-powered money to GDP of less than 1 percent. Similarly, Kyrgyzstan's new currency, the Som, had an extremely tenuous role in the economy upon its introduction, with an M2:GDP ratio of about 4 percent in 1994.

In these cases, there is a strong argument for an internationally provided stabilization fund to help back the new or newly stabilized currency for the first year or two. The $1 billion Polish Stabilization Fund in 1990 had a powerful positive impact on confidence in and political support for Poland's ambitious reform program. Estonia, fortunately, was able to create its own stabilization fund to support the new Kroon in 1992, using repatriated gold reserves that had been held by Sweden and the U.K. since World War II. Other countries, however, have not been so fortunate.

In most cases, the short-term pegging of the exchange rate should be viewed as a temporary stage that continues until confidence in the currency is established and partial remonetization of the economy is achieved. Therefore, a pegged rate might last for about one year, to be followed by a more flexible arrangement such as a crawling band exchange rate system. Long-term pegged rates are realistic only in very small, open economies, such as those in the Baltic States, which may viably choose a currency board arrangement.

Banking Crises

During a banking crisis, the basic international arrangement is that central banks are responsible for the oversight and prudential regulation of their nation's banks, whether those banks are operating domestically or as subsidiaries in foreign countries. This division of labor may break down, however, when domestic banks have extensive short-term liabilities denominated in foreign currencies. In this case, the central bank may need substantial foreign exchange reserves to meet a sudden withdrawal of funds denominated in a foreign currency. Lacking adequate foreign reserves, the domestic central bank may be unable to play the role of lender of last resort.

There is, at this point, no international regulatory regime governing the use of foreign exchange–denominated accounts in national banking systems. When Argentina's dollar-based banking system succumbed to crisis early in 1995, Argentina required an emergency international infusion of funds to stabilize the banking sector because the Argentine central bank lacked the instruments and adequate reserves to serve as lender of last resort on its own. This was especially true as a result of the currency board rules that have prevailed in Argentina since April 1991. The central bank is enjoined from extending domestic credit, even to illiquid commercial banks. And even if the central bank were to violate its operating principals, the market's confidence in Argentina's exchange rate peg would be rapidly undermined. In the event, the central bank eased various reserve requirements, which amounted to a modest extension of credit to the banks. Reserves fell from some $18 billion to $14 billion in a couple of months. To staunch the continuing hemorrhage of withdrawals from the banking system, Argentina arranged a roughly $10 billion international package of official and private support for the banks.

As described earlier, the most important way to reduce the frequency of this kind of crisis would be for governments and central banks to restrict the use of foreign currency deposits or other kinds of short-term foreign liabilities of the domestic banking system. At a minimum, the regulators should require that commercial banks' short-term foreign liabilities (deposits and CDs) should be matched by short-term and liquid foreign assets. Of course, in a world of derivatives, swaps, and other off-the-balance-sheet means of converting the currency denomination of assets and liabilities, regulators will occasionally be caught short even if there are strong restrictions on open positions.

In addition to these regulatory changes, there will be the need, from time to time, for emergency cross-border lending to support banking systems under siege as the result of the abrupt withdrawal of foreign-denominated funds. As in any lender-of-last-resort operation, the governing principle for emergency international support should be a combination of ex ante prudential standards to avoid moral hazard; strong conditionality in the event of a bailout; timely lending to avert or stem a panic; and provisions for emergency renegotiation of private sector debts, in lieu of bailouts, when that is feasible. Probably the greatest shortcomings in proceeding with a general international system of support are the lack of adequate prudential supervision in most developing countries and the lack of detailed attention at the level of the IMF and the BIS to the state of banking regulation in the developing countries. This suggests that it should be a high priority for the BIS and IMF together to establish a far more rigorous system of prudential monitoring (e.g., of capital adequacy, reporting and disclosure, portfolio diversification, risk ratings, reserve provisioning, off-balance-sheet monitoring, risk management, and deposit insurance) of developing countries, as a prelude to enhanced international facilities for emergency lending operations.

References

Diamond, D., and P. Dybvig. 1983. "Bank Runs, Deposit Insurance and Liquidity." *Journal of Political Economy* (June).

Eichengreen, B., and R. Portes. 1995. *Crisis? What Crisis? Orderly Workouts for Sovereign Debtors.* London: Centre for Economic Policy Research.

Hanke, S. H., and K. Schuler. 1994. "Currency Boards for Developing Countries." Sector Study No. 9. San Francisco: International Center for Economic Growth.

IMF (International Monetary Fund). 1995. *International Capital Markets: Developments, Prospects, and Policy Issues.* Washington, D.C.: International Monetary Fund.

Jao, Y. C. 1992. "Monetary System and Banking Structure." In *The Economic System of Hong Kong,* edited by H. C. Y. Ho and L. C. Chau. Hong Kong: Asian Research Service.

Obstfeld, M. 1996. "Models of Currency Crises with Self-Fulfilling Features." European Economic Review 40(3–5):1037–1047.

Obstfeld, M., and K. Rogoff. 1995. "The Mirage of Fixed Exchange Rates." Working Paper No. 5191, National Bureau of Economic Research, Cambridge, Mass..

Radelet, S., and J. Sachs. 1998. "The East Asian Financial Crisis: Diagnosis, Remedies, Prospects." *Brookings Papers on Economic Activities,* forthcoming.

Sachs, J. 1994. "The IMF and Economies in Crisis." Paper presented at the London School of Economics, July, London.

——. 1995a. "Do We Need a Lender of Last Resort?" Paper presented at the Frank D. Graham Lecture, April 1995, Princeton University, Princeton, N.J.

——. 1995b. "Theoretical Issues in International Borrowing." In *International Debt,* edited by G. Bird and P. N. Snowden. Vol. 2. Edward Elgar. Originally published in *Princeton Studies in International Finance,* no. 54.

Sachs, J., A. Tornell, and A. Velasco. 1996a. "The Collapse of the Mexican Peso: What Have We Learned?" *Economic Policy,* no. 2:15–63.

——. 1996b. "Lessons from the Mexican Peso Crisis: What Have We Learned?" *Economic Policy,* no. 22:15–63.

Wigmore, B. 1987. "Was the Banking Holiday of 1933 a Run on the Dollar Rather Than the Banks?" *Journal of Economic History* 47:739–756.

Index

Abramovitz, Moses, 241
Agosín, Manuel, 147
Alfiler, F. Enrico, 101, 109
American depository receipts (ADRs): price determination, 80–84; of Russian companies, 229, 240–41
Argentina: banking crisis (1995), 254; capital inflows (1990–1994), 130; currency board arrangement, 252n. 1; currency board system, 150, 154; lending boom in (1989–1994), 151–53
Armijo, Leslie, 79
Asia: capital inflows (1990s), 48; current account balance (1978–1993), 43–44; fiscal deficit (1978–1993), 44–45; foreign direct investment flows (1990s), 49; market response to news, 86–89
Aziz, Zeti Akhtar, 109, 118

Bachetta, Phillippe, 111
Baker Plan (1985), 24, 43
Balance of payments: capital account measures in response to capital inflows, 117–22; capital account restrictions in Poland, Hungary, and Czech Republic, 211t; effects of shocks in Latin America on (1981–1983), 41–43; reserves, trade and current account balances of Czech Republic, Hungary, and Poland, 221–22. See also Capital account; Reserves, international
Banerjee, Neela, 232, 243
Bank for International Settlements (BIS), 38
Banking crises: effect on emerging market countries, 248, 251; IMF response to, 260–61

Banking systems: commercial bank lending in central and eastern Europe (1990–1996), 191–96; lending booms, 149–53; Mexico, 56; regulation and supervision of capital inflows, 120, 122; Russian, 237–40; Thailand, 56
Bank of China, as lender-of-last-resort, 254
Bankruptcy court, international, 63
Barrera, F., 148
Belchere, William C., 109
Bercuson, Kenneth, 115
Berezovsky, Boris, 237
Blasi, Joseph R., 240
Bond markets: Hungary and Czech Republic, 210; U.S. market (1920s, 1930s), 23–24, 27–38
Borgés, Jorge Luis, 93
Brady, Nicholas, 1
Brady Plan, 1, 12, 43
Brahmbhatt, Milan, 180
Brainard, William, 75
Brandmeyer, Michael, 70
Brazil: capital inflows (1990–1994), 130; lending boom in (1989–1994), 151–53; restrictions on capital inflows (1994), 62
Budnevich, Carlos, 95, 110
Bufman, G., 137
Bush, Keith, 230

Calvo, Guillermo, 4, 47–49, 77, 94, 98, 99, 105, 110, 141, 143, 146, 193, 212, 221
Calvo, Sara, 52, 77
Capital: controls in Chile and Mexico, 146–49; controls on, 154–55; uses of inflowing, 223
Capital account: balances in Hungary, Czech Republic, and Poland (1990–